Black is a Church

Black is a Church

*Christianity and the Contours of
African American Life*

JOSEF SORETT

OXFORD
UNIVERSITY PRESS

OXFORD
UNIVERSITY PRESS

Oxford University Press is a department of the University of Oxford. It furthers
the University's objective of excellence in research, scholarship, and education
by publishing worldwide. Oxford is a registered trade mark of Oxford University
Press in the UK and certain other countries.

Published in the United States of America by Oxford University Press
198 Madison Avenue, New York, NY 10016, United States of America.

Library of Congress Control Number: 2022058621

ISBN 978-0-19-061513-0

DOI: 10.1093/oso/9780190615130.001.0001

Printed by Integrated Books International, United States of America

Thank you to Columbia University Press, *Public Culture*, and the University of Notre Dame Press
for the permission to reprint the following previously published materials:

A selection of chapter three appeared in a different form as, "The Answers were Aprocryphal:
Protestantism and the Politics of Pluralism in *Phylon's* Early Years," in Darren Dochuk, Editor,
Religion and Politics Beyond the Culture Wars: New Directions in a Divided America.
(South Bend, IN: University of Notre Dame Press, 2021).

A selection of chapter four appeared in a different form as, "A Fantastic Church? Literature, Politics and
the Afterlives of Afro-Protestantism," *Public Culture* (81: Volume 29, Number 1, January 2017), 17–26.

Selections from the introduction and chapter four appeared in a different form as, "Secular Compared
to What? African American Religion and the Trope of Sacred & Secular," in Jonathan Kahn and
Vincent Lloyd, Eds., *Race and Secularism in America* (New York: Columbia University Press, 2016)

Contents

Contents

Preface and Acknowledgments

Black is a Church is a book filled with ideas that have been with me for far too long. Years before I ever imagined that such thoughts might become a book. Much of it was written alongside my first book, *Spirit in the Dark*. Both books reflect my efforts to better understand an overlapping, entangled set of questions that have been refined over the years since I began graduate school at Harvard in the Fall of 2001. In truth, one of the first places I found some provisional language for these concerns was, several years earlier, in Dr. Leonard Lovett's Theology and Black Identity class, which I took during the Spring semester of my junior year at Oral Roberts University. I've moved through too many classrooms, and read too many books, in pursuit of clarity regarding these questions during the nearly three decades that have passed between then and now. Yet a series of everyday episodes, of much less formal conversations and commentary, have been just as formative to my thinking on these topics. I make brief mention of three such episodes here, insofar as they help to set an everyday context for the arguments that unfold on the pages that follow.

Episode 1: May 2002 (Boston, MA). Near the end of my first year of Ph.D. coursework I was invited by State Senator Dianne Wilkerson to sit on the closing panel of the State of Black Massachusetts conference, which she was convening in Boston at the Reggie Lewis Center on the campus of Roxbury Community College. That day I joined an incredible panel that included, among others, one-time Boston Rainbow Coalition mayoral candidate Mel King; Deborah Prothrow-Stith, the state's former Commissioner of Public Health; and then editor-in-chief of the Hip Hop magazine *The Source*, David Mays. My task was to speak to the resources that religion had provided to black communities over the years. After a round of presentations, the conversation was opened to the audience, and the first person to grab the microphone was a middle-aged man who directed his question to me. His question, which was actually more of a comment (and a call to conversion), went straight to the point: "When will the black community realize that none of the problems we face will be solved until we all accept Jesus Christ as our Lord and Savior?"

Episode 2: July 2010 (New York, NY). In the summer following my first year on the faculty at Columbia University, I was enlisted by the Arcus Foundation to convene a group of scholars, clergy, and activists to discuss the sexual politics of black churches and what they meant in the context of a growing movement for marriage equality. Following a public-facing panel the night before at Union Theological Seminary, roughly twenty of us gathered downtown at the Bishop Desmond Tutu Conference Center for a closed-door, if not private, roundtable discussion. Most of the presentations made that day evolved into chapters in an edited volume, *The Sexual Politics of Black Churches*, that was finally published in February 2022. One thing in particular stands out in my memory from that initial gathering. One of the presenters began their remarks with a rather casual comment (that does not appear in the book) about their own social location: "Culturally-speaking, I'm a part of 'The Black Church.'"

Episode 3: April 2017 (New Haven, CT). Toward the end of a year in residence at Yale's Institute for Sacred Music, I had the privilege of organizing a two-day event discussing religion and black music in the Post-Soul era. The convening wrapped up with a masterful talk that was both a conference capstone, synthesizing all of the presentations, and a keynote lecture that invited everyone in attendance to think in new ways about the place of religion and music in the context of black life—past, present, and future. The address began with a bit of auto-biography, as the speaker situated their presentation in the everyday experience of coming of age in the 1970s. At the end of their prefatory remarks, the keynote speaker confessed, somewhat jokingly, "I may be a heathen, but that doesn't mean I'm unchurched."

Each of these rather casual comments reveals much about the complex inner workings of the power and persistence of Christianity in the making of individual black lives and black social worlds. Each is also evocative of the different kind of logics at play in everyday and academic understandings of the role of "The Black Church"—as a social institution with material and symbolic significance in the context

of American life. And each illumines the complicated ways that racial authenticity and religious orthodoxy work together, while also
often pulling in unpredictable directions, to inform and animate the
ways that we feel, move, and think in the world. In the first episode,
Christian salvation was presented as a prerequisite for collective black
flourishing. Here blackness finds its true meaning (in fact, its social
salvation) only in alignment with a version of Christian orthodoxy.
The second episode suggests that membership roles are not the only
metrics for suggesting who participates in, belongs to, or lays claim to
church. And the third clarifies as much even as it suggests something
more. That is, the lack of a professed Christian commitment—whether
measured through attendance, membership, belief, or practice—
should not be confused for either an unfamiliarity with The Black
Church or for the absence of its influence on the way one makes their
way in the world. In both the second and third episodes, a certain black
Christian orthodoxy is seen to have an organizing power, regardless of
whether or not one chooses the tradition, or the church, for oneself.
Together, these episodes illustrate just a few of the many possibilities
that result from the peculiar convergences of racial authenticity and
religious orthodoxy in (black) America. Together, they also powerfully illustrate both the ironies of American secularism and the still
unfolding tradition of Afro-Protestantism. It is these traditions that
Black is a Church sets out to understand.

In the years spent working on this book, I accrued an abundance
of debts that are impossible for me to fully account for here. Protocol
requires, nonetheless, that I give it a go.

I often refer to myself as a grandson of The Black Church. I was not
raised in a family context where the weekly routine involved our presence in the pews of institutional Afro-Protestantism every Sunday. For
my mother, however, this was very much the norm growing up. That is,
before she became one of the many spiritual seekers of her generation,
a quintessential daughter of the 1960s who fled, following her high
school graduation, the church of her childhood. Prior to that, however, my mother was raised in the belly of Boston's black Methodist
community, at the historic Charles Street African Methodist Episcopal
Church in Roxbury. Off to college at the age of seventeen, she promptly
left the church of her youth, never to return. She eventually came back

to the Christian faith, but not to the AME church in which she had been raised. Except on the occasional Mother's Day when she, with my younger brother, Tarek, and me in tow, went to worship at that church she had left long ago. These trips were for her, above all, a sign of love and respect on that highest of Black Church holy days. And that is because her mother, Belva Wallace, remained a member at that same church until 2017, when she made her transition from labor to reward at the age of ninety-three. My grandmother served her church faithfully for over six decades—as an Usher, Missionary, Stewardess, and more. During the final decade of her life, she was also, somewhat reluctantly, consecrated as a Deaconess—a title that the AME Church reserves for church mothers observed to embody a certain, and special, spiritual virtue.

As a recent college graduate in the mid-1990s, I returned to my grandmother's church and joined of my own accord (much to my mother's dismay, I would later learn). As far as I could tell, my grandmother took great pride in my presence at her church. It was a small prize, perhaps, in the face of her daughter's departure decades earlier. Her church became my spiritual home for a few years during an incredibly challenging, yet formative time in my young adult life. Charles Street AME helped me salvage a sense of Christian faith, not long after my adolescent faith had begun to fall apart and just as I was graduating from Oral Roberts University. It was largely my experience in that congregation that propelled me in the direction of becoming a professor. For that welcome home, without which this book would never have been written, I remain grateful to Mother Belva Wallace—or as she will always be to me, simply, Grams.

The deepest debt of gratitude, of course, goes to those who have no choice but to deal with me the most. This daily dealing intensified all the more during the past few years, following the onset of the COVID-19 pandemic in 2020. I finished final edits to this book during the Omicron surge, but much of the writing and revising was done under the terms of lockdown and long days of remote education. I was fortunate that my sons, Elliot and Jacob, after logging off from their own virtual schooling, would pull me away, not without my resistance, from staring at the computer screen, where I was busy book writing, drafting emails, teaching classes online, or Zooming from one meeting to the next. Home-cooked meals followed by multiple rounds of Uno became our family ritual. Before then I never imagined that seventy-plus straight nights of dinner together, occasionally prepared with their assistance, was a remote possibility. We are more than lucky that this is our story to share. As those home-cooked meals have grown fewer and farther between, approaching something like the pre-pandemic rhythms, I am even more thankful for their presence and personalities through it all. Certain kinds of gratitude feel cheapened when put to pen, but I cannot express enough appreciation for the one who already knows. More than words, Ayanna, most of all.

A special thank you goes to my father, Howard, and his wife, Mabel, as well as to my mother-in-law, Marlyn, and late father-in-law, Orbert, who made his transition from this life to the next in August of 2022. They each, in their own way, offered consistent encouragement with their regular inquiries into how my writing was coming along.

Steady conversations with friends and colleagues have sustained me through the ups and downs of putting words on the page, and especially during those periods when there were no words coming: Fred Davie, Warren Dillon, Jamil Drake, Babanina James, Vivaldi-Jean Marie, Lerone Martin, Iman Oakley, Shaun Robinson, Jerome Sealey-Ashford, Nicole Thomas, and Jonathan L. Walton. Thank you all for talking me through matters of life and death, for walking with me through the everyday rhythms of work and play, and for sharing plenty of laughter along the way.

Intellectual and other kinds of support for the research and writing of this book came from an incredible group of colleagues, many of whom have also become friends. Given that much of this book was written alongside *Spirit in the Dark*, a measure of gratitude goes to everyone I named in my acknowledgments to that book. Four colleagues, in particular, carefully read a way-too-long manuscript several years ago and provided feedback that helped me realize what I had written would do much better if separated into two books. For close readings and considerable feedback, special thanks go to Gil Anidjar, Courtney Bender, Eddie S. Glaude Jr., and Farah Jasmine Griffin.

It's a lucky thing to find intellectual community in the form of one's primary professional affiliation. I feel fortunate to be able to say this about Columbia University, and especially concerning my colleagues in the departments of Religion and African American and African Diaspora Studies. It is indeed a privilege to share space (virtual and physical) on a regular basis with so many generous human beings. An extra measure of gratitude goes to Gil Anidjar and Mark C. Taylor, both of whom read and commented on this manuscript in its penultimate form. I've also benefited from discussing many of the book's arguments with Robert Gooding-Williams. Obery Hendricks's sage advice and outsized sense of humor has helped me return to writing after many a long day. Andrew Jungclaus tracked down issues of *Phylon* and provided insightful annotations, which helped me write much of chapter 3. Andrew also put an invaluable extra set of eyes on the manuscript during the copyediting process and on the final proofs. Derrick McQueen's administrative acumen kept CARSS on track during long spells when I was otherwise occupied with the book. Derrick also helped me see the connections between our collaborative work and my "independent" scholarship. Edwin Torres, Shawn Mendoza, Sharon Harris, and Katrina Dock have each made the work go much smoother than it would have otherwise on all too many occasions.

As this book entered production, I moved to a new office near the center of Columbia's Morningside campus and, in doing so, gained a host of new colleagues. Much appreciation goes to the Columbia College community (students, staff, faculty, and alums), and especially the Senior Leadership Team and the team in 208 Hamilton.

I have benefited from feedback from numerous colleagues who either read part of the manuscript or invited me to give talks and, in doing so, provided me with readers and audiences for the work in progress. In addition to being a trusted confidant, friend, and mentor, Barbara Dianne Savage read the entire manuscript early on. Barbara also invited me to give a talk at Oxford University in 2019, while she was in residence there as the distinguished Harmsworth Visiting Professor. Attendees at the Rothermere Institute's American History Research Seminar, which Barbara led that year with Stephen Tuck, provided helpful feedback on a much shorter version of chapter 3. I also received valuable questions and critique during presentations of various parts of the book at the University of California at Santa Barbara, University of Virginia, Washington University in St. Louis, Wheaton College, and Yale University. Thank you to Jeffrey Barbeau, Joseph

Blankholm, Darren Dochuk, R. Marie Griffith, Claudrena Harold, Lerone Martin, and Sally Promey for those invitations. I also benefited from a year of conversations with the Black Studies and the Study of Religion working group, made possible with support from the Luce Foundation and ably guided by Monique Bedasse, Tiffany Hale, Joseph Winters, and Alex Alston. An additional anonymous review, courtesy of Oxford University Press, was especially helpful at just the right time.

So many others contributed in ways big and small. Conversations with David Daniels about Charles Price Jones deepened my understanding of the early history of black Pentecostal traditions (which · I know well, on experiential terms, in the present) discussed in chapter 2. Rapping with Joshua Bennett about the theoretical and aesthetic resources of Afro-Protestantism was both inspiring and enlightening. An email exchange with Pamela Klassen very early in the writing helped clarify, more than she could have known, what I was trying to get at in my thinking about Afro-Protestantism in relationship to the broader spectrum of black Christianity/ies. Larry Murphy dug into the archives of the Society for the Study of Black Religion and sent me a CD of Charles Long's 1980 state of the field address. Mayra Rivera's feedback on an earlier version of the introduction helped me clarify several of my claims, especially concerning the idea of Afro-Protestantism as a North American story and a formation of the nation-state (i.e., the United States).

A year spent as a visiting fellow at Yale University's Institute for Sacred Music provided the space (physical and intellectual) necessary for me to begin thinking about this book on its own terms, as well as to begin considering what might come next. Thank you to Martin Jean, Sally Promey, and the ISM community for their hospitality.

For a second time, Jana Riess's developmental and copyediting skills both reshaped and sharpened the content and form of the entire manuscript. Thank you, Jana! And a second thank you also goes to Kate Babbit, for indexing and, yet again, another pair of editing eyes.

Working with Oxford University Press has been just as much a pleasure the second go round too. Theo Calderara and his team shepherded this book, from acquisition through production, with tremendous care and great patience. For that I'm grateful.

Introduction

On the Life and Death of "The Black Church"

In February 2010, the *Huffington Post* went public with its plans for a new dedicated section on the popular political news website. A blog post authored by the site's founder opened with a revelation. "I've always been fascinated by religion," Ariana Huffington confessed. As if breaking popular dinner table decorum, she proceeded to wax nostalgic about the religion of her youth, providing images of the material cultures and sensory memories—"of summer wool and candle smoke" and "widows in black kerchiefs"—from the churches of her native Greece. As an adult, a publisher, and a public figure, Huffington was no less convinced of religion's continued importance. Moving from her own religious past to the purpose of her media empire's newest venture, she preached, "I believe that we are hardwired for the sacred, that the instinct for spirituality is part of our collective DNA."[1]

This new web portal would provide a democratic space for reasoned discussion, facilitating, Huffington explained further, "an open and fearless dialogue about all the ways religion affects both our personal and our public lives." In this way, it aimed to serve as a corrective to a climate defined by divisions between Right and Left, which had long been noted as reshaping the American religious landscape during the latter half of the twentieth century.[2] Things had only become more divisive in the new millennium, especially in the years after 9/11. Not only would *HuffPost Religion* feature informed commentary about the role of religion in public life; it would offer resources for spiritual formation. The new site was to be a place where critical analysis would be complemented by the pursuit of self-actualization. And it behooved readers to take note. Huffington ended her introduction with an exhortation to participate in the dialogue. She borrowed her invitation from the German-Swiss artist Hermann Hesse: "Ask your soul!"[3]

Black is a Church. Josef Sorett, Oxford University Press. © Oxford University Press 2023.
DOI: 10.1093/oso/9780190615130.003.0001

Though Ariana Huffington announced the new spiritual instal-
lation of her grand media vision, she would not oversee day-to-day
affairs. For this role she enlisted an individual whose very DNA
suggested that he was predestined to preside over the de facto Judeo-
Christian culture that had come to define American public life since
World War II. Paul Raushenbush, an ordained Baptist minister and
then chaplain at Princeton University, was hired to lead *HuffPost
Religion*. Raushenbush was the inheritor of what is imagined to be
the very essence of "good religion" in the United States. He was born
into a mixed-faith family of progressive and reasoning Protestants
and Jews, aligned with the political norms of American democracy.[4] In addition to his academic training at Union Theological
Seminary in New York, Raushenbush is the great-grandson of Walter
Rauschenbusch, who authored the signal text of the Social Gospel,
Christianity and the Social Crisis (1907). He is also a great-grandson
of Louis D. Brandeis, the progressive legal crusader who, in 1916, became the first Jewish justice on the U.S. Supreme Court. By birthright,
then, with Paul Raushenbush at the editorial helm, *HuffPost Religion*
was well equipped to help right the wrong role that religion had come
to play in fomenting America's culture wars.

Despite its clear liberal commitments, Ariana Huffington's an-
nouncement was relatively nonpartisan. Raushenbush's introductory editorial began in a similar fashion. *HuffPost Religion* would be
a platform for perspectives from "across the religious spectrum," he
explained. However, Raushenbush clarified, it would by design provide
a "forum for how religion is and *should be* functioning" (italics mine).[5]
Here a clear prescriptive concern began to emerge alongside the site's
commitments to description and analysis. Raushenbush's first blog as
editor, as if a postmodern epistle, was tellingly titled "Dear Religious
(and Sane) America." *HuffPost Religion* would provide a "sane middle
way" between the excessive passions of the Religious Right and Islamic
extremism, on one hand, and the New Atheists, on the other. These two
competing camps were cast here in familiar terms, as vitriolic foes in
the most recent staging of religion versus the modern world. Standing
in this gap, the civilizing logics of an unnamed liberal Protestantism,
updated as Judeo-Christian democratic norms, would provide the
bridge of civil discourse that *HuffPost Religion* aimed to build.

HuffPost Religion, to be sure, was by no means founded as a Christian blog. Nor was it simply a platform to disseminate the views of the interfaith preacher serving as its editor. In this regard, the roster of writers featured at the time of the launch exemplified the portal's liberal Protestant commitments even as it confirmed that religious diversity would be valued over an exclusively Christian vision. Included in this inaugural group of essayists were the evangelical author and political organizer Jim Wallis, a leading advocate for an evangelical Left whose essay named the recent "Great Recession" as a spiritual crisis. The self-help guru Deepak Chopra claimed that "Only Spirituality Can Solve the Problems of the World." Eboo Patel, president of Interfaith America (then Interfaith Youth Core; where, just a few years later, Raushenbush would begin working), offered a practical portrait of "The Pluralist Next Door." Activist nun Sister Joan Chittister diagnosed a "changing" Catholic Church. Rabbi Or Rose put forward a Jewish environmental ethic. And meditation expert Sharon Salzberg offered a Buddhist reflection on a middle way between overindulgence and self-hatred. From the site's initial content and contributors, the presence of persons from a variety of religious, racial, and ethnic backgrounds was clear. So was their shared interest in speaking across discrete religious traditions and the prevailing cultural divide. An interreligious project was an explicit priority for *HuffPost Religion*, as was pushing back against the political gains of the Religious Right.[6]

Princeton professor Eddie Glaude was the only participant in the launch who directly focused on African American religion and culture.[7] His contribution, "The Black Church Is Dead," proved to be the most popular in the inaugural series, garnering roughly twice as many "likes" and "shares" on Facebook as Chopra's essay, which was a distant second. Glaude's was the lone black voice in this liberal religious virtual launch. Yet it did the lion's share of the work of promotion and social media engagement.[8] Perhaps none of this is surprising, given the disproportionate weight of the nation's moral vision that black people—and African American Protestants specifically—have long been expected to shoulder. By far the least optimistic in this first ensemble of essays, Glaude's contribution was also quite different from the others. While fellow contributor Patel mobilized Martin Luther King Jr. to make a claim for religious pluralism and drew upon W. E. B. Du Bois to sketch the contours of religion writ large, Glaude focused squarely on the inner workings and historical evolution of a very specific Christian (and black) tradition. He made no mention of any "great world house," to borrow Patel's phrase, which was borrowed from King. Nor did he call for an ecumenical model of interfaith (or interracial) engagement. Instead, Glaude zeroed in on one particular house that race and religion conspired to build—namely, Afro-Protestantism—and its relationship to Black America and the nation as a whole. In doing so, he presented "members and preachers" of "The Black Church" with what he hoped was "an opportunity to breathe new life into what it means to be black and Christian."[9]

On Elegizing "The Black Church"

Beyond the pages of *HuffPost Religion*, Glaude's elegy sparked a new, if familiar, conversation concerning the role of "The Black Church" in the United States. Rather than a call to engage with the practices of religious pluralism, Glaude diagnosed what he took to be the decline of a single sacred institution, religious and racial at once. Such an observation would seem somewhat counterintuitive. Scholars of American religious history have long noted the decline of mainline (read: white) Christianity without documenting any similar development within black churches. To the contrary, African American religion has long figured as a vibrant religious foil to the larger narrative of a secularizing West. Appeals to King, like the one made by Patel, as well as the appeal of black artistic traditions and the embodied worship forms (i.e., gospel music, the shout, call and response) associated with Afro-Protestantism, worked to substantiate such claims. Yet things were not as they might seem, Glaude suggested, and persistent pleas to King might even be part of the problem. They obscured the complicated and multifaceted history of black Christianity, as well as the evolving demands made on churches in the contemporary moment. Glaude urged readers to reconsider the terms of their present existence, to "find their prophetic voices" and to "work on behalf of those who suffer most."[10]

The essay struck a nerve with black Christians, clergy and lay, of all variations. It also provoked a response from scholars of American religion across the country. Along the way, it created a firestorm of media interest. What is (and was) "The Black Church"? What of its relationship and responsibilities to black communities? And the nation and the world? By the standards of a pre–"Black Twitter" period, Glaude's essay went viral, as it was linked to roughly two thousand times.[11] It sparked a plethora of rejoinders across the blogosphere, including an online academic forum—featuring six scholars plus a response by Glaude—on the popular religion-themed website *Religion Dispatches*.[12] Eventually, the debate made its way onto the pages of the *New York Times*, where Samuel Freedman wrote about it in his "On Religion" column. Freedman's story, in turn, inspired additional interviews and stories on several public radio stations.[13]

In the interest of full disclosure, this recounting is not simply a dispassionate recording of a now decade-old debate. I, too, threw several irons in this fire. I participated in the *Religion Dispatches* roundtable and engaged in a one-on-one dialogue with Glaude on the virtual platform bloggingheads.tv. Several months later, with colleague Fredrick Harris, I helped organize a panel at Columbia University. *Is the Black Church Dead? A Roundtable on the Future of Black Churches* featured, alongside Glaude, several prominent preachers and scholars, including Anthea Butler, Eboni Marshall Turman, Obery Hendricks, and Otis Moss III. My purpose in outlining these exchanges, to be clear, isn't to settle a score or rehash old news. I have no desire to defend any position I took back in 2010. Nor do I wish to rekindle the debate in the present moment.

Instead, my aim here and throughout this book is to invite a closer consideration of the terms through which "The Black Church," as an institution and an idea, has been conceived of within black social life and beyond. My goal is also to explore how Afro-Protestantism has proven to be a special problem for black thought. With regard to the former half of this equation, I am especially interested in tracking, across the long arc of American history, the ways that Afro-Protestantism has provided a set of logics—academic and everyday—through which blackness has been, and continues to be, imagined and embodied, theorized and practiced. As for the latter, my concern is with how "The

Black Church" has figured (or not) within academic discourse, especially in the context of the interdisciplinary form of inquiry known as Black Studies. Of course, these overlapping concerns—between past and present, sacred and secular, scholarly and popular, the American and the black—are always already entangled. And in both cases, my most fundamental question concerns how "The Black Church"—Afro-Protestantism, as I refer to it throughout this book—has enchanted and informed, defined and delimited the contents and forms of modern black subjectivity and social life.

What was so remarkable about the entire exchange that ensued in the wake of Glaude's *HuffPost Religion* article in 2010 is that what was for a long time primarily an academic problem somehow transformed into a popular debate. So much for the long-standing divide between town and gown. If only for a brief moment, here the public stakes of a scholarly argument became clear. Indeed, scholars of religion in the United States have long been interested in the special place of black churches in the nation's political and social landscape. As one interlocutor highlighted, Glaude's observations extended a set of ongoing critiques leveled by black intellectuals across the twentieth century, including theologians James Cone and Gayraud Wilmore, sociologists C. Eric Lincoln and E. Franklin Frazier, and the writer-activists Richard Wright and W. E. B. Du Bois, to name just a few. Each of these men (a not insignificant point), as well as many others, have in different ways announced the decline of The Black Church.[14] Yet, if the argument was already so familiar—old news, one might say—then why the vociferous response in 2010?

Certainly, a significant number of members and leaders of black churches took offense at Glaude's hyperbole. Some dismissed his arguments as those of an out-of-touch academic. Others argued that their own churches and ministries were ample evidence that the institution was alive and well. Still others asked, *Even if black churches had work to do, who was he, as an Ivy League professor, to turn a private argument—about the intramural dynamics of black life—into a public affair?* Yet this was more than a matter of dirty laundry being aired. After all, scholars of religion in America—and various kinds of presumable outsiders to black churches—were no less captivated by and critical of his claims. Perhaps what was so exciting about the public response to Glaude's elegy was that, for some of us scholars, our research questions were being taken seriously by the very communities that were the subjects of our works, but that were also, quite often, the very people and communities that first set us on a scholarly path. Suddenly expertise in and experience within black churches had popular cachet. A claim to knowledge—intellectual but also intimate—of Afro-Protestantism was, for a moment, a credential for public relevance. The lines between theory and practice, or between intellect and identity, were, it seemed, powerfully fused.

The only consensus, if any, that emerged in this most recent iteration of a century-long conversation was that "The Black Church" was not, nor had it ever been, a monolith. The singular rhetoric was, rather, an umbrella term and a trope for a plurality of black Christian experiences. Additionally, black churches were forthrightly named as not necessarily being the politically progressive institutions they are often assumed to be. Instead, the endless invocations of Martin Luther King Jr. that still prevail in American public life were identified as masking a much more complicated reality. As Glaude put it, "too often black churches and those who pastor them have been and continue to be quite conservative." In truth, King was more the exception than the rule of black Christian life. If nothing else, this conflation of Afro-Protestantism with progressive activism would be put to rest, once and for all. Or maybe, as Glaude hoped, his provocation would encourage others to advance a new prophetic politics for the twenty-first century from the institutional bases of black churches. Ironically, if absent a coherent political vision, the continued vitality of black churches was witnessed to in the cacophony of (contradictory) voices that contributed to these conversations.

For a few months, African American religious life was afforded a peculiar public platform. Popular media outlets took notice, and not because of a sexual transgression, a financial scandal, or the exigencies of an election season. In short, "The Black Church" was *the* story, and a decade before Henry Louis Gates Jr.'s PBS mini-series on the subject. Never mind that the context for the debate was the *Huffington Post* launching its expansion into the virtual worlds of religious pluralism. Neither Ariana Huffington nor Paul Raushenbush could have predicted that Glaude's essay would create a groundswell. For once, the media seemed genuinely interested in something that typically occupied the attention of only a small subfield of scholars and practitioners. To be sure, academics are often as skeptical of media inquiries as we are of grand decrees—whether announcing the decline of mainline Protestantism or declaring the death of God. Here, however, was an instance in which a media investment appeared to be aligned with academic interests, either concerned with or confused by the complexities of the black Christian experience. Indeed, a public audience was primed for the conversation. A provocative claim placed in the right platform, Glaude's essay appeared to be an instance of an academic idea that had found its time.

Black Studies and the Problem(s) of "The Black Church"

When the *Huffington Post* inadvertently reignited a long-standing debate about the special significance of the church, within both the American cultural imaginary and in black social life, a public portal was also opened to the academic study of religion. Within the context of religious studies, Christianity had been the target of a sustained set of critiques since at least the 1960s. And for several decades scholars had been invested in undoing what has rightly been identified as Christian hegemony, and with decentering, more specifically, "The Black Church."[15] In more recent years, scholarship in this vein has done much to demonstrate that, empirically speaking, there is no such thing as *The* Black Church—as Barbara Dianne Savage averred in her 2008 book, *Your Spirits Walk Beside Us: The Politics of Black Religion*. In its most hyperbolic forms, this argument has taken the form of elegy, such was the case with Glaude's 2010 *HuffPost Religion* blog. This tradition of critique, in a strange turn, even led some scholars to call for a "moratorium" on the very phrase "The Black Church."[16] More commonly, however, the aim has simply been to historicize the emergence of the term—that is, to explain the historical and political contexts that gave rise to the idea of "the Negro Church"—and to make clear how a particular idea of "The Black Church" constrains, to this day, what we see (or fail to see) in the social world.

In this regard, perhaps no scholar has been more influential than the late historian of religion Charles Long. In his now classic essay, "Perspectives for a Study of Afro-American Religion in the United States" (1971), Long issued a clarion call for scholars to study black religion "outside the normative framework of Christian theology."[17] For Long, under the rubrics of the "extra-church," studying religion outside "the Christian theological tradition" required examining black culture in ways that defied the binary logics of sacred and secular. One might examine African-derived spiritual traditions like the Yoruba religion in Brazil, Vodun (or Voodoo) in Haiti, and Conjure (or Hoodoo) in the southern United States. Yet one could also attend to religious ideas as they circulated in presumably "secular" forms of black cultural expression, such as folklore, music, and the arts. In Long's formulation, both the latter and the former constituted "extra-church" forms of religious ideas and practices as they animated black life in the Americas.

Christianity, Long explained, constituted "the cultural categories of the American reality." As such, it hindered the study of black social life not just by limiting the sources and sites of study. As a methodology, vis-à-vis theology, it imposed and reinforced a set of colonial logics that rendered opaque a significant portion—that is, the non-Christian dimensions—of the African American experience. In this view, for Long, any division between sacred and secular was less important than the manner in which Christianity worked through a set of colonial frameworks to make a vast array of ideas and practices illegible—at least as what we identify as "religion." Accordingly, Long's definition of religion—as "orientation in the ultimate sense, that is, how one comes to terms with the ultimate significance of one's place in the world"—served to counter the categorical limitations of Christianity and to clarify, with regard to the black community, "the hermeneutical problem."[18]

All of black life, "experience, expression, motivations, intentions, behaviors, styles, and rhythms," were to be plumbed for religious meaning(s). Yet by placing the ideas and practices made legible by his broader definition of religion under the shared umbrella of "extra-church," Long both challenged and confirmed the colonial logics of the Christian and theological terms that he sought to challenge. Locating African-derived religious traditions alongside presumably "secular" cultural forms under the sign of the "extra-church" effectively blurred together questions of geographic and religious difference. It also left unaddressed the question of what comprised the "extra-church" other than alleged alienation from or opposition to Christianity writ large. Further, Long argued that anything identified under this rubric constituted a more authentic reflection of the black experience. That is, he asserted that any religious form found outside of churches better revealed "the true situation of the black community."[19] While Long's critique of the dominance of a Christian lens—in both black and white—was well-warranted in the 1970s (and remains so today), what holds as "true" in his account begs for interrogation. The analytical blurring—under the sign of the "extra-church"—witnessed here between black secular formations, on one hand, and matters of religious and geographic difference, on the other, merits much closer consideration.

All of the issues that Long outlined in the 1970s were at stake, even if unnamed, in Glaude's 2010 black church elegy. The omission of such scholarly specifics was, perhaps, a product of the context in which his claims appeared: that is, a new website focused on the role of religion in public life. Accordingly, Glaude's contribution was described as "an obituary for the black church . . . the Digital-Age equivalent of nailing a set of theses to a church door."[20] As much as Glaude's essay befitted an audience interested in religion, his claims concerning the declining relevance of the church in modern black life fit squarely within a broader body of scholarship on the black experience—namely, Black Studies. Rather consistently across the contexts of literature, politics, and scholarship, the decline of religion has been a—if not *the*—primary theoretical premise of the modern world and a special problem for black thought. As persistent as it is imprecise and often unsubstantiated, this has been no less true (in fact, is perhaps *more* true) for the rise of Afro-modernity. And Black Studies, on this matter, has been no exception to the rule. During the first half of the twentieth century, Du Bois, Frazier, and Wright, as was noted earlier, and many other black intellectuals offered some version of Glaude's diagnosis of black church decline. Yet despite Glaude's prime academic post as chair of Princeton's Center for African American Studies, the broader field of Black Studies barely seemed to take notice.

Even with its robust history of oppositional politics, Black Studies has generally, if uncritically, adopted the orthodoxy of academia's ostensibly secular lens. Within the interdisciplinary context of Black Studies, religion—and Afro-Protestantism in particular—has remained undertheorized. To be sure, due attention has been given to African American religious thought and practice. Even still, within Black Studies, religion has remained largely marginal in terms of how the cultural, intellectual, and political tradition is construed and contested. Moreover, an acknowledgment of the historic significance of religion (and the church, specifically) has coexisted alongside a strident critique of religion as *the* impediment to black progress. Religion, one could say, has been everywhere and nowhere at the same time. Yet rarely, if at all, have the kinds of critical questions posed by Long concerning religion made it into what might be considered the major debates within Black Studies. While by no means a monolithic intellectual endeavor, a range of competing camps within Black Studies, if by default or disinterest, seem to agree on this matter. And this apparent consensus prevails even in the face of a set of intellectual positions that animate the field today (under a variety of names), including conceptual approaches that attribute a certain kind of spiritual or sacred value to black subjectivity and social life, theories that interpret the structural and racial logics of modernity on terms that might best be understood as religious or theological, and criticism that enlists religious sources and practices to underwrite a theory and performance of blackness.[21]

Perhaps the best evidence of this orthodoxy, which also has a large measure of popular currency, is the term "Intersectionality." With her roots in legal education and critical race theory, Kimberlé Crenshaw developed the term to account for the ways intersecting identities shape policy agendas and, as such, increase (or decrease) access to resources and degrees of social marginalization under the presumed (racial) neutrality of the law. In doing so, Intersectionality helps to map how a range of identities, including race, gender, class, sexual orientation, age, and disability, shape experience in the social world.[22] Yet strikingly, the term and its typical usages stop short of accounting for different kinds of religious identities, practices, and traditions, all of which mark social difference—marginalization and inclusion—in similarly powerful ways. Is one to draw the conclusion, then, that the spiritual is socially insignificant? Or that the religion(s) one identifies, affiliates with, or practices has no bearing on access to resources and opportunities or the protections of citizenship granted by law? Does the social world or the state not take notice when one identifies, or is marked as, for example, either Christian, Jewish, or Muslim? And what of those who don't fit within the rubrics of the popular "trifaith" model?[23]

Within the context of black studies, perhaps the closest that these questions have come to a broad hearing is within debates about the place of religion (really, Christian churches) in the modern civil rights movement. To be sure, images of Martin Luther King Jr. and black clergy loom large in the histories and the iconography of the 1960s. As has already been noted, such imagery has led to an association of black churches with progressive politics. In his 1986 book *The Jesse Jackson Phenomenon: The Crisis of Purpose in Afro-American Politics*, political scientist Adolph Reed squarely challenged this sentiment. Reed argued that the political role played by churches was more symbolic than it was substantive or statistically significant. While black churches certainly served an organizing role in the movement, Reed notes, most were not aligned with an emancipatory politics and resisted radical change. Indeed, to the contrary, the cohort of clergy who marched with King were in the minority with regard to the predominant political ethos of black churches. As Reed surmised then (and similar to what Glaude broadcast in 2010), the idea of black churches as a site of progressive politics was more myth than fact.[24] As has been pointed out many times in the intervening years, the relationship between religion and politics in African American life has been much more complicated than a matter of "accommodation vs. resistance."[25] Even still, radical politics—and black radicalism more specifically—have more often than not been understood in opposition to religion, or as originating outside of "The Black Church."

A particular investment in churches on the part of black Americans, for that matter, has been cited by the historian Winston James as a mark of distinction from black people in other diasporic contexts, such as the Caribbean. James cites churches as more than symbolically significant in sourcing a tradition of black American political conservativism (in terms of comfort with the status quo). Black radicalism, in his view, is posited as secular, if not antireligious, or as grounded in religious traditions (albeit unnamed) other than Christianity and/or in geographies outside the United States. Given the centrality of Christianity (Protestant and Catholic), past and present, across the Caribbean, this is a striking claim. Yet, once again, black radicalism (and a capacity for political resistance more broadly) is associated with secularism and/or non-Christian religious traditions that are imagined as somehow foreign to Black America.[26] Ironically, we might note that both Reed's and James's arguments are in keeping (or, at least, not at odds) with what Long asserted back in 1971—namely, that the "extra-church" was more aligned with "the true situation of the black community."

Be it Reed's observation (drawing on historical and social scientific evidence) regarding black church mythologies or the unsubstantiated identifying of black radicalism by James as foreign or opposed to Afro-Protestantism, my point here is not to superficially highlight a couple of isolated assertions of individual scholars—here, by a political scientist and historian, respectively. These two examples (from the 1980s and 1990s) are significant insofar as I take them to still be indicative of a tacit (and often explicit) secularism that has occupied the position of orthodoxy in black studies. Religion as assumed, elided, and an afterthought—or better yet, religion as a problem for black politics—all at once.

One important exception to this rule is Robin D. G. Kelley's 1996 essay in the *Journal of American History*, "We Are Not What We Seem: Rethinking Black Working Class Opposition in the Jim Crow South." Here Kelley raised a series of questions that invited historians of the black experience (and the black South specifically) to consider more carefully the ways in which religious ideas and practices, including prayer, "belief that God is by one's side," "talking in tongues," Conjure, and a "sign from above," might be understood as part of a "strategy of resistance." On Kelley's account, only one historian since Du Bois—the late Vincent Harding—had "been bold enough to assert a connection between the spirit and spirit world of African Americans and political struggle."[27] A good number of historians have since heeded Kelley's call, as have some Black Studies scholars working in other disciplines and (interdisciplinary) methods. Yet rarely, if ever, has religion been viewed as a major trajectory in Black Studies more broadly. Nor has it yet to produce a rethinking of the larger conceptual questions that Long posed. For a more contemporary example, one might consider the 2014 "States of Black Studies" issue of *The Black Scholar*, which featured an interdisciplinary roster of some of the leading Black Studies scholars, who work with a variety of theories, methods, and foci in the interdisciplinary field. Just as Intersectionality's omission regarding the social significance of religion raises a set of questions, the absence of religion in this important special issue reveals much about the state(s) of the field.[28] There is, perhaps, reason to think that this trend is changing, given the growing interest in the work of the late political scientist and scholar of black radicalism Cedric J. Robinson. As Erica Edwards has recently noted, throughout his body of work Robinson wrote incisively of the political power of religious traditions, including Christianity, in shaping black political and cultural activism.[29]

My point here, to clarify, is not to claim that religion, or "The Black Church," has been an unequivocal force for black good, be it cultural and political resistance, radical social transformation, collective affirmation, or personal resilience. It is only to suggest, following Kelley circa 1993, that black studies might benefit from a rethinking of its secularist assumptions. To put it another way, as this book tries to do, there is still much to learn from interrogating the relationships between the theoretical maps of secularism (and, necessarily, religion) and the cultural territories that they claim to apprehend in the context of black life—and for the field of black studies.[30] By highlighting a prevailing secular orthodoxy, *Black Is a Church* aims to show that, contrary to prevailing orthodoxies, Afro-Protestantism has for centuries comprised the center of a tradition of black theory and practice even as it has been relegated to margins of black studies.

Black Is a Church

Black Is a Church is one of the first books to linger at the nexus of the religious/secular entanglement within the context of African American culture.[31] In doing so, it tracks a persistent logic, evident in Long's 1971 essay, and follows the evolving relationship between racial (black) authenticity and religious (Christian) orthodoxy across three centuries. This pairing has been anything but exclusively one of oppositions, as Long seemed to suggest. That premise, instead, might be flipped on its head and restated in the form of a question: Are religious orthodoxy and racial authenticity (really, the Christian and the black) necessarily at odds? Or, better yet, how best to understand the complex entanglements of blackness and Christianity in time and space? This most basic question provides an entree into debates about "the secular" even as it complicates common assumptions about what the category of "black religion" is taken to represent, stand in for, and contain.

In taking up these concerns *Black Is a Church* tries to distill a set of more specific arguments that are often up for grabs in debates around the religious/secular binary as they have shaped scholarly and popular interpretations of black cultures and communities. In doing so, this book attends to the ways that race and religion coalesced early in American history under the sign of black subjectivity and social life and the collective formation that later came to be known as "The Black Church." *Black Is a Church* foregrounds "religion" (and accordingly, the secular) alongside categories (i.e., nation, gender, class, sexuality) that have been more readily employed to theorize "the black"—and the forms of difference within blackness—on more precise terms.[32] Here the aim is to account for the entangled logics of European Christianity, white supremacy, and colonialism that converged to define the modern category of religion and make the social order of the "New World," which then also created the conditions of possibility for the emergence of black subjectivity and social life, at least in North America, on decidedly Protestant terms.[33]

As has already been suggested, the problem with "The Black Church" is, at least in part, the assumption of singularity, as postmodern critiques have produced a healthy skepticism toward any metanarrative. In this view, the theological and political shorthand of "The Black Church" both elides difference across a variety of black churches and reinforces the idea of particular kinds of black churches and specific kinds of black Christian practice as normative. That is, appeals to "The Black Church" have essentialized race (blackness) and religion (Christianity) toward the end of rendering mainline

Afro-Protestantism (i.e., Methodist and Baptist denominations) as the *true* black church. All other black churches and black Christians, in this view, are aberrations. This particular entanglement, then, has worked to determine, for scholars and practitioners, a normative vision of "The Black Church" as what truly counts as black religion—and blackness, in general, for that matter.[34] In this way, a particular Christian orthodoxy and a politics of racial authenticity came together to set the terms for the study of "The Negro Church," such that it privileged an Afro-Protestantism, aligned with democracy and oriented to confront Jim Crow, as both the object of study and the norm for practice. The force of the conjoined logics of (racial) authenticity and (religious) orthodoxy also left scholars reluctant to engage with what were perceived as less legitimate displays of black Christianity.[35] Here one might note, as this book tries to show, how narrating the history of "The Black Church" brings to light the normative reasoning of religious liberalism—and liberal Protestantism more specifically—that shaped both race politics *and* the politics of studying religion in the United States during the first half of the twentieth century and beyond.[36]

The problem of Christianity, to be sure, is not simply the suggestion that black churches are monolithic. What also comes to the fore is the implicit, yet no less significant, national cast of this normative narrative of Afro-Protestantism. Unpacking the trope of "The Black Church" requires recognizing that the phrase also participates in (and is the product of) a discourse of citizenship, American nationalism, and perhaps even empire. Talk about black churches, even in the plural, typically assumes the geographic locale of the United States. What follows from this, then, is the recognition that Afro-Protestantism—and black Christianity more broadly—has never been representative of the entire repertoire of religious practices, ideas, and organizational arrangements that comprise the spiritual worlds of the African diaspora. Black churches ought not be conflated with or confused with black religion. And the United States has never been the sole, or even the primary, province in which black people in the Americas have practiced their "religion"—Christianity included.

Long-standing transnational networks and perpetual (forced and chosen) migration and movement have facilitated, sustained, and transformed black social life in ways that frustrate a privileged narrative of "The Black Church" in the United States. Black religions have been practiced both within and across the borders of various nation-states, such that hemispheric frames and "Africana religions" are helpful analytical rubrics—at least in clarifying precisely what is conjured, vis-à-vis the nation-state, by the term "The Black Church."[37] Otherwise put, black religions comprise an array of complex, multivalent ideas and practices, which often bend and blur the boundaries of specific traditions while, in real time, traversing the borders of various nation-states. Moreover, even within the bounds of a specific nation-state (even, yes, the United States), black religions—under the terms of modernity—are always practiced, by definition, under conditions of dislocation and diaspora.[38]

Ultimately, in troubling "The Black Church" a proverbial diaspora (of black Christianities and black religions) comes to the fore. Together these intellectual currents clarify the ways that race, religion, and nation (but also class, gender, and sexuality) have worked together to construct and circumscribe the field—of practice and study—in particular ways. That is, they work together to map and make the church in the likeness of a particular kind of North American (middle-class, male, heteronormative) story. And each of these discursive logics is at play, even as they are often left unnamed, in every appeal to "The Black Church." At the same time that we can observe the modern, presumably secular logics that animated the "The Black Church" from its beginnings, Christianity was, conversely, made constitutive to the formation of blackness. By this I do not mean to assert a constructive claim for any particular version of Christianity as normative for black life. Nor do I mean to suggest that black people have any kind of claim to (or monopoly on) an imagined authentic or true Christianity.

As *Black Is a Church* tries to illustrate throughout the pages that follow, the mutually reinforcing discourses of racial authenticity and religious orthodoxy came together, over time, in such a way that Christianity (largely, although not exclusively, some form of Protestantism) was made constitutive of the contents and forms of blackness. As such, we might ask: If "The Black Church" is not to be taken for granted as normative, and if "extra-church traditions" are not taken to be more "true," and if the idea of a black secular is not deemed implausible, then how are we to understand the relationship between

Christianity, never a single thing, and the entirety of African American life, in all of its diversity? One might ask: How did Afro-Protestantism become instantiated in and shape the contours of black subjectivity and social life across time and space, distilled through a range of institutional configurations, political ideologies, and cultural imaginings? And how is it that across a variety of contexts, in various registers, appeals to "church" have often constituted a conjuring of blackness? These questions, and others, sit at the center of the arguments and examples that organize *Black Is a Church*.

As much as this book aims to unpack a bundle of questions entangled at the nexus of theories of secularism and the study of black culture, it does so by narrating what might, more helpfully, be understood as the heterodox history of Afro-Protestantism. To be clear, I have no sense that a turn to the "extra-church" lends itself to an evasion of the creative and critical powers of Afro-Protestantism's hegemony. Indeed, looking outside Christian churches and examining the broader cultural and political landscape of black social life would seem only to confirm the persistent and pervasive powers of "The Black Church" and the disciplining logics of Christianity more generally. Again, to be clear, I mean such a claim neither as a normative proposition nor as an apologetic in support of black Christian privilege. Nor do I mean to suggest that all of black life displays an institutional allegiance to "The Black Church," or that black people think in ways that neatly adhere to the categories of Christian orthodoxy. Rather, what I hope the episodic account put forward in this book illustrates is the fact that Afro-Protestantism—even in its essential difference(s)—is both part and parcel of the modern West and a distinctly American experiment. Otherwise put, black subjectivity and social life (in its individual and corporate forms)—that is, blackness or the black—is illustrative of a set of prevailing logics that recall, to paraphrase the literary theorist Sacvan Berkovitch, the Protestant origins of American selfhood and social life.[39] Afro-Protestantism, then, is decidedly black even as it is distinctively American.

In my first book, *Spirit in the Dark: A Religious History of Racial Aesthetics*, I tried to tell a story that mapped the complexity and diversity of religious ideas that animated a debate about black art and culture across much of the twentieth century. At the same time, I asserted—without full or sustained argument—that Afro-Protestantism was never unseated or decentered in what I named as the history of racial aesthetics, from the New Negro era to the age of the Black Arts. Instead, I argued that black artists and intellectuals both undermined and reinscribed the prominence of Afro-Protestantism by advancing a grammar of spirit under the sign of an aesthetic that was imagined—albeit not without debate—to serve the ends of race politics. By following the frequent pairing of church and spirit, *Spirit in the Dark* attempted to play with tensions between the literary possibilities of a nascent religious pluralism and the abiding significance of "The Black Church." As a follow-up and follow-through—but more prequel than sequel—to such claims, *Black Is a Church* offers an extended argument that demonstrates the abiding powers of Afro-Protestantism from the late eighteenth century up through the present day.

Going one step further, a basic contention of this book is that the modern secular notion of "the black" is, in fact, a religious idea, the product of a distinctly Christian genealogy. Moreover, "The Black Church" is made legible by (and becomes legible in) its adherence to the registers of (American) secularism, that is, as a practice of (or a failure to achieve the disciplines of) citizenship and democracy. Accordingly, *Black Is Church* is a theory of black religion, by which I mean Afro-Protestantism. And by this I mean that blackness, more simply, is a Protestant formation. Otherwise put, the contents and forms of Christian faith were encoded, through the forces of history, within the practices of blackness. Each of the chapters that follow serves to illustrate the claim that implicit, and often explicit, in most talk (even so-called secular talk) of blackness in the United States one can identify a constitutive measure of Protestant Christianity. Across the spheres of literature, politics, and scholarship, modern articulations of blackness—evangelical in their propensity for expressive enthusiasm and capacity to demand allegiance even while appealing to the authority of literacy and reason—have, at the same time, generally held to an orthodoxy of heterodoxy. That is, "the black"—which is to say, Afro-Protestantism—is by definition a hybrid formation, a product and performance, an idea and practice, resulting from (and dependent upon) contact and exchange, colonization and creolization, black and white, sacred and secular, race and religion, Christian and "extra-church."

Heterodoxy has been definitive of the whole that is Afro-Protestantism. In the same way, blackness has never been a single thing. Indeed, blackness, née Afro-Protestantism, has attempted to hold difference together. In other words, the terms under which Afro-Protestantism became constitutive of "the black" were at once consistent with the processes of a secularizing and Christianizing form of citizen-making. Blackness itself is inextricably tied and remains indebted to the story of this nation's Protestant iteration of secularism.[40] As has been true of the Black Arts, "The Black Church" (or black religion, or "the black") was made to bear the burdens of race politics, which has provided the conditions of possibility for a range of ironies. The discourse and practices of racial authenticity and religious orthodoxy have worked together in such a way as to obscure this heterodox history of Afro-Protestantism, or at least the ways in which it is commonly understood and imagined. Moreover, adherence to a particular alignment of orthodoxy or authenticity—what some might identify as a species of literalism—has often contained and obscured the presence of a quite robust heterodoxy. Conversely, an abiding investment in allowing for a heterodox set of ideas and practices to exist together (and perhaps even flourish) has often required and demanded a public espousal of what is often deemed to be a rigid (or literalist) orthodoxy. Otherwise put, sometimes the most public professions of what seem to be "conservative" or "fundamentalist" strains of Christian orthodoxy have coexisted alongside—and, one could argue, created the conditions of possibility for—some of the most queer social arrangements within the context of black churches and communities. Afro-Protestantism, which is to say blackness—as subjectivity, social formation, and discursive terrain—has facilitated, disciplined, and provided a stage for these seemingly contradicting possibilities.

Whether as a source of pride or the site of shame, "The Black Church" has overwhelmingly been figured as a political formation, rendered legible when made to align with a vision of progressive racial politics, that is, when in service to the political interests of "the race." This effectively secular politics of religious recognition prevailed even as black churches were often diagnosed as failing to achieve its aims. Instrumentalist interpretations and functionalist accounts have long held sway with regard to black cultural, intellectual, literary, and religious life alike. And Afro-Protestantism has been a powerful and persistent thread across these terrains. To clarify, I am not using the language of Afro-Protestantism (rather than "The Black Church") to suggest some entirely different phenomenon than the church. Rather, I appeal to Afro-Protestantism to provide some analytical distance from the overdetermined associations attached to "The Black Church," namely, the independent black church movement (i.e., black Baptists and Methodists starting in the early nineteenth century) and the institutions and denominations that followed. Afro-Protestantism, here, is still meant to reference actual churches, but also to acknowledge a pervasive set of ideas, affects, and affiliations that circulate beyond and in relationship to the physical space and place of "The Black Church."[41] It recognizes that the line between black churches and the communities they serve is difficult to draw without crooks, breaks, and fissures. Nor is it easily policed by professed (or denied) belief, confession, dogma, or revelation.

Interpreting Afro-Protestantism, again, requires us to pay attention to the discourses of class, gender, nation, sexuality, and all kinds of difference that have been managed and mobilized through the entangled logics of racial authenticity and religious orthodoxy. Altogether, then, the heterodox history of Afro-Protestantism evolved so as to imagine, name, make, and mark form(s) of modern black subjectivity and social life such that they responded to the vicissitudes of white supremacy while also refusing to reduce blackness to the limits of the interpretive horizon associated with Christian doctrinal orthodoxy. To my mind, modern black literary and cultural expression, activism, organizing, and intellectual life—each of which is often presumed to be secular— reflect a peculiarly Afro-Protestant mode of inquiry, inheritance, and repertoire. Afro-Protestantism, as such, is an ethical apparatus, institutional form, and aesthetic performance that animates (all) black subjectivity and social life, especially, but not solely, in the United States. Otherwise put, Afro-Protestantism constitutes a theory and practice of "the black."

Afro-Protestantism has figured centrally within a history of practices developed to conjure a black corporate identity and a collective sensibility.[42] Within a climate of national ambitions during the eighteenth and nineteenth centuries, independent black

churches participated in, and were infused with, the fervors of national aspirations. As the late historian James Melvin Washington
once observed, black churches possessed "the soul of a nation."[43]
Accordingly, black denominationalism was part and parcel of the
work of nation-building. Yet the circle of influence between race, religion, and nation was anything but unidirectional. Religion helped to
make the nation, just as religious institutions and racial identities were
made in the image of the nation. Black churches made citizens out of
members even when black people were not recognized as such under
the law. Black churches also helped to make gendered and classed
subjects. Citizenship, and consonantly "The Black Church," was thus
often imagined as a space allowing for the achievement of manhood
and "middle-class" status.[44] In this vein, Afro-Protestantism unfolded
as both political project and aesthetic vision, marked as modern by
its weaving together—under the sign of "The Black Church"—a
distinct account of race, religion, class, gender, and nation. That is,
Afro-Protestantism developed as a quintessentially American institution, assemblage, and episteme at once—a set of discursive logics,
structures of feeling, and social relations.

To the point, in noting the certain outward-extending influence of
Afro-Protestantism into the sphere of black social life, one can also
discern the making of a nation with the soul of a church. One might
aptly paraphrase Amiri Baraka's observation regarding the geographies that animate black imaginaries—which is to say, if "black is a
country," then most certainly, black is a church![45] To be clear, by positing blackness as a religious formation—a church, as it were—I do
not mean to reinscribe the logics of a romantic racialism wherein
African Americans are imagined as naturally religious or spiritual by
birthright. Nor do I mean to affirm or endorse the hold of a Christian
hegemony on black bodies and imaginations in everyday life or in lin-
gering theological visions for a field of academic inquiry. Instead, my
goal is to illustrate how, through the forces of history, the cultures and
structures of Afro-Protestantism were woven into the very fabric of
modern black subjectivity/ies and social life. *Black Is a Church*, as such,
is an account of how Afro-Protestantism came to constitute both the
terms of order *and* the order of things.[46] And to do so, the chapters
that follow turn from black churches proper—namely, "The Black

Church"—to the presumably "secular" annals of African American literary, political, and intellectual life.

Book Overview

Black Is a Church attempts to track the privileged place of Afro-Protestantism as it has simultaneously made and occupied the cultural, intellectual, and political maps of modern black life. Rather than following a tight chronology, *Black Is a Church* moves through a series of episodes located across the span of four centuries (from the late 1700s through the early 2000s). The narrative is held together by the play between close readings, theoretical concerns, and historical questions. Each of the episodes is organized around a concrete case from one of three arenas of African American life—the literary, the political, and the intellectual—that work together to illustrate the book's larger argument. To be clear, I recognize that each of these spheres remains entangled with the others in all of the moments that I examine. The division I am outlining, by way of chapter organization, is for emphasis and illustrative purposes. Each episode provides a distinct approach to the questions at hand. Together the episodes that comprise each chapter narrate a story about the ways in which black (American) culture and identity have been (and remain) animated by a particular Protestant logic that is often left unmarked even as it is assumed. Even the most ardent articulations of a black secularism, I argue, have extended and reinscribed an Afro-Protestant logic. Conversely, the terms of secularism have provided the conditions of possibility for Afro-Protestantism's public recognition. As such, *Black Is a Church* offers a theory of a black secularism that has frequently been enacted through a call for a renewed or reformed church, hence shedding light on the (racial) ironies of the American secular.

In chapter 1, I argue that Afro-Protestantism harbored literary ambitions and relied upon literary strategies to enunciate itself since the earliest years of its formation. To put it another way, African American religion emerged as a literary practice, and Afro-Protestantism was forged as and formed by a set of literary performances. Here I offer a reading of several slave narratives and spiritual autobiographies, especially as they have figured in standing theories of African American literary history. Calling attention to the tacit (and often proactive) embrace of a narrative of secularization, chapter 1 shows how the content of Protestant Christianity was essential to (and inseparable from) the establishment of the earliest black literary forms. Significantly, Christianity and colonialism are seen to coalesce in the working out of a (literary and reasoned) Afro-Protestant tradition, which took shape under the terms of conquest, contact, and enslavement in the early Americas. A close reading of the slave narratives helps to reveal how Christian and literary commitments came together to establish a New World tradition of Afro-Protestantism. The argument here is that, most concisely, black literature began on Afro-Protestant terms, and Afro-Protestantism was initiated as a literary performance. And it was in and out of this milieu that black subjects first emerged.

Chapter 2 moves from the emergence of Afro-Protestantism, as it was worked out in the slave narratives, to track its heterodox history in the convergence of literature, politics, and religion at the end of the nineteenth century. To do so, the chapter moves across a set of social movements to reveal how religious (Christian, really) aspirations animated the earliest calls for a "race literature," and "the color line" provided an organizing logic, even if not explicitly named as such, for religious innovations as divergent as the practices of pluralism on display at the first World's Parliament of Religions (1893) and the novel forms of Christianity associated with a Pentecostal movement emerging at the time. Examining a period that was described as both a "nadir" and a "renaissance" for black life in the United States, chapter 2 highlights how Afro-Protestantism evolved in at least two distinct— but not disconnected—trajectories: in the burgeoning institution of "The Negro Church" as it took on a more robust form *and* through nascent ideas about what is now commonly referred to as "African American literature," such as Victoria Earle Matthews's 1895 speech, "The Value of Race Literature." Finally, chapter 2 offers a reading of W. E. B. Du Bois's *The Souls of Black Folk* (1903), a text that thinks across and through these developments to offer a theory of religion for modern black life and that is also a distinctly Afro-Protestant performance.

In many respects the academic study of African American religion reached a point of critical maturity during the 1930s and early 1940s with the publication of such works as Benjamin E. Mays and Joseph Nicholson's *The Negro's Church* (1934), Mays's *The Negro's God as Reflected in His Literature*, Zora Neale Hurston's folklore writings, and Arthur Huff Fauset's *Black Gods of the Metropolis* (1944). Chapter 3 offers a novel entree into this key moment in the formation of the field. To do so, I turn from the literary and political traditions of Afro-Protestantism to more fully explore how a similar politics of religion impinged upon the scholarly pursuits of black intellectuals. More specifically, this chapter follows the founding and early years of *Phylon: An Atlanta University Journal of Race and Culture* during the 1940s, as a case study in how race politics and academic ambitions converged to privilege a particular form of Afro-Protestantism as the true site, source, and subject of black religion.

Finally, in chapter 4 I bring the book's long narrative from the late eighteenth century up through the new millennium with a discussion of three more recent episodes that illustrate the persistence of the art and politics of Afro-Protestantism in the three spheres discussed in chapters 1, 2, and 3. Moving from scholarship (black religious studies) during the 1980s to literature (black cultural criticism) in the 1990s and ending with politics (via #BlackLivesMatter and black writing) in the 2010s, *Black Is a Church* comes to a close with an illustration of, and ode to, the afterlives of Afro-Protestant modernity.

1

The Literary Beginnings
of Afro-Protestantism

Reading slave narratives reveals a literary culture through which
enslaved Africans and their descendants helped to fashion a novel
tradition that was definitively American and decidedly black. These
first-person accounts provide an early example of what would become a long-standing practice of engaging the nation's dominant religious idioms from the particular social location of subjects living on
the racial undersides of slavery and colonization and their aftermath.
That is, the authors (and communities) that produced these narratives
inhabited and authorized a tradition of Protestantism that signified—
resisted, reimagined, and valorized, all at once—something as distinctively black as it was quintessentially American. In this regard, as a
genre extending from, as well as entangled with, the form of spiritual
autobiography, slave narratives illustrate the degree to which literary
forms can be, and often have been, animated by existential, political,
and religious concerns even as they are evidence of aesthetic practices.[1]
As this chapter will show, the slave narratives helped to inaugurate and
set the parameters for a particular set of practices that came to define a
tradition of Afro-Protestantism in the United States. Additionally, the
slave narratives provided a critical space for and played an early and
crucial role in establishing a genealogy of ideas that eventually gave
rise to the terms "The Black Church" and "black religion" as they would
come to be understood in the twentieth century.

To acknowledge the racial order and religious landscape in which
the slave narratives took on social significance is not to deny the genre's
literary merits. Indeed, the idea of extracting aesthetic meaning from
the political context of a work of art or literature is an anachronism
by the measures of late eighteenth- and early nineteenth-century
America.[2] From the vantage point of race politics, in twentieth-century

Black is a Church. Josef Sorett, Oxford University Press. © Oxford University Press 2023.
DOI: 10.1093/oso/9780190615130.003.0002

parlance the slave narratives provide a prehistory to a vision of "race literature" that Victoria Earle Matthews would more fully enunciate in 1895, as will be discussed in detail in chapter 2. On religious terms, the genre made an early contribution, as Yolanda Pierce has argued, to black engagements with "the signs, symbols, and stories that comprise Christian dogma."[3] Yet they were no less artistically significant for their political, religious, or racial aspirations. Indeed, Theodore Parker, a Metaphysical Club contemporary of Ralph Waldo Emerson, noted in 1849 that the writings concerned with the "Lives of Fugitive Slaves" comprised the only cultural form that was "wholly indigenous and original." The slave narratives, for Parker, contained within them "all the original romance of Americans."[4] Anticipating W. E. B. Du Bois's assessment of the Spirituals as novel Americana, the Boston-area theologian and Unitarian clergyman's reading of the slave narratives paired religion and aesthetics decades before Matthews asserted that "race literature" would render an authentic and "real Christianity."[5] In this view, it becomes increasingly clear that, in the form of the slave narratives, Afro-Protestantism developed as a literary practice.

Indeed, literary and religious aspirations converged in the slave narratives. As one scholar has noted, "from the chaos of colonization and slavery" these enslaved authors enunciated "new identities, new communities, and new American literary traditions."[6] Even outside the genre of the slave narrative, literature was a site in which religious and racial as well as gender and national identities were contested. Literacy served as a social currency that religious and racialized subjects were required to demonstrate as evidence to support (or at least make the case for) their inclusion in the American community. On one hand, the Puritans produced a literature that proved key in constructing a narrative of American culture as distinctly Protestant that persists, if a bit more ambiguously, to the present day. Yet the nation's Puritan origins were forged over and against religious and racial others—namely, transplanted Africans and native peoples—who were subjected to the violence of the Christian Europeans who "settled" the New World.[7] To be sure, survival required that these subjects, enslaved and free, understood the nascent national (literary and religious) culture even as they were mapped outside the moral boundaries of the developing nation. And though they were rendered other—as objects, commodities, and savages—by every imaginable measure, black and native peoples developed a range of strategies through which to assert their selfhood, affirm their autonomy, maintain and establish community, and set their sights on freedom.

Positing that Afro-Protestantism had its beginning as a set of literary practices is, by most counts, a counterintuitive claim. Rather, via the Great Awakenings of the eighteenth and nineteenth centuries, American revivalism is typically credited with creating the conditions through which most black people, enslaved and free, first embraced the Christian gospel in large numbers. If efforts at catechism comprised the earliest attempts to convert Africans in the New World, the enslaved made Protestant Christianity their own through the practices associated with evangelicalism and its powerfully induced experience of conversion.[8] That is, African American Christianity—and Afro-Protestantism specifically—emerged as a national phenomenon primarily in an expressive and affective register. Black religion, more generally, has been (and still is) understood as, first and foremost, emotional and embodied rather than literary or reasoning. In short, Afro-Protestantism, by origin and definition, is most commonly understood as a popular (or vernacular) form.

It is true that evangelical revivalism provided the platform and practices through which enslaved Africans and their descendants became Christians—and Americans, for that matter—en masse. In the process, evangelicalism became the preeminent narrative of African American religious history and the primary corporate story of a people as it took shape across the long nineteenth century, moving from slavery toward freedom. Many of the details of this dominant narrative are recounted and confirmed in the individual testimonies detailed in the slave narratives. During the same time period (and even earlier), however, the slave narratives also put in place a set of discursive practices through which black subjectivity was enacted as a performance of a particular kind of literary (and literate) Protestantism. In turn, this literary expression of Afro-Protestantism provided the structures through which to imagine "the race" as a whole: a corporate racial sensibility alongside an individualized sense of a black self. As much as specific sacred texts (i.e., the stories in the Hebrew and Christian Bibles) provided a language for collective racial identity, the

literary Afro-Protestantism worked out in the slave narratives established the terms through which black people came to understand, imagine, and present themselves as American and New World—that is,
modern—subjects.[9]

Otherwise put, the literary practices of Afro-Protestantism encoded
a set of disciplining logics that formed black subjects and social
worlds. And Afro-modernity was made to adhere to the conceptual
logics of this literary Protestantism. As such, Afro-Protestantism—
as a set of performances, practices, social arrangements, and imaginative possibilities—provided a culture and structure that both
animated and oriented black lives in the New World. In this view,
the literary genre of the slave narratives (which grew out of and
deepened the more overtly "religious" tradition of spiritual autobiographies authored by enslaved people) offer a window into the
circumstances, the conditions of possibility, and the terms through
which black people came to apprehend and inhabit the Americas and
the modern world.

Talking about African American religion, first and foremost, as such
(i.e., as a literary practice) does not mean ignoring or obscuring the
fact that efforts to catechize black people in antebellum North America
were relatively unsuccessful. It is true, in terms of sheer numbers, that
many more black people made inroads into Christianity by way of
evangelical revivalism. Highlighting Afro-Protestantism as literary
performance also does not require reifying a rigid divide between
the emotional terms of evangelical conversion and the rationalistic
rules of catechism (e.g., as a simultaneous demonstration of literacy
and doctrinal knowledge). Rather, this shift in emphasis calls attention to ways in which "low/popular" (i.e., emotional, experiential) and
"high/elite" (i.e., literate, reasoning) are co-constituted in religious
practice and intertwined in normative definitions of both race and
religion. Catechesis and conversion were, in short, always entangled
and co-constitutive. The respectable (and literary) rules of catechism
shaped the terms in which "true" Christianity, in both black and white,
was imagined even as the very categories of authenticity and orthodoxy were themselves racialized, as respectively black and white. What
is now often thought of as blackness, as (individual and corporate)
identity and practice, was forged in this matrix: Afro-Protestantism,

a peculiar performance of religious orthodoxy and racial authenticity at once.

This logic, of course, cast a normative literary and reasoned piety as Western and white, while evangelicalism's affective practices came to be understood both as distinctive to and definitive of the faith of black folk (the ring shout, the chanted sermon, "the frenzy," etc.) and as undesirable relics of a bygone era. Yet an inverse logic has also often held with regard to African American religion and culture, wherein the undesirable has been valued for its air of authenticity or opposition to the norm. In this view, the spiritual vitality and heightened emotion apparent in Afro-Protestantism were perceived to resist both the violently racist order (i.e., chattel slavery) as well as the move, over time, in modern industrial society toward mechanization and standardization. In this view, the alterity associated with black religion was a buffer against the normative logics of white supremacy and modernity's spiritual decay and decline. At the same time, a masterful performance of "good" or "true" religion (i.e., catechism, the "high" forms of literary Protestantism) was understood as able to provide African Americans with the keys to the (American) kingdom.

Again, rather than mutually exclusive modes of religious practice, catechesis and conversion required each other. Low (i.e., conversion) authenticated high (i.e., catechesis), and the latter authorized the former. Conversion created the conditions of possibility for and a pathway toward catechism. Catechism, then, confirmed and provided evidence of, as well as extended from an authentic conversion. Yet the relationship between these two forms was neither exclusively linear nor chronological. A heterodox set of ideas and practices apparent within (and often exceeding the limits of) the variety of New World Christianities was delimited and disciplined by the orthodoxy of a normative literary and reasoned Protestantism. And a working out of the relationship(s) between these two kinds, trajectories, or traditions of Christianity was on full display in the slave narratives—and from this working out, a synthesis: Afro-Protestantism.[10]

More broadly, the diverse set of religious ideas and practices that have been apparent across the history of modern black life was made to adhere to the ruling logics of a publicly performed Afro-Protestantism. In turn, Afro-Protestantism (often unnamed by literary critics) both underwrote a (presumably secular, universal) racial subjectivity—that is, blackness—and provided a rubric expansive enough to contain and order the collective imaginings of Afro-modernity. Ultimately, the genre of the slave narrative—itself a product of the literary conventions, politico-racial concerns, and religious cultures of its day—helped instantiate this particular brand of Afro-Protestantism as at once normative for black religious life and determinative of black subjectivity and social life, more generally.

Scholars of American literature have identified the slave narratives as a genre that was key for both the development of an original American literature and culture and the formation of a distinctive black literary tradition. That these texts reflect the religious landscape of the period in which they were composed—including specific practices, historical events, and theological claims—has not been lost on critics. Many, especially the earlier slave narratives are alternatively described as "spiritual autobiographies" because the genre is riddled with themes, questions, and concerns typically conceived of as overtly religious or spiritual. To be clear, the spiritual here functions as a synonym for Christianity, as many of these texts tell the story of the respective narrators' journeys to Christian faith. While the best place in history to start may be contested, histories of African American literature share a position of downplaying, even while conceding, the genre's religious beginnings.[11] Even more, scholars and critics have rarely considered how this body of literature helped set a course for African American religious history, or how it both reflected and shaped the politics of Christianity's place in black cultural, political, and social life more broadly.

The story of the slave narratives is not simply a history of secularization, the occasion of a secular racial and literary identity triumphing over, superseding, or transcending the constraints of a more parochial religious or spiritual orientation. The emergence and evolution of this genre should not be understood as a singular narrative of linear progress, wherein a modern and secular racial present supplanted an always already primitive African and sacred past, with American Christianity just a stop along the way. Rather, reading across the slave narratives one is made witness to the instantiation of a form of black subjectivity that is a distinctly religious performance of, more precisely, Protestant

Christianity. Indeed, the forging of this modern racial subjectivity, typically rendered as a secular formation, was akin to the making of blackness as an orthodox monotheism, which would come to preside over and discipline the heterodox, pantheistic, and pagan sensibilities that preceded it (and which never entirely disappeared). Otherwise put, to borrow Gauri Viswanathan's argument regarding secularism, Afro-Protestantism provided a set of conditions under which a great deal of heterodoxy continued to thrive.[12] To the point, the tradition of Afro-Protestantism that developed (and continues to be underread by scholars) in the slave narratives would grow to public (even hegemonic) prominence and to preside over a black social life marked by a good measure of religious and cultural pluralism. Through a reading of several eighteenth- and nineteenth-century slave narratives, this chapter simultaneously sheds a more precise light on the varying "religious" content of this literary form, the normative Afro-Protestantism that this tradition helped to produce, the religious difference(s) disciplined by this tradition, and the degree to which Afro-Protestantism produced and became constitutive of black subjectivity and social life.[13]

Re-Forming James Gronniosaw: Literacy and the Pretense of Afro-Protestantism

The ascent of a privileged Afro-Protestantism becomes evident as early as the late eighteenth century. In his now classic theory of the African American literary tradition, *The Signifying Monkey* (1988), Henry Louis Gates Jr. identified *A Narrative of the Most Remarkable Particulars in the Life of James Albert Ukawsaw Gronniosaw, An African Prince, As Related by Himself* (circa 1770), as the first text in the tradition of the slave narrative. Gronniosaw is generally considered to be the first African published in Great Britain. Born in West Africa, according to his narrative, he was sold to a Dutch trader; brought to Barbados, where he was purchased and sold again; and brought to New Jersey, where he was first introduced to Christianity. The narrative follows Gronniosaw's journeys throughout the Atlantic World, from slavery to freedom, and from pagan to convert and, eventually, to Christian maturity.

Gronniosaw's narrative is generally recognized as falling within the genre of the spiritual autobiography. However, it should also be read as a primary source and starting point for the particular sort of normative Afro-Protestantism produced under the sign of a secular modernity in the New World. As Gates rightly notes, the "Anglo-African narrative tradition" inaugurated with Gronniosaw's narrative begins within West African cultural worlds wherein distinctions between sacred and secular were nonexistent. Yet Gronniosaw's narrative also drew upon a "tradition of Christian confession." After all, Gates observes, "[i]t is his ability to read and write and speak the Word of the Lord which motivates Gronniosaw's pilgrimage to England."[14] Though Gronniosaw's growing Christian faith is seen to propel his narrative forward, for Gates (and the field of black literary studies more broadly), religion is decidedly not *the* story. However, published at the start of a decade that saw the founding of the first independent black Baptist and Methodist churches, the narrative also provides a different starting point for African American religious history.[15]

Unsurprisingly, the primary investment of scholars of African American literature has been in Gronniosaw's "concern with literacy." Literacy is especially significant because, for Gates, the slave narratives reveal how, "[i]n the black tradition, writing became the visible sign, the commodity of exchange, the text and technology of reason."[16] It is through a demonstration of literacy, then, that Gronniosaw would seem to shed his animist African origins, pass through the portal of Protestant Christianity, and enter into the Western world of letters as a modern, rational, European, white, secular subject. In the process of pursuing literacy, Gates explains, Gronniosaw undergoes a "secular or cultural cleansing or inundation that obliterates (or is meant to obliterate) the traces of an African past."[17] In short, Gronniosaw is transformed through literacy from African savage into Enlightenment secularist, at least in Gates's telling. Gronniosaw, by contrast, presents himself as on a pilgrimage.

To be fair, Gates neither overlooks nor denies that religion is significant to Gronniosaw's life and narrative. However, Gronniosaw's Christian faith is depicted as ornamental—as accidental, in the philosophical sense. That is, the "warp and woof of Protestant Christianity," to quote Gates, appears to be only incidental in Gronniosaw's "strange passage from black man to white." My point here is less about Gates's reading of Gronniosaw, which assiduously tracks language and literacy, both figuratively and literally, to illumine how the "trope of the talking book" emerged in the slave narratives to prefigure an African American literary tradition.[18] More important, here, is that Gates reads Gronniosaw's narrative through a secularizing lens that has been taken for granted in modern literary studies writ large.[19] In doing so, Gates both participates in and advances a set of secularist assumptions—an interpretive paradigm that tends to view religion not necessarily with antipathy but rather with indifference—that continues to animate and organize the orthodoxies of African American literary history.

More generally speaking, the orthodoxies of American literary theory have privileged a subjectivity enacted through a performance of secularity. Though scholars present Gronniosaw as a secular man in the making, he represented himself as a person in pursuit of good religion.[20] Declaring that he and his wife were but "very poor Pilgrims," his narrative is one in which they are "travelling through many difficulties towards our Heavenly Home."[21] Significantly, Gronniosaw's self-fashioning was entirely in keeping with most writers in the slave narrative tradition. As much as reason and literacy were means for authorizing (black) humanity in the New World, the humans being authorized (and doing the authorizing) overwhelmingly came to identify as Christian. The slave narratives demand to be read more closely with a concern for how the politics of religion—and Christianity's special place therein—shaped both formal and thematic concerns, as well as the tropological forms, of the tradition.[22] Literary demonstrations of reason often required, and took the shape of, an overtly religious performance even well after the onset of modernity. Yet not all kinds of religiosity or religious practices were considered equal. The slave narratives do not supply readers with evidence of a generic or universal religious performance. Rather, these texts provided a discursive space in which a particular kind of Christian faith was worked out and made normative for and constitutive of blackness, even as other religious performances and practices were moved to the margins or rendered undesirable and invisible.

Gronniosaw's narrative records much more than the process of securing a racial (read: modern, secular) self. It is also his testimony concerning Christian conversion, sanctification, and catechism. Indeed, pilgrimage is the animating impulse—whether as providential design or human compulsion—that drives the entire narrative.[23] For instance, Gronniosaw compared himself to John Bunyan, the English preacher and author of *Pilgrim's Progress*. And the text most often cited in the narrative is the popular Puritan devotional by Richard Baxter, *Call to the Unconverted*.[24] From one perspective, Gronniosaw's desire to have "the Talking Book" speak to him might give literacy (and literary form) a certain priority over the content of specific books. However, the letters over which he sought to demonstrate mastery were decidedly religious and specifically Protestant. As Gronniosaw underwent a literary transformation (from black to white), he mapped out his New World pilgrimage primarily through encounters with Christian texts, including devotionals, doctrinal tracts, prayers, and scriptures. It was, in fact, through an engagement with the contents of these texts that Gronniosaw's racial self was formed as Protestant. As he traveled the transatlantic routes of "the triangle trade" en route to freedom, selfhood, and Christian salvation, the discourses of race, reason, and religion were unevenly entangled. One must at least ask, to borrow a phrase from religious historian David Wills, "What is the relation here of the Christian self to the racial self?"[25]

Throughout his narrative, Gronniosaw's growing knowledge of self and the world are paired with his ongoing acquisition of Christian doctrine. At the outset, in Africa, he describes himself as "curious" and "lost in wonder," establishing his identity as different from family members because of his distinctive theological questions. All of his "wonderful impressions" suggest, at the outset, both a capacity to reason and a disposition toward Christian answers. Yet they also confirmed him to be innocent and naïve, unaware of human motives, economic interests, and denominational differences.[26] Gronniosaw's "simplicity" made him a fit target for mercantile avarice and missionary zeal alike. On one hand, he represented a source of material value in the form of potential slave labor. On the other, he was a potential receptacle for religious knowledge in the form of Christian doctrine. Indeed, as Gronniosaw steadily becomes increasingly anchored in orthodoxy, his story is one of growing spiritual sophistication *and* social discernment.

As the narrative unfolds, Gronniosaw gradually learns the finer points of Christian doctrine (e.g., creation, sin, grace) and discards cruder ideas about religion (e.g., God as a "Great Man of power" in the sky, evil as personified as "a black man called the devil that lives in hell"). En route to conversion he also moves toward emotional maturity, experiencing a complex affective spectrum of misery, happiness, confusion, humility, and more, all of which work together to prepare him well for the rigors of a reasoned Christian life. Additionally, Gronniosaw eventually comes to understand the meanings of racial difference, the significance of monetary value, and the range of human motivations, while also becoming aware that there are many kinds of Christians. Before meeting the famed revivalist George Whitefield or mastering the mysteries of Christian doctrine, he must first acquire more mundane forms of literacy. Readers stand by as Gronniosaw, somewhat humorously, learns to "curse and swear surprisingly."[27] This more profane performance of an Anglo identity initially augments his African past. Only over time does Gronniosaw move from an anthropomorphic sense of wonder to monotheism and from empty profanities to an elaborate system of Christian ideas. Indeed, only after proceeding through these successive steps of maturation in the faith—what some might call "sanctification"—does his narrative culminate with a set of encounters with a committee of Protestant clergy.

Only much later in the narrative, after readers have followed his path of spiritual growth, does Gronniosaw successfully negotiate seven consecutive Thursdays of meetings with a panel of forty-eight "Calvinist ministers." Following the completion of their examination, he observes that these preachers "were all very well satisfied, and persuaded I was what I pretended to be."[28] In this view, whiteness and Protestantism are figured as coterminous in the process of conversion. That is, Gronniosaw's racial reformation *and* his demonstration of literacy are signaled by his satisfactory completion of Christian catechesis.[29] To be sure, his transformation involved a negation. Gronniosaw proved himself no longer to be African, as Gates argues, culturally speaking. Nor were his choice words, in the King's English, still profanities. Instead, in the affirmative, he performed literacy by proclaiming the Word of the Lord. His "modern" difference was measured in the metrics of religious devotion and through a mastery of Christian doctrine. In short, the demonstration of Gronniosaw's new racial self involved—in fact required—the performance of mature Christian orthodoxy. If literacy and reason are to be understood as secular, then Gronniosaw's was a thoroughly Protestant secularism.

Gronniosaw's process of sanctification, as represented in his narrative, equipped him well for the social world he came to inhabit. As Tracy Fessenden has noted, to convert to Christianity was to gain entrance to the Americas "as socially recognized beings in a world where shared scriptural and narrative forms (i.e., the spiritual autobiography) could be appealed to and circulated." Insofar as their conversions were encoded in the form of the slave narratives, for black subjects these texts also achieved the end "of positioning them, as critics, outside of that center where whiteness, Christianity, and access to the Word were neatly aligned."[30] That is, Christianity simultaneously facilitated inclusion within and critical opposition to the social, religious, and racial order of the day. As such, the emergence of Afro-Protestantism revealed black people's ambivalent (or multivalent) attachment to Christianity. It offered them social recognition within a dominant religious order even as it created space for a social identity distinct from white Christians and source material to critique Christianity's role in ordering their enslavement and domination.

This ambivalent investment in Christianity can be observed most powerfully near the end of Gronniosaw's exchange with the forty-eight ministers, where he writes, "*So I stood before 48 Ministers every Thursday for seven weeks together, and they were all very well satisfied, and persuaded I was what I pretended to be.*"[31] Here, his choice of the word "pretended" clarifies the performative quality of conversion in general. He is not to be dismissed as engaging in a subtle act of spiritual subterfuge. Rather, catechism provided the evidence of his conversion. It was a public expression presumed to accompany, or substantiate, a qualitative change in interior status. Gronniosaw's performance of orthodoxy over a period of seven weeks (numerically signaling and symbolizing the completion of his conversion) authenticated his achievement of a new self.

In this case, Gronniosaw's public confession was intended to prove that he had been fully (re)formed as a Christian. His catechesis was persuasive enough to convince the ministerial panel. However, readers are still left asking whether his conversion, to which they have been made witness, was just pretense. Did Gronniosaw genuinely believe all that he confessed? Or was he, perhaps, "passing" as Christian? Significantly, the power and perils associated with "passing" as a racial performance would eventually come to occupy a special place in the black literary tradition, and in American life.[32] With regard to religion, however, such queries are unverifiable with no recourse to DNA, familial claims, or genealogy. Instead, this line of reasoning calls attention to the limits of what the category of professed "belief" does or does not reveal.[33] At a minimum, accenting the interpretive breaks in the process and performance of catechism—between Gronniosaw's evolving understanding of the Christian faith and that of his examiners, as well as those who would later read his narrative— confirms (his) conversion to be necessarily multivalent.[34]

Gronniosaw's assertion of a novel subjectivity—his new Protestant self—was presumed to be predicated on his ability to, in effect, erase or obscure any evidence of his African past. This performance presents itself, fundamentally, as an either/or proposition: past/present, black/white, African/European, primitive/modern, sacred/secular, pagan/Anglican, old/new. His conversion and subsequent catechism suggested a complete alteration of his religious and racial identities. As noted above, the exchange of the old for the new—from ignorant savage to literate subject—involved both negation and addition. However, Gronniosaw's performance did not necessarily require a radical break from the past. Success before the panel of forty-eight clergy, as well as with the slave narrative's reading public, required only the pretense—which is to say, a public performance—of just such a break. This, in fact, is the central premise of the structure of conversion: an observable demonstration that "old things are passed away, all things are made new."[35] Such logic nonetheless begs the question of what constitutes the new in Gronniosaw's performance of a "secular" self and the reformed interiority it was meant to confirm. It also leaves open the possibility, indeed the likelihood, that things presumed to have passed away persist. Whatever constituted Gronniosaw's old self was effectively obscured or reordered, but this does not mean that it was not erased.

Just as the clergy panel appeared to be persuaded by his performance, if one concedes that Gronniosaw's new and modern self was Christian, such a proposition also invites more precise consideration of the form(s) of Christian faith that Gronniosaw performed. On the one hand, his conversion highlighted how a mastery of literacy, as evidence of reason, entailed a performance of a particular kind of Christian catechism. Though conversion always implies admittance into a new (religious) community, it is clear here that the context of Gronniosaw's transformation was oriented by a racial logic wherein religious salvation and social inclusion were not easily disentangled. That is, Gronniosaw's African past (defined by animist beliefs), followed by the experience of enslavement, lends itself to a close reading of the religious form(s) (i.e., testimony, confession, scripture reading) that helped advance him into the racial present. This is all the more true given that his performance took place in the presence of examiners who, in assessing the authenticity of his conversion, exercised significant power over his social fate. Indeed, even in the Age of Independence, the line between slave and free, and the protections of the social contract, were often secured by the sign of Christian faith.[36]

Gronniosaw's attainment of a literate, religious subjectivity also stands in contrast to the fact that a majority of Africans (and, later, African Americans) who converted to Protestant Christianity did so short of achieving literacy or theological orthodoxy. Rather, most embraced Christian faith under the experiential, embodied, and participatory conditions of evangelical revivalism. Not incidentally, Gronniosaw's pursuit of salvation led him first to meet the renowned provocateur of evangelical fervor, George Whitefield, in England. Indeed, it was the charismatic Whitefield who later approved Gronniosaw's decision to travel onward to Holland, where he eventually persuaded the bureaucratic panel of Calvinist clergy of his conversion. Here evangelical expressiveness appears akin to a developmental step, or a way station, on the road to reasoned catechism. Gronniosaw's successful performance abetted his social inclusion in the Christian West, and in doing so, it inaugurated a tradition of black letters. More important, at least in this context, it helped establish the parameters for a nascent literary and reasoning Afro-Protestantism as the normative script for black religion in the New World.

Early Slave Narratives, "Good Religion," and the Politics of Difference

Not simply an isolated individual literary event, Gronniosaw's narrative helped to establish (and was indicative of) the orthodoxies of an emerging religious, racial, and cultural tradition: Afro-Protestantism. In this view, the slave narratives can be seen as participating in and providing a discursive context for the making of a prescriptive pluralism that set the terms for relationships among three things within the context of black social life: the established literary forms of Protestantism; the embodied and affective practices of evangelicalism; and, of course, religious identities and practices outside the bounds of institutional Christianity—itself never a single thing, to be sure.[37] To revisit an earlier point, it is important to keep in mind the degree to which all three of these entities, in time and space, have been entangled with and required each other. For instance, in the context of Afro-Protestantism, evangelical expressiveness and non-Christian practices have deferred to the registers of religious literacy in terms of public authorization, even as they provided those literary forms with the competing authority of authenticity. Indeed, the emerging racial order in North America mapped alterity and authenticity onto black (and non-Christian) bodies and would facilitate the development of a black subjectivity that was at once secular and Protestant.

The modern racial subjectivity articulated in the slave narratives emerged not simply in opposition to an imagined "primitive" and "pagan" African past. Rather, these privileged performances of a reasoned Afro-Protestantism were developed through a deliberate disciplining of a range of religious "others" that were no less significant to the multiple contexts of contact and exchange in the Americas. The version of Protestantism that Gronniosaw proclaimed proved critical to his new social status in the Atlantic world. He exchanged the animism of his African past for the catechism of his Euro-American present, even as his narrative projected his monotheistic present onto his past as a mark of distinction within his original African context.[38] More generally, the kind of Protestantism that Gronniosaw performed adhered to what has commonly been identified as "good religion"—that is, a form of religion that is "rational, word-centered, nonritualistic, middle-class, unemotional, compatible with democracy"—and that was in keeping with the norms of an emerging modern, "secular" public sphere.[39]

Though Gronniosaw's story is but one narrative, it effectively provides a window into the cultural contact, racial asymmetries, and religious difference at play in the formation of the modern world. Tracking the racial and religious transformations that are on display in the slave narratives—en route to conversion and catechism and as indicative of an emerging Afro-Protestantism—helps reveal the limits of overly simplistic binaries such as African/European, pagan/Christian, black/white, or Protestant/secular. Such a reading of the slave narratives highlights how the desire to master a performance of Afro-Protestantism (and the privileges it could provide) followed from an astute reading of the entangled asymmetries of race and religion in the New World. The possession and demonstration of such religious faculties were fundamental to the founding of a black literary tradition and to the emergence of a modern racial imaginary.[40] More pointedly, the slave narratives effectively illustrate the early workings of how black religion would come to be synonymous with a version of Christianity that aspired to the status of "good religion" even as Afro-Protestantism was a hybrid, creolized form, by definition. Gronniosaw's narrative, then, provided an early, and exemplary, template for black life "in the contact zone," to borrow Mary Louise Pratt's phrase. In following these developments via the slave narratives, one can observe how black subjectivity itself emerged as a Protestant formation.[41]

Conversely, "bad religion" was not exclusively associated with an emotional evangelicalism or an uninstitutionalized form of wonder, as was described in Gronniosaw's account of his earlier years in Africa. Rather, Afro-Protestant performances, like Gronniosaw's before the clergy panel, worked prescriptively to order a variety of other kinds of religious sensibilities. This prescriptive work comes even more to the fore in other slave narratives, such as those of John Marrant and Quobna Ottobah Cugoano, both of which were published not long after Gronniosaw's.[42] What follows here is not intended as a full or exhaustive reading of each account. Instead, these selective engagements with the narratives of Marrant and Cugoano are meant to illustrate how the disciplinary logics of what has come to be known as religious pluralism—previously described as an achievement of a secular racial self—contributed to the rise of a privileged Afro-Protestantism.[43] In this regard, the slave narratives offer a detailed portrait of the map of religious and racial difference in an Atlantic World where Protestantism won the day. Moreover, much of what is found in these narratives confirms that Christian literacy specifically was prized over the faculties of literacy or reason generically. Recall that it was Gronniosaw's persuasive exchange with the forty-eight Calvinist ministers that signaled the culmination of his transformation.

The Narrative of the Lord's Wonderful Dealings with John Marrant, the Black, is an excellent example in this regard.[44] First published in 1785, Marrant's narrative is unique in that he was never a slave. In fact, slavery does not even appear as an ancillary topic in his story, which is more properly understood as a tale of Indian captivity.[45] As such, Marrant's account does not mirror Gronniosaw's pairing of the pathway from slavery to freedom with the pilgrimage of a sinner toward salvation. Instead, he offers an account of evangelical conversion, his unorthodox missionary training and travels, and his eventual ordination into Christian ministry. More than racial oppression, Marrant's narrative seems especially concerned with the ability of spiritual power to surmount social and cultural difference for the purpose of Christian salvation. When Marrant is faced with an impasse of communication, providence intervenes in ways both mundane and miraculous. Ultimately, Marrant's narrative is a story of "dangers and deliverances," all of which work together as he journeys toward a mature "Christian experience."[46]

What most readily stands out is Marrant's adeptness at weaving stories of the Christian Bible's most celebrated heroes into his own biography. Born free in New York, Marrant moved south as a child with his family and spent his formative years in South Carolina, Florida, and Georgia. At the age of thirteen he attended one of the revivals spreading throughout the eastern seaboard and converted to Christianity after hearing Whitefield preach. The long arc of Marrant's narrative loosely mirrors the parable of the Gospel of Luke's prodigal son, a young man seduced by vice who sets out on a course away from his family. As the biblical tale proceeds, the prodigal eventually returns to his homeland, where he is initially unrecognized and later jubilantly reclaimed by his father. Marrant's narrative does not follow the prodigal's path to the letter. Marrant depicts himself entering into the wilderness of Indian lands—like the Israelites before their entrance to the Promised Land and like Jesus in preparation for his ministry. Along the way, he fashions himself as similar to Moses, Joseph, and Daniel, each of whom rose to power in a foreign kingdom. And Marrant's Indian lands are fashioned after the biblical Egypt and Babylon. After straying from his divine purpose, he is thrown from a boat like Jonah. When he is imprisoned and threatened with death by execution, he sings his way to freedom like Paul and Silas. He even subtly likens himself to Jesus on the cross, as he prays, "[T]hy will be done." Marrant's biblical imagination may have been eclectic, but it was by all accounts prolific.[47]

Yet this series of sacred stories were all located within a single, more familiar story of American evangelicalism. Marrant's narrative recounts how he was converted while hearing a sermon preached by Whitefield. In fact, Whitefield's delivery was so powerful that it left Marrant on the ground, "speechless and senseless near half an hour."[48] As the narrative continues, he frequently fasts (at times, not of his own volition), and is found "tarrying" in prayer until receiving a revelation. Marrant eventually finds his vocation as a missionary—first, to the Cherokee nation, whose language he slowly learns to speak "in the highest stile," and later to his own family. After several successful missions to the Indians, Marrant returns to the same family that had initially rejected his newfound evangelical fervor, propelling him into the wilderness. Like the prodigal son's father, Marrant's family fails to recognize him, believing him to be dead. Only upon being kissed by his youngest sister is he "made known" to the others. Rather than a simple or sentimental reunion, Marrant describes being reunited with his family as another successful religious mission. Once again "the dead was brought to life; thus the lost was found," Marrant declares.[49]

Capturing the centrality of missionary work/evangelism to his entire account, Marrant concludes his narrative with a prayer for the salvation of all people: "that strangers may hear of and run to Christianity; that Indian tribes may stretch out their hands to God; that the black nations may be made white in the blood of the lamb. . . . Amen and Amen." For Marrant, literacy itself mattered less than a *mastery* of language, which his narrative figures as a sign both of Christian maturity and of his competence as a missionary to the Indians. The ability to learn and speak a foreign tongue was important insofar as it enabled him to translate the Christian Gospel and do the work of the Lord. Repeatedly he emphasizes his ability to take on the forms of Cherokee culture, but only for the purposes of communicating the content of Christian faith. At one point he explains, "I had assumed the habit of the country." On another occasion he writes, "My dress was purely in the Indian stile." In each case, the point is clear: language, wardrobe, and culture were just media in service to the message, which demanded fluency for its dissemination. They were simply technologies that made translation possible, enabling the spreading of the Christian gospel.

Eventually Marrant's ability to "pray in their tongue" led to the conversion of his would-be Indian executioner and gave him an audience with the Cherokee "king." Initially, however, his linguistic skills caused the king to confuse him for a "witch." Marrant's ability to read from the Bible in the Cherokee language and to pray in such a way that moved them emotionally led the king to accuse him of sorcery—a potentially tragic case of misinterpretation. Yet his prayers were so efficacious that, Marrant observed, eventually "the Lord made all my enemies to become my great friends." Throughout his narrative Marrant emphasized raw emotion as much as formal mastery. Feelings figure as prominently as, if not more than, literacy as readers witness the author "burst out into a flood of tears" on five separate occasions.[50]

Emotional displays in conversation, prayer, and song often provide the occasion for transformation in Marrant's narrative. For instance, he relays a time during his imprisonment when his would-be executioner overhears him praying (again, like Paul and Silas but also like the Hebrew boys in the fiery furnace). According to Marrant, the guard "looked about the room, and said he did not see him [Jesus]; but I told him I *felt* him. The executioner fell upon his knees, and entreated the king, and told him that he had *felt* the same Lord."[51] Here, affect rather than eloquence elicited the change in Marrant's circumstances, persuaded others of his spiritual power, and bridged the gaps between their respective social worlds. Ultimately, not only did his earnest prayers secure his safety, but they became salvation for the "Indian tribes" as well. Whether through emotion or reason, Marrant's message to readers remained clear: "A great change took place among the people; the king's house became God's house."

Even still, Marrant's investment in Indian culture was ambivalent at best. He did what was necessary to learn the language and culture "in the highest stile" (even if initially under the coercive terms of being kidnapped by an Indian hunter). In time he grew to regard the Cherokee people as "friends." Nevertheless, "Indian stile" is described as decorative, a foreign form that had to be filled with Christian content. It required Marrant's formal mastery for its proper administration. In short, cultural familiarity and social intimacy with the Indians served the singular aim of their conversion to Christianity. Friendship was not a goal in itself. Marrant was prepared for missionary work only by pairing a "[f]uller knowledge of the Indian tongue" and "sweet communion . . . with God." In this formulation, acquiring the former was appropriate only if it facilitated the latter. "Indian stiles" mattered insofar as they allowed him to communicate the same evangelical message that was his salvation—namely, the Christian gospel preached by Whitefield, who had died just fifteen years prior to the publication of Marrant's narrative in 1785.

Two years later Quobna Ottobah Cugoano (later baptized with the Christian name John Stuart) published his first book, *Thoughts and Sentiments on the Evil of Slavery*. Cugoano, who had been born in Ghana before being captured and taken to the Caribbean, eventually became one of the most prominent Africans in England during the first half of the nineteenth century. As suggested by his title, Cugoano's early narratives focused mostly on the evils of slavery. As such, *Thoughts and Sentiments* might be read as a secular refutation of the leading apologists for slavery and colonization of his day. The publication was both history and autobiography, and a short excerpt from the narrative was later republished as an appendix to Thomas Fisher's *The Negro's Memorial, or Abolitionist's Catechism*. The context—a claim for abolition—of this reprinted excerpt provides a clue, granted after the fact, of Cugoano's interest in religion, albeit from a different angle than Marrant's.[52] Cugoano's narrative was a polemic against the institution of slavery, as well as the various forms of intellectual authority that were made to support it, including Enlightenment reason and Christian theology.

Through his narrative, Cugoano pairs reason and religion as part of a single sacralized social order. Both were to blame as the primary "pretences for enslaving the Africans," which is not to suggest that Cugoano valued reason and religion on equal terms. Even as *Thoughts and Sentiments* advanced a strident critique of slavery as an evil institution, Cugoano provided a theodicy for his own enslavement. Reason and literacy were important, but Christianity was to be valued "above all." He explained in greater detail: "I have both obtained liberty, and acquired the great advantages of some little learning, in being able to read and write, and, what is still infinitely of greater advantage, I trust, to know something of HIM who is that God whose providence rules over all."[53] He then likened himself to a hero of the Hebrew Bible, Joseph, who was enslaved in Egypt only to rise to prominence at the right hand of Pharaoh. All of the evil that was done to him in slavery, Cugoano observed, "the Lord intended for my good."[54] As much as it was a polemic against slavery, Cugoano's narrative is also a personal testimony of divine "providence." The value of "liberty" and "learning," in general, was that they allowed Cugoano to have access specifically to religious knowledge. Similar to Marrant, literacy was simply the medium for Cugoano. It was a means to a more significant end—namely, the message of Christian salvation.

In *Thoughts and Sentiments* Cugoano elevated religion as more valuable than reason. Throughout the narrative he suggests that literacy found its purpose in Protestantism. Somewhat paradoxically, his narrative also gave voice to an explicit rejection of Christian authority, at least in its Catholic form. In recounting a sixteenth-century confrontation between the Inca king Atahualpa and Father Vincente de Valverde of Spain, chaplain to the colonizers, Cugoano presented an altercation in which Christian reason—in this case, a claim to papal authority over the "New World"—proves unpersuasive. Here his language resembled that of Gronniosaw after his examination before the clergy in Holland. In Cugoano's account, Father Valverde approaches Atahualpa, "*pretending* to explain some of the general doctrines of Christianity."[55] (italics mine) Where Gronniosaw's performance persuaded the Calvinist ministers that he was who he "pretended to be," Valverde's efforts at persuasion were unsuccessful. Atahualpa declined to "embrace the Christian religion, acknowledge the jurisdiction of the Pope, and submit to the Great Monarch of Castile." Additionally, he refused to "renounce the religious institutions established by his ancestors . . . in order to worship the God of the Spaniards." Finally, Atahualpa rejected the authority of Valverde's breviary, which the "fanatic monk" held up to verify the truth of his jurisdictional claims.[56]

When the Incas threw the priest's prayerbook to the ground "with disdain," Valverde announced that the word of God had been insulted and promptly declared war. From Cugoano's perspective, this dramatic exchange revealed the false pretense of colonial Christianity for what it was: a cover for a call to arms and violent enslavement. It also confirmed his definition of "true religion" and left space for a potential measure of religious pluralism. The wedding of conquest with missionary concerns was a non sequitur for Cugoano. In his view, Atahualpa had every right not to relinquish his lands, which were claimed by the rights of "hereditary succession" and ancestral rites. Nor did he need to "forsake the service of the Sun, the immortal divinity whom he and his people revered."[57] Christianity, as he saw it, was incommensurate with colonization and enslavement. Yet, ironically, it was entirely consistent with the modern doctrine of the rights of man. Cugoano's argument was simple: these rights ought to be extended to all men, irrespective of religion, race, ethnicity, or nationality.

In Cugoano's narrative, Atahualpa figures as a critique of both Enlightenment reason and Christian exclusivity, even though the author's own definition of religion did not depart from what are typically identified as the central precepts of these traditions. Moreover, underlying Cugoano's argument is the assumption that the Incas' gods must require them to adhere to ideas similar to what he took to be Christianity's core precepts.[58] To be sure, he classified religious practices associated with the precolonial Americas (and Africa) as "errors of superstition and idolatry."[59] However, Cugoano's willingness to grant Atahualpa's sun god recognition marked a significant departure from the unformed "wonder" that Gronniosaw attributed to Africa. Additionally, Cugoano's narrative can be read as leaving space for indigenous religious traditions, or allegiance to non-Christian deities, as legitimate sources of spiritual authority.[60]

Regardless of whether they were Protestant, Catholic, or "Mahometan," the "enslavers of men" belonged to the "synagogue of

Satan" and were aligned with "that most dissolute sorceress of all religion." For Cugoano, the slaveholder was truly "the Antichrist."[61] True religion, he insisted—and true reason, for that matter—was an antislavery, ethical, and reasoning Protestantism, in contrast to Valverde's Catholicism. Yet he also left open the possibility that each of these religious traditions, insofar as they rejected the practices of slavery and colonization, might be true. Even still, Cugoano's *Thoughts and Sentiments on the Evil of Slavery* attributed "greater advantage" to knowing the Christian God over "being able to read and write." In short, his Christianity was singularly antislavery, though not necessarily theologically exclusive.

In general, these early slave narratives by Gronniosaw, Marrant, and Cugoano seem to be in agreement that Christianity provided literacy with its reason(s) and rightful content. While an emotional evangelical conversion experience was often considered an appropriate introduction to Christianity, a mature faith was literary and reasoning. A seasoned Afro-Protestantism was then demonstrated persuasively through emotional expression and eloquence in oral and written forms—such as Gronniosaw's catechism, or the slave narrative itself— but also by its antislavery commitments. For both Gronniosaw and Marrant, an encounter with Whitefield was a necessary step, but not the final stop, in the formation of their Afro-Protestant selves. For Cugoano, true religion was conceived of as a brand of Christianity consonant with Enlightenment ideals about human rights, yet only insofar as those ideals were extended to enslaved Africans and their descendants. In all cases, reason in service to a disciplining religion— making, forming, and extending Protestant Christianity specifically— was the literary rule. On all counts, the practice and affirmation of black freedom was the sign of true faith. And this vision of Christianity was encoded in—and a sign of—a fully formed and "proper" black subjectivity.

The range of slave narratives ultimately stopped short of consensus in their varying portraits of how best to understand the "greatest advantages" attendant on "some knowledge of the Christian religion."[62] Moreover, these texts displayed divergent understandings of the relationship between Protestantism and Catholicism, or any of the other religious traditions present in the social worlds that surrounded the slave narratives. On the one hand, Marrant's explicit missionary ambitions overdetermined his exchanges with native peoples in North America. On the other, Cugoano cast the indigenous peoples of South America as more than targets for conversion. The Incas presented a spiritual alternative to the "barbarous inhuman" form of Christianity practiced by Catholic colonizers. As such, Atahualpa was not obliged to recognize their sacred texts or their sovereignty claims, as his ancestors and their "religious institutions" possessed their own spiritual authority.[63] Even still, Cugoano might never worship the sun god for himself.

From Marrant's perspective, effective translation of the "good news" of the Christian gospel toward the goal of Indian conversion was all that mattered. And for Cugoano, owing to the overwhelming asymmetries of colonial contact that mediated every encounter between Europeans and Natives (African and American alike), the Christian mysteries failed to translate. Nevertheless, in both cases, Protestant Christianity prevailed, whether by bringing outsiders into the fold or through embracing the other by means of an ethical (i.e., antislavery) definition of religion that assumed itself. Religious difference was reined in and disciplined—in ways less obvious and more explicit— by the literary, reasoning Protestantism that ordered the English-speaking social worlds of the slave narratives.

In this regard, Gronniosaw's was the first, and perhaps the most fully formed, performance of an Afro-Protestantism that was ascending to organize modernity's imaginative possibilities and constraints. His account was consistent with Marrant's Christian teleology, wherein a masterful performance of Christian literacy simultaneously facilitated social inclusion and spiritual salvation. At the same time, the chronology and moral geography interwoven into his transatlantic travels were of a kind with what might be described as Cugoano's comparative theology.[64] Gronniosaw's journey culminated with an elaborately sophisticated Calvinist catechism in Europe, but recall that early on he described an unformed sense of "wonder" within himself, well before he had any knowledge of specific doctrines. Though Gronniosaw did not grant spiritual authority to African gods, he nonetheless posited a Christian potentiality in otherwise "pagan" Africa. His story is one of both coming into an awareness of his racial self and coming out as the Protestant subject he always was—even before he himself knew it.[65]

In Gronniosaw's narrative, racial secularization and Christian sanctification assume one another. The author/subject—once enslaved, now free—was secular insofar as it is assumed that a literary and reasoning Christianity now presided over the local relics, primitive rituals, and antiquated cosmologies associated with social life prior to the onset of modernity, specifically Gronniosaw's Africa, Marrant's Indians, and Cugoano's Incas. More generally, these accounts presume a universal category of religion that still required the catechizing of a particular kind of modern—Protestant, precisely—subjectivity *and* was premised upon the erasure, obfuscation, or reinterpretation of each of these premodern pasts.[66]

Afro-Protestantism, as seen in these early slave narratives, was thus defined by and tied to both its Euro-Christian and "Native" prehistories even as it became constitutive of a modern, secular, and racial imaginary—and a distinctly black selfhood—that colonized those religious pasts in specific ways. That is, the forging of Afro-Protestantism required that "bad religion," in a variety of forms, be excised from the historical record and occluded in the present. Ultimately, the slave narratives were essential to the enactment of an Afro-modernity— namely, a peculiarly Protestant, black subjectivity—that assumed and obscured the persistence of religion (and diverse forms of spiritual authority) all at once, and all under the sign of a racial secularism (e.g., reason, rights of man). Even when religious difference was plausibly affirmed, as it was by Cugoano, it was achieved through an archetype of good religion that presupposed the Protestant norm.

Afro-Protestant Alterities, Within and Without

Roughly twenty years after the publication of Gronniosaw's autobiographical statement, *The Life of Olaudah Equiano, or Gustavus Vassa, an African* was published in 1789. Gronniosaw had authorized his account, in part, by identifying himself as "an African prince." Yet it was Equiano, simply "an African," who became the model for most slave narratives written in subsequent decades. Like Gronniosaw's and Cugoano's, Equiano's narrative moves back and forth across the Atlantic Ocean—from freedom to slavery and back. However, Equiano outdid both of his literary predecessors, as his narrative tracks him then leaving Europe and returning to Africa. He eventually moved from England to Sierra Leone, where a significant group of black émigrés from the United States had begun to settle, with British assistance, starting in the 1780s, after the American Revolutionary War.[67]

Equiano's narrative also adhered to the familiar pairing of religion and reason established by those who wrote before him. For Gronniosaw, literacy found its fullest form in his masterful performance of Christian catechism before the panel of Calvinist clergy in Holland. Readers witness Equiano, like Gronniosaw, grow in doctrinal knowledge as his narrative unfolds. Yet Equiano shared more in common with Cugoano, who privileged what was akin to a form of Christian reasoning commensurate with the doctrine of "the rights of man." In fact, the two men were commonly thought to have collaborated on Cugoano's book, which was published just four years prior to Equiano's. Both men also became prominent in the abolitionist movement, the network of activists (and readers) that provided a primary audience for the slave narratives. Their accounts were effectively enlisted in the cause as literary evidence in support of emancipation, and helped set the course for future narratives published during the nineteenth century.

For Gronniosaw, as well as for Marrant, reason and literacy clearly served the ultimate ends of conversion and catechism. In contrast, Cugoano and Equiano conceived of reason on more expansive terms than as solely in service to securing Christian salvation. In doing so, it would seem, they relegated religion to a lesser role. Yet they also emphasized Christianity's social currency in greater measure. Both of their narratives more explicitly construe religion as one form of reasoning, as a source of authority, in a broader antislavery discourse. Religion was an important evidentiary example, yet it was not the only source of argumentation. Nor was Christian salvation, or catechism, the end of the story. More precisely, Equiano affirmed Cugoano's assertion that all forms of slavery were fundamentally at odds with "true Christianity." Yet Equiano's narrative also displays a pragmatic theological lens in which the "truth" of various religious ideas and institutions are assessed in light of their perceived ability to advance his own varying interests, which included the abolition of slavery, support for commercial enterprise, *and* responses to specific theological questions. For example, Equiano considered Quaker teachings, Roman Catholicism, and Judaism, but none of them proved satisfactory. Later he heard Whitefield preach, which "impressed" him deeply and led him to affiliate with Methodism. As much as reason more generally became the ruling logic of the slave narratives, Equiano came to have his own experience of confirmation in the Christian faith.[68]

If Equiano became the model for future slave narratives, then it may be fair to say that the genre increasingly adhered to a narrative of secularization. As Equiano's narrative recounts a series of encounters with various religious ideas and practices, including his conversion to Christianity, reason is figured as more significant than these subtle distinctions. However, his apparently secularizing plot line should not be conflated with a trajectory of religious decline. Equiano's observation of and engagement with a variety of religious traditions and his eventual Christian conversion foreground the individual's ability to choose a religion through comparison and reasoned deliberation. Across the nineteenth century black people in the United States increasingly embraced Protestant Christianity, as another wave of revivalism spread across the nation.[69] In this way, the early slave narratives—which mediated literary, political, and religious traditions at once—reflected the growing significance of Christianity throughout the Americas during the Age of Independence and, subsequently, as the nation moved incrementally toward emancipation.

Protestantism's central, if contested, place in American culture could be seen, for instance, in the significant role evangelicalism played within abolitionist movements that gained momentum in the decades prior to emancipation. It was also apparent in the theological line that Frederick Douglass drew in his first autobiography, *Narrative of the Life of Frederick Douglass, an American Slave* (1845), between "Slaveholding Religion and the Religion of Christ." Douglass explained, "I love the pure, peaceable, and impartial Christianity of Christ: I therefore hate the corrupt, slaveholding, women-whipping, cradle-plundering, partial and hypocritical Christianity of this land."[70] As Douglass makes clear in several of his narratives, the debate over true religion was often waged as a struggle over the meaning of Christianity itself, which was nonetheless understood as synonymous with religion writ large. And the essence of Douglass's "Christianity of Christ" was a theology and politics that sided with society's most vulnerable people (although not deemed fully human at the time, by law), including slaves, women, and infants.

In this way, the early accounts of Gronniosaw, Marrant, and Cugoano, and later Equiano and Douglass, participated in the construction of a literary (ethical and reasoning, and antislavery) Afro-Protestantism as the sine qua non of black religion. At the same time, these authors also helped establish a set of tropes regarding "true religion" that would continue to hold the center in the slave narratives up through Douglass and beyond. Even as a normative Afro-Protestantism secured and sustained its centrality to this literary tradition, the margins—that is, non-Christian religions and less literary iterations of Christianity—remained no less significant to the diverse religious imaginings apparent in the genre. The later cases of Shaker convert Rebecca Cox Jackson and the enslaved Muslim Omar ibn Said, respectively, illustrate the possibilities for religious alterity—within and without the borders of Christian orthodoxy—and the difficulties attendant on forging and sustaining such identities in North America. These narratives also display a greater degree of attention to differences within Christianity, beyond the good/bad binary determined by one's position on slavery, as well as to the relationship between Christianity and "other" religions. Yet, as powerful exceptions, they each also reveal the enduring power of the literary rule of Afro-Protestantism in ordering the prospects for black subjectivity and social life in the age of slavery and freedom.

The Life of Omar ibn Said (1831) was unique on at least three counts. For one, it is the only autobiography of an African slave written in Arabic in the United States. Said was also different from other enslaved authors in that he learned to read and write prior to his enslavement.[71] And in Said's narrative, readers don't witness the enslaved author realize the promise of freedom. In most cases, the slave narrative itself exemplified the act of writing one's way out of bondage, as the authors acquired literacy. Indeed, attaining literacy is what enabled them to author(ize) their own emancipation, demonstrating their humanity through an achievement of literacy. Said, on the other hand, was literate (and learned, for that matter) in Arabic prior to being taken captive. He did, however, learn English after arriving in North America. That Said referred to English as the "Christian language" reveals much about how he understood the relationship between religion, language, and nation in the new land where he was conscripted into slavery.

In this regard, *The Life of Omar ibn Said* offers a glimpse of one man's efforts to negotiate his identity as an African Muslim while enslaved in the United States, which he also refers to as "the Christian country."[72] According to Said, "[I]nfidels took me unjustly and sold me into the hands of a Christian man." Readers are once again introduced to an unstated norm in which true religion (be it Christianity or Islam) and chattel slavery are figured as necessarily opposed. During his time in America, Said was made the property of two different men, both of whom he identified as Christians. The first "Christian man," observed Said, "did not fear Allah at all, nor . . . read or pray." His second master, however, "fears Allah . . . [and] loves to do good deeds." This "righteous man," he explained, "does not beat me, nor call me bad names, nor subjects me to hunger, nakedness, or hard work. I cannot do hard work for I am a small, ill man."[73] The difference between whether one was "evil" or "righteous," in Said's account, appeared to be more a matter of ethics, and of reading and praying, than identification with a specific religious doctrine. Here the Christian master is recognized as fearing Allah because of his fair treatment of Said, the Muslim slave who would come to "pray in the words of our Lord Jesus the Messiah."[74] Said appeared to adopt what might be described as a comparative religious ethic, or a theology of religious pluralism. Not unlike Cugoano's narrative, *The Life of Omar ibn Said* implies that Christians and Muslims share the same God, which makes Said's conversion in the narrative all the more curious.

That Said was educated prior to being enslaved troubled the traditional plot line of the slave narrative. Typically the passage from wonder to reason was evidenced in the acquisition of literacy, as established first in Gronniosaw's narrative. Moreover, the slave narrative's standard movement toward a reasoning subject was generally mapped onto a journey from Africa to the Americas and/or Europe, a re-formation of the author's spiritual self from pagan to

Protestant and, of course, the passage from slavery to freedom. Over the course of Said's account, the geographic and religious movement is apparent: he is taken from Africa to the southern United States and appears to embrace Christianity. The first (i.e., the acquisition of literacy), however, is impossible since Said already knew how to read and write in Arabic; the second—his Christian conversion—is not entirely clear.[75] For instance, Said referred to his prayers to Allah in the past tense, adding, "[N]ow I pray . . . in the words of our Lord Jesus the Messiah." Yet his religious transformation was more ambiguous than those recorded by other authors, such as Gronniosaw and Equiano. Some clues in the narrative suggest he did convert, and others imply otherwise. Indeed, Said's contemporaries debated the authenticity of his conversion.[76] That his narrative was written in Arabic would suggest that it remained his primary language (and Islam his primary religion, perhaps) even after he professed to embrace Christianity—in the "Christian land" among a people who spoke the "Christian language," not insignificantly.[77]

Several concerns emerge with regard to the potential meanings surrounding Said's contested conversion. His narrative evokes the question of Christianity as performance and pretense, raised previously by both Gronniosaw and Cugoano. Recall Gronniosaw's claim after being examined by the clergy panel, that they were "persuaded I was what I pretended to be." Did Said also "pretend" to convert to curry favor from his Christian master? Did Christianity present the best prospect for a coherent spiritual community in a Christian land? Or did Said not understand that an embrace of Christianity was a necessarily mutually exclusive proposition against maintaining fidelity to Islam? To be sure, Said's narrative was by no means an erasure of his Muslim, African, or Arabic past. Neither did it entail a neat exchange of Islam for Christianity, and Arabic for English.[78] One wonders whether such a comparative frame is itself the result of the coercive terms of social existence within a "Christian nation," and all the more so for enslaved black subjects in the American South. Whether *The Life of Omar ibn Said* was evidence of a definitive conversion, a rejection of Christianity, or an early example of "multiple belonging," is unclear. What is clear is that, as a slave narrative, it was indelibly shaped by the prescriptive powers of a Protestant hegemony aligned with the institution of New World slavery—otherwise put, by racial capitalism.[79]

Questions of interiority, belief, and authenticity are perhaps unresolvable, and not just in the case of Said. It is clear that he operated within the rules of an ethical and literary definition of religion, which carried authority in both Islam and Christianity, which in the Americas was the product of a particular Protestant genealogy.[80] In this regard, the possession of a persisting Arabic and Islamic alterity—subjected to the scrutiny of public confessions and their presumed interiorities—made Said no less a subject of the prevailing Afro-Protestantism. If *The Life of Omar ibn Said* was marginal because its author maintained a Muslim identity, the distinctions Said drew between "evil" and "righteous" Christians were consistent with other slave narratives during the middle decades of the nineteenth century. Notably, he leveled little outright criticism on the institution of American slaveholding, or the slave trade, as a whole. This is unsurprising given that slavery, albeit under dramatically different terms, was a social fact in his homeland. Instead, Said's narrative focused on the specific terms of enslavement and varying treatment that the enslaved received from their masters.[81]

In contrast to Said's, the writings of Rebecca Cox Jackson were more in keeping with the conventional connections between the genre of the slave narrative and abolitionist politics.[82] Like Marrant, she was never enslaved, but grew up in the hotbed of Afro-Protestantism that was Philadelphia during the nineteenth century. However, Jackson's proto-feminist theology caused her to fall out of grace with the overwhelmingly male leadership of institutional Afro-Protestantism—specifically, the African Methodist Episcopal Church—and instead, eventually, embrace life as a Shaker. Yet her firm commitment to bringing the gospel to black people, in particular, over time also put her at odds with an overwhelmingly white Shaker community, with whom she experienced commonality in terms of her status as a woman, her theology, and her interest in ecstatic religious practices. Though Jackson remained within Christian congregations throughout her life, her heterodox beliefs and practices often relegated her to the margins of both the Afro-Protestant and Shaker communities. While Said appeared to at least put on the "pretense" of his masters' Christianity, Jackson submitted to the authority of her "inner voice" rather than compromise with religious institutions or clergy leaders. Though Shaker leadership eventually supported her mission to the black residents of Philadelphia, she first had to strike out on her own. As the founder and leader of an independent spiritual community, Jackson created a ministry quite distinct from the small number of itinerant black women preachers at the time, such as Jarena Lee, whose ministries were authorized by Afro-Protestant denominational structures.[83]

The singularity of Jackson's ministry set the trajectory for her literary work as well, as her writing did not adhere to the standard literary structure of most slave narratives. Ultimately, her mission was to her own people and in her native tongue (unlike Marrant). Indeed, Jackson founded her Shaker mission in Philadelphia, the very city in which she was raised. Additionally, her path to literacy did not come through the embrace of Christianity. She was born into a family where literacy was common, and her older brother was an ordained minister in the founding church, Mother Bethel A.M.E. Church, of a denomination that prized learned clergy and helped to define the literary rule of Afro-Protestantism. Still, struggles over literacy—better yet, for literacy—were no small part of what eventually led to her estrangement from her family and the A.M.E. Church. Education was a privilege most often afforded only to men. And only in middle age did Jackson teach herself to read, through an arduous process that she described as miraculous. Indeed, literacy was one of her "gifts of power." Though not a literal captive, in pursuing her call Jackson repeatedly ran up against the constraints of the gender, racial, and religious orders of her day.

Jackson's path to spiritual maturity also did not follow the customary plot lines apparent in most slave narratives. The degree to which she was even familiar with these texts is unclear.[84] In contrast to Gronniosaw's elaborate catechism, Marrant's "highest stile," or Cugoano's and Equiano's historical sensibility and literary sophistication, Jackson's writing was rather unpolished. Never mind that she never received the benefit of a formal editorial process, as was the case for almost all of the other authors, before her death. In this regard, her *Gifts of Power* perhaps shared more in common with the significantly shorter *Life of Omar ibn Said*. Yet, where Said's literary limitations were more a matter of linguistic difference, Jackson's unsophisticated prose was a product of the gendered exclusions of a normative Afro-Protestantism that reserved formal education (and the pulpit) primarily for men.

Jackson's literary difference was further heightened by the specific forms of religiosity to which she subscribed. For one, she maintained a commitment to her own "inner voice" in ways that, ironically, foregrounded physical bodies.[85] For instance, Jackson's Shaker practice included technologies of the body that encouraged intimate asceticism (celibacy), excessive public expressiveness (shaking), and esoteric possession (spiritualist mediums). All of these practices revealed a form of reasoning that confounded the body politics of established black churches in the North, despite the fact that Jackson's life and literary imagination were all the while quintessentially Afro-Protestant. That is, Jackson departed from the path that her male literary predecessors cleared, which moved from emotionalism to reason on the way to spiritual maturity. Over against the rule of textual mastery as the outward sign of salvation, established by the successful pretense of Gronniosaw's catechism, Jackson's religious vision embraced evangelicalism's embodied expressiveness and simultaneously privileged the authority of women.

Jackson's unique combination of religious heterodoxy and literary simplicity perhaps helps explain why her writings were not published until more than a century after her death in 1871.[86] In this regard, the aesthetics of her writing and religious practice both confirmed and clarified the boundaries of the respectable version of Afro-Protestantism to which most independent black churches aspired during the nineteenth century.[87] Such churches were often the primary sites for black collective deliberations and political organizing, and Jackson's Christianity refused to abide by their rules of public reasoning.[88] To be clear, insofar as education and literacy (and ordination) were privileges reserved primarily for men, institutional Afro-Protestantism also refused her. Moreover, while part and parcel of nineteenth-century revivalism, Shakerism—whether black or white—embodied the antithesis of the modern, reasoning Protestantism that was central to the nation's literary culture during the period.[89] For Jackson, true religion was stubbornly disciplined by black women's interiority and asceticism even as it encouraged, if not required, excessive displays of bodily expression (and black women's bodies, no less!), which unsurprisingly ran afoul of the Afro-Protestant establishment of her day.

Summary

Together these slave narratives simultaneously reveal both a significant measure of fluidity and clear normative fault lines within an emerging Afro-Protestant social world. If by refusal and excess, perhaps none clarified the boundaries of this Afro-Protestantism as powerfully as Jackson's *Gifts of Power*. These narratives also help to illumine a certain porousness between Protestantism and a range of other religious traditions (e.g., Said's Islam) and spiritual authorities (e.g., Valverde's Catholicism, Atahualpa's ancestors) that animated the early Americas. Some narratives featured a variety of practices within Christianity, including speaking in foreign tongues, critiques of biblical justifications for slavery, appealing to the power of prayer, ecstatic worship, spirit possession, and much more. Other accounts contrasted Christianity in general with indigenous religious traditions in both North and South America, as well as in Africa.[90] To be sure, the authors' strident critiques of colonialism called Christianity into question. Yet such criticisms did not amount to an erasure of Afro-Protestantism or facilitate the adoption of a secular black subjectivity in its stead. Rather, to borrow a phrase from Henry Louis Gates Jr., a "mastery of the text of God, alone of all other texts," remained the most widely embraced path from slavery to freedom. And, conversely, freedom was the sign of true Christianity, and real religion in general. At the same time, however, an incredibly rich milieu of cultural and religious diversity was effectively disciplined by masterful performances of a literary and reasoning Afro-Protestantism—which is to say, a performance of black subjectivity.[91]

In this regard, Afro-Protestantism can be identified as the text within the text of blackness. Christianity put flesh on the bones of an Enlightenment reason and an emerging racial subjectivity even as doctrinal orthodoxy provided the normative scripts for evaluating the practice of blackness. That is, an Afro-Protestant orthodoxy was stitched into the very fabric of black subjectivity and thus was made

constitutive of the various forms of racial authenticity that would develop in its wake. Though black writers developed literary traditions on
necessarily formal terms, they were also formed by the constraints and
possibilities of the particular social contexts that colored all of their
literary visions in the shades of a persistently racial and Protestant secularism. Even as these authors (and their texts) rejected the conflation
of Christianity with the colonial enterprise, they often assumed an ethical, reasoning core to Christianity that furthered the era's notion of
"good religion." In short, the literary aesthetic of Afro-Protestantism
that emerged in the slave narratives was critical of colonialism even as
it was consistent with an emerging conception of religion that reflected
the logics of colonialism.[92] In this view, the slave narratives offer an
early portrait of a prescriptive religious pluralism that—by simultaneously revealing and obscuring diversity within Christianity and
rendering marginal "other" religious traditions—helped instantiate
Afro-Protestantism as definitive of a New World black subjectivity and
social world then taking form.[93]

The slave narratives were never simply a literary practice solely dependent upon the logics of racial (black/white) or religious (sacred/
secular) binaries. Rather, these spiritual autobiographies were emblematic of the undeniably entangled kinds of social practices that
took place under colonial contact and chattel slavery in the Atlantic
World. Moreover, they illumine the inherently hybrid nature of black
subjectivity and social life in the Americas. "To be a subject means
to activate the network of discourse from *where one stands,*" Barbara
Johnson argued, ". . . to take nourishment from more than one source,
to construct a new synthesis."[94] And to be a black subject in the
Americas was to inhabit—both emerge out of and exist within—the
inheritances of multiple worlds mediated all the while by gross asymmetries of power.[95]

Even as black people, both enslaved and free, embraced Christianity
in growing numbers, performances of Afro-Protestantism in the
Americas were always tinged with the tragic terms of their formation.
This is the central irony of black religion: as a New World phenomenon, Christianity provided a set of resources for personal affirmation and social dissent, access to rituals of collective identification and
communal celebration, and space for the assertion, most basically, of

a self. Yet the process by which black people were evangelized and the means through, and terms under, which they embraced evangelicalism was, simultaneously, nothing less than a "spiritual and cultural holocaust."[96] While hybridity is now widely lauded, its earliest embodied performances by enslaved Africans recognized, if but intuitively, that the acquisition of power and privilege—and even the capacity to survive—was often contingent upon one's ability and willingness to bind the lifeworld of one's enemy deep within one's own body and soul.

Christianity, as it was received and re-formed by black people in countless instantiations—what has been referred to here as Afro-Protestantism—can be understood, to borrow a phrase from Ashis Nandy, as the "intimate enemy."[97] Afro-Protestantism both encoded the traumas of the wholesale slaughter that was enslavement and colonialism and cultivated an immeasurable degree of ingenuity directed toward survival, identity formation, and social and cultural coherence, if not wholeness. Persistent and impenetrable bonds were formed between Christian theology and the practices of colonialism. This invidious pairing then set the course for organizing modern social life and death and for the categories modernity made to interpret and organize the world. These social facts—the facts of living and dying in "the contact zone"[98]—were often observed and argued through and against by the authors of the slave narratives. Yet they were also reproduced in the inverse as race politics and religious history were bound together in the formation of African American literary and religious traditions. The Afro-Protestantism being worked out in the slave narratives was then necessarily a novel, creolized, and creolizing formation: a strange admixture of African and American, sacred and secular, high and low, literary and oral, unruly and disciplined, embodied and esoteric, oppressive and enabling, reasoning and unreasonable. Afro-Protestantism as the black.

To put the matter otherwise, in the slave narratives Afro-Protestantism emerged as a peculiar secular performance within a growing repertoire of fundamentally religious forms. In this context, Afro-Protestantism came to constitute a set of structure(s) and form(s) for thinking and feeling black and the conditions of possibility for (Afro) modernity. This seeming contradiction stands at the center of Afro-Protestantism's heterodox history, which is also the central irony of black subjectivity and American secularism. As should be clear, just as catechism and conversion were entangled in the slave narratives, so too is it difficult to draw a clear boundary between spiritual autobiographies and the genre as a whole. Some of the later narratives would seem to suggest a secularizing telos for African American literature. However, the earnest pretense—that is, a good faith performance—of Afro-Protestantism, as witnessed first in Gronniosaw's narrative, continued in full form well into the decades that followed emancipation.

Indeed, as the slave narratives were superseded by a growing literary culture that emerged out of the soil of Reconstruction—as well as its demise and the subsequent legal codification of racial segregation—the idea of a "race literature" was born. As the independent church movement, primarily enacted by black Baptists and Methodists, rapidly expanded during the latter half of the nineteenth century, formerly enslaved people continued to assert their independence with appeals to the written word. As with the slave narratives that preceded it, the new race literature—and the moment and movements in which it took root—would continue to bear the marks of the particular Christian genealogy that shaped the way blackness—as subjectivity and social life—was imagined from the very beginning.

2

Afro-Protestantism, Pluralism, and the Problem of the Color Line

Catechesis was the religious rule that helped to write the literary origins of African American religious life in the New World, as seen in several of the slave narratives published near the end of the eighteenth century and as the end of slavery approached. By the turn of the twentieth century, however, Afro-Protestantism had become a religious and racial tradition as well as a set of structural arrangements, a social order defined simultaneously by a commitment to independent institution-building (i.e., churches), a set of literary practices, and an embrace of the emotional fervor of revivalist Christianity, with its intense, affective registers of conversion.[1] To be sure, the literary aspirations that defined the beginnings of black religion never disappeared. Indeed, the heterodoxy that animated Afro-Protestantism across the nineteenth century persisted, despite (or because of) an increasingly robust literary rule that was rearticulated within the emerging rubrics of appeals to a "New Negro" following the rise of Jim Crow. However, the tributaries through which this literary, religious, and racial tradition flowed were reconfigured by a range of developments during the second half of the nineteenth century. Significant among these changes were the legal end of chattel slavery, the overwhelming bloodshed of the Civil War and its aftermath, Reconstruction and its subsequent demise, the not unrelated rise and rule of white supremacist campaigns of terror and violence (especially) in the American South, the disenfranchisement of recently freed black men and women, and the legal triumph of racial segregation in the United States.

The final years of the nineteenth century dramatically encapsulated the contradictions that defined the nation's cultural aspirations as well as its political and philosophical ambitions. On the one hand, the 1890s was a decade that has been referred to as the "nadir" in terms of

Black is a Church. Josef Sorett, Oxford University Press. © Oxford University Press 2023.
DOI: 10.1093/oso/9780190615130.003.0003

the country's long and vexed history of race relations.[2] Though slavery had come to an end, the long-standing racial hierarchy was recodified through an elaborate system of Black Codes—actively enforced by the threat (and ritualized practices) of the lynch mob—that ensured black people would not come close to approximating freedom, social equality, or full citizenship. After a series of legal setbacks in several southern states, the cause of equality for the formerly enslaved was effectively undone when, in 1896, the nation's highest court affirmed the rule of legal segregation. The Supreme Court's ruling in *Plessy v. Ferguson* established the doctrine of "separate but equal," signaled the institutionalization of Jim Crow, and marked a definitive end to the promise of Reconstruction.

On the other hand, during the very same years that the United States witnessed the ascendancy of Jim Crow, word began to travel about a "Negro renaissance" in both literature and politics. Black writers, race leaders, and preachers alike called for "a New Negro for a New Century"—an apt phrase that was the title of an ambitious book published by Booker T. Washington, N. B. Wood, and Fannie Barrier Williams in 1901. The cross-section represented by this team of authors—a race leader, a historian, and a club woman—was indicative of a select, if statistically small, group of black elites who fashioned themselves as part of a New Negro movement. The poets, novelists, critics, and political leaders of this Negro renaissance galvanized each other and made a powerful claim on the attention of a liberal, largely white readership at the turn of the twentieth century.[3] As the new century dawned, figures like Ida B. Wells, Charles Chesnutt, W. E. B. Du Bois, Paul Laurence Dunbar, Sutton Griggs, Charles Price Jones, and Victoria Earle Matthews contributed to the beginnings of what Matthews would refer to, in an 1895 speech, as "race literature." If not all directly in dialogue with one another, each of these individuals made important contributions to the cultural, intellectual, and political ferment of the era. Moreover, their writings captured the complicated ways that religion, race, and literature coalesced in a set of social movements during the final years of the nineteenth century.[4] Together they participated in the construction of "the New Negro" as a mythic, and heroic, figure in the midst of a period of dramatic racial violence.

Giving focus to their literary aspirations, most of these authors were actively involved in a variety of activities that were then grouped under the rubric of race politics. Indeed, it is impossible to imagine a "negro renaissance" in the arts without a sense of the political activism with which race literature was entangled at the time. Negro writers were often assigned and expected to bear (as well as taking upon themselves) the burden of race politics. Matthews was active in the settlement house and women's club movements.[5] Chesnutt and Du Bois both participated in the early gatherings of the Niagara movement, as well as the founding of the National Association for the Advancement of Colored People (NAACP), as did Wells, although she is best known for her journalistic crusades against lynching. Much of the racial activism and writing of the day was also interwoven with the rhythms, rituals, and institutional resources of Afro-Protestantism. As they did when they were first formed, black churches continued to serve as a space for pursuing spiritual and social equality at once—as well as they figured significantly as a sign of black freedom. And now, notably, churches also provided a publishing base for race literature.[6]

On the heels of Emancipation and the revivalist fervors of the Great Awakenings, the numbers of black people who embraced the Christian faith had grown exponentially during the decades that preceded the twentieth century. Accordingly, the number of independent black churches, especially Baptist and Methodist congregations, had also grown significantly.[7] Unsurprisingly, then, one of the first people to deploy the term "New Negro" was a Baptist clergyman, Sutton Griggs, who did so in his 1899 novel, *Imperium in Imperio*.[8] The activism of another one-time Baptist minister, C. P. Jones, occurred largely through an emerging network of Afro-Pentecostal churches that he helped to establish. The fact of his rootedness in nascent black Pentecostal and Holiness movements perhaps helps to explain why Jones is the least familiar figure in this group.[9] Although most overtly in the careers of clergy such as Griggs and Jones, race literature and politics was, more often than not, entangled with church-based organizing in a period that was defined by outsized religious ambitions.[10]

Indeed, the turn of the twentieth century was a moment of grand spiritual aspirations in North America. Early American Pentecostals insisted on worshiping in ways that resisted the modern logics of racial segregation and religious dispensationalism. At the same time, a primarily Protestant vanguard of liberal elites attempted to expand the boundaries of human brotherhood by imagining a global community not divided by religious difference. While the NAACP was inaugurating a new era of interracial organizing for black citizenship across the nation, similar developments were underway within the realm of American religious life—most notably, with the inaugural World's Parliament of Religions in 1893. Accordingly, each of the above-named figures enunciated a racial sensibility that also bore the markings—and contributed to the making—of a moment that has been hailed as "the dawn of religious pluralism."[11] Under the guise of the New Negro, once again Afro-Protestantism, alongside the emerging practice of religious pluralism, gave shape to the form and substance of black subjectivity and social life and helped to underwrite how New Negroes participated in several distinct but interconnected social movements of the day.[12]

Victoria Earle Matthews and the Religious Value of Race Literature

There is perhaps no better exemplar of America's entangled religious and racial aspirations at the end of the nineteenth century than Victoria Earle Matthews. Club woman, settlement house activist, and author, Matthews brought all of these commitments together in a speech she delivered to the First Congress of Colored Women in Boston on July 30, 1895. "The Value of Race Literature" was received as a credo for the Negro women's club movement even as it inaugurated a critical conversation about the substance and form of a tradition now commonly referred to as African American literature. Matthews's writings offer a window into more than the emergence of a novel genre of writing. Her work (along with that of her peers) illustrates just how central, if contested, Christianity was to the very first imaginings of a literary tradition she then named "race literature," as well as to the social religious, racial, and political movements of this particular moment in history.[13] As was argued in chapter 1, the slave narratives bore witness to the ways in which Afro-Protestantism both harbored and was defined by literary aspirations from its inception. The same was certainly true of African American religion during the 1890s, when Matthews delivered her now classic speech. Conversely, from the moment of its earliest articulation near the end of the nineteenth century, race literature was also imagined as a religious practice.

As envisioned by Matthews, race literature would represent "real Christianity" and serve as an effective counter to the problem of the color line. Better yet, in her formulation, both race literature and religion—in keeping with the normative logics worked out in the slave narratives—were necessarily opposed to slavery and the newer form of social inequality: racial segregation under the legal rubric of "separate but equal." In tandem with the nascent New Negro movement, race literature would counter the injustices of Jim Crow. In this regard, Matthews echoed an earlier era in American history (and in black writing) by wedding a notion of "real Christianity" with a form of reasoning that affirmed black humanity and positioning literature as a religious resource in service to the social and political struggle for racial equality.

Matthews was one of the first people to give language to—to theorize, as it were—the phenomenon of race literature. In "The Value of Race Literature," she offered a provisional definition of the genre as "writings emanating from a distinct class—not necessarily race matter; but a general collection of what has been written by the men and women of that Race." Race literature would bear witness to the full range of experiences of the formerly enslaved and their descendants. Indeed, Matthews called for a body of writing that would reflect the "very marked difference in the limitations, characteristics, aspirations and ambitions of this class of people." Race literature would be produced by "the race" even as it might not focus exclusively on, in her words, "race matter"—all of the matters that comprised black life, even when they failed to align with a normative vision of race politics. In making her case for the significance of this nascent literary project, Matthews assigned to race literature an explicitly religious purpose. It would "represent an original school" that reflected the Negro's social status as a second-class citizen, to be sure. Yet race literature, Matthews continued, would also "rightly interpret our unappreciated contribution to Christianity."[14]

Matthews elaborated further on how she understood the connections between Christian virtue and her activism on behalf of "Afro-Americans," and black women specifically.[15] In "The Value of Race Literature" she explained that "the prejudice of color" and the nation's "unchristian disposition" were "the source of an original school of race literature, of racial psychology, of potent possibilities, an amalgam needed for this great American race of the future." The manner in which whites practiced Christianity revealed a moral deficit and made race literature a necessity. Their faith, in her view, was decidedly not "real Christianity." As such, Matthews imbued the genre with spiritual purpose and granted it the capacity to generate social change. Race literature would help the cause of black social equality while also providing "the race" with a much-needed outlet for their "unnaturally suppressed inner lives."[16] Race literature would be a source and site through which "real Christianity" would put the lie to the hypocrisy of religiously sanctioned racism and the unnatural conditions it imposed on black life. In this regard, Matthews affirmed the line that Frederick Douglass had previously drawn, discussed in chapter 1, between the "Christianity of this land" and the "Christianity of Christ."[17] Race literature would be a means through which to simultaneously achieve the social and spiritual—at once racial and religious—end of bridging the gap between the two.

As Matthews's most famous speech suggested, Christianity figured prominently in the writing and theorizing of race literature from the outset. Moreover, institutional Afro-Protestantism, particularly black Baptist and black Methodist churches, had come to play a primary role in the production and circulation of black writing during the nineteenth century. In fact, it was on the pages of the *A.M.E. Church Review*—a leading black journal of the day published by the African Methodist Episcopal Church—that a critic first declared that a "New Negro literary movement" was underway.[18] The *A.M.E. Church Review* also published at least three of Matthews's short stories, including the popular "Aunt Lindy: A Story Founded on Real Life" (1889).[19] In "Aunt Lindy," Matthews wove together the tale of a formerly enslaved woman who gained renown for her healing work as a nurse. The story takes shape after the scene of a great fire. Aunt Lindy is asked to care for one victim of the fire, whom she soon discovers to be her former master, an evil man who years ago sold all of her children into slavery. Unsurprisingly, upon recognizing her patient, Aunt Lindy found herself in a frenzied anger and contemplating murder. Constrained by the recollection of Christian scripture, "Vengeance is mine, ses de Lawd," Aunt Lindy recalls. Accordingly, she wards off her rage, praying for the strength to do so, and proceeds to gently nurse the old man back to health.

In "Aunt Lindy's Tale" and elsewhere, Matthews used the popular genre of sentimental fiction to challenge the dominant racial discourses of her day. Her short stories illustrated the complexities of black social life and offered complicated portraits of black women specifically as agents in the world with rich interior lives.[20] Even more significant here, in "Aunt Lindy's Tale" Matthews introduced the idea of "Afro-Americans"—and black women in particular—as the embodiment of an ethical, reasoning Christianity. In this view, black people were required to love their enemies and to do so despite a flood of contrary emotions and regardless of the ends such actions might yield. Matthews's story, however, presents the possibility that such faithfulness might produce rewards in life. Readers observe Aunt Lindy's refusal of rage, figured as evidence of the integrity of her faith, and the chain of events that her act of apparent forgiveness triggers. In her care, Aunt Lindy's former master, "Marse Jeems," steadily returns to good health. He then confirms that an unidentified young preacher who unexpectedly arrives in town is indeed Aunt Lindy's firstborn son, whom he long ago had stolen from her arms and sold into bondage.

Within the constraints of a short story, Matthews manages to advance several arguments that together elevate a Christian norm for race literature. Readers are made aware that some black people are "real" Christians. Early in the narrative Aunt Lindy announces that both she and her husband, Uncle Joel, "ain't heathins." To the contrary, they both demonstrate a deep knowledge of the Christian Bible, discussing between themselves the mandate to care for "de stranger widin thy gates."[21] Christian morality—as demonstrated here through biblical literacy—functions to affirm Aunt Lindy's and Uncle Joel's humanity even as it demands that they "love their enemy." Additionally, the narrative arc of the story suggests that Lindy's capacity (which stands in for the capacity of "the race" writ large) to be disciplined by and demonstrate Christian virtue—ethical and forgiving rather than emotional or vengeful—promised rewards for black and white folk alike. Indeed, the once evil master is healed, and the former slaves and grief-stricken parents are reunited with their firstborn son. Past sins appear to be redeemed in the present through Aunt Lindy's embrace of an Afro-Protestant subjectivity and the form of reasoning—namely, forgiveness—it would seem to require. The entire exchange hinges upon Aunt Lindy's willingness to refuse what is, by all accounts, a well-warranted, and quite rational, act of vengeance.[22]

Ultimately in "Aunt Lindy," Matthews presents a literary and reasoning Christianity as the key to reconciling the United States' racially divided past and present. Just a few years later she would make this claim more directly, and more grandly, in a speech at the 1897 Annual Convention of the Society of Christian Endeavor in San Francisco. There Matthews presented herself as, like her audience, "clothed in the garments of Christian womanhood." Having established a shared "we" with the primarily white women in her hearing, she then called upon them to "join with us in elevating the head, the heart, and the soul of Afro-American womanhood."[23] Across her activism and writing, Matthews's notion of "real Christianity" made a religious mandate of the racial uplift ideology prominent at the time.[24]

In "Aunt Lindy" the heroine's choice to submit her emotions to Christian duty is the very condition of possibility for physical healing (for Marse Jeems) and familial restoration (for Aunt Lindy and Uncle Joel). In this way, "Aunt Lindy" effectively illustrates the role accorded Christianity in a tradition of sentimentalist literature that was popular during the latter half of the nineteenth century. A decade before Du Bois singled out the "problem of the color line" in *The Souls of Black Folk* (1903), the religious aesthetic apparent in Matthews's vision for race literature fit within a longer tradition that was imagined as intervening in social problems.[25] Exactly forty years earlier, Harriet Beecher Stowe's *Uncle Tom's Cabin*, which began as a serialized short story that trafficked in similarly sentimental depictions of race and religion, provided an apt prototype in its critique of American slavery.[26]

In both her speeches and her short stories, Matthews elaborated an ethical, reasoning, and literary Afro-Protestantism that also undergirded her activism in the women's movement. A closer reading of the politics of religion apparent in "Aunt Lindy" reveals the particular kind of religion(s) that Matthews privileged as an organizing logic and telos for race literature. Indeed, if Lindy adopted for herself a form of Christian subjectivity, the social world that she inhabited was animated by a range of religious traditions, as well as the competing authorities of modern science and medical materialism. Upon closer inspection, the singularity of Christian truth in Matthews's story is less certain. Along with her appeal to Christian scripture, the story's heroine avails herself of unspecified "desired herbs" to supplement her prayers and the prescriptions of the local doctor. It would seem that the esteemed Lindy's healing prowess resulted from something other than (or in addition to) her Christian virtue and nursing acuity. The storyline suggests as much.

Matthews's appeal to herbal remedies hints at the presence of alternative healing practices and indigenous spiritual resources that were cultivated alongside the authorized and respectable discourse of Protestant Christianity (and the nascent authority of the medical sciences). While Lindy declares that she and Joel are not heathens, the story makes no normative claims about her other attachments or competencies. To be sure, it is Lindy's Christian faith that chastens her rage and narratively frames the return of her firstborn son. Yet readers are left to wonder what role the herbs played, along with prayers and medicine, in the old man's healing. It's not so much that Christianity subdues or converts a nebulous "secular" threat in "Aunt Lindy." Rather, it is the Protestant rule—in this case, Aunt Lindy's performance of an Afro-Protestant selfhood—that presides over and organizes the terms under which other identified agents (i.e., "desired herbs") are mobilized. In this way, Matthews's readers were made witness to a subtle form of the kind of religious pluralism that abided within black communities as they negotiated America's (white) Protestant establishment in the Gilded Age. Matthews's Protestant vision of pluralism was distinctive in its "Afro-American" iteration of racial and religious difference. Yet it was also of a kind with a version of racial difference and religious pluralism on display elsewhere at the time. Indeed, "Aunt Lindy" was republished in pamphlet and book form in 1893, the same year of the first World's Parliament of Religions, an event which will be more fully discussed later in this chapter.[27]

Prominent among the "alternative" spiritual practices present within African American communities at the end of the nineteenth century was the hybrid folk tradition known as Conjure or Hoodoo.[28] If the invocation of "desired herbs" might be overlooked by present-day readers, Matthews's audience would have recognized its significance. By the time "Aunt Lindy" first appeared in the pages of the *A.M.E. Church Review*, the African American Conjuring tradition had been a familiar trope in American literature for some time. Perhaps most famously, Conjure figured at a pivotal moment in the *Narrative of the Life of Frederick Douglass, an American Slave* (1845). In this account, as an enslaved youth en route to securing his freedom, Douglass found an audience with an "old adviser" by the name of Sandy Jenkins, who instructed the young Douglass to take "a certain *root*" with him as he planned to confront Edward Covey, a ruthless overseer. With the aid of this root, in Douglass's telling, he engaged in a two-hour physical struggle with Covey, who got the "worst end of the bargain." Noncommittal concerning the source of his newfound "resolve to fight" (much like Matthews's passing mention of the "desired herbs"), Douglass confesses, "[F]rom whence came the spirit I don't know." What is clear in the narrative is that his successful confrontation with Covey was the "turning-point" in his "career as a slave."[29] Separated by over four decades, the "Aunt Lindy" story and Douglass's narrative are quite different on several counts. In both, however, the receipt of a natural remedy associated with the spiritual tradition known as Conjure—rather than, or alongside, an appeal to Christianity—enables the path toward freedom.

Adding to Hoodoo's literary history, the Conjuring tradition received an extended treatment in the 1890s by Charles Waddell Chesnutt. A lawyer by training, Chesnutt became the first Negro novelist published in the United States when *The House behind the Cedars* went to press in 1900. Two collections of his short stories, *The Wife of His Youth and Other Stories of the Color Line* and *The Conjure Woman and Other Conjure Tales*, were released one year earlier.[30] Where Douglass's *Narrative* and Matthews's "Aunt Lindy" subtly suggest the significance of Conjure, *The Conjure Woman* portrayed more fully the indigenous spiritual tradition, which had an especially strong presence in the American South. Chesnutt's short stories present Conjure as a repertoire of cultural practices that formerly enslaved Africans and their descendants accessed as alternative sources of spiritual and social power. Conjurers, in turn, are cast as powerful figures revered (and often feared) for their spiritual faculties and ability to advise on, possibly even solve a variety of real-world problems. If not explicitly stated, Conjurers are imagined as ancestral presences who derive their powers from ties to an African past. They are also portrayed, in the present, as well suited—perhaps better than Christian clergy—to deal with day-to-day affairs, such as personal relationships and business dealings. Often disparaged as "black magic," Conjure figured, for black practitioners and their clients, as both a source of opposition to the dominant Protestant religion of their white neighbors (and former masters) and a practical resource for resolving "race matter"—to borrow Matthews's language—more mundane than those addressed by the doctrines and creeds of Christian theology or the literary rituals of catechism discussed in chapter 1.[31]

Chesnutt's writings help to map out a literary history of two parallel, if interwoven and at times competing, traditions of cultural and spiritual authority—Christianity and Conjure, respectively—in African American life. In shorter form, Matthews offered a fictional portrait of these traditions entangled in the character of Aunt Lindy, an image supported with historical evidence.[32] The idea and representation of Conjure and Hoodoo would persist, all the while reconfigured and reinterpreted, as black writing evolved over the course of the twentieth century. Although never overturning the Afro-Protestant rule articulated in Matthews's theory of race literature, both she and Chesnutt (and Douglass before them) placed the indigenous black American spiritual tradition of Conjure in plain sight as the genre emerged and the new century took shape. Conjure was, in practice, a constitutive ingredient in the history and performance of a heterodox Afro-Protestantism, a religious tradition expansive enough to abide a good deal of theological and cultural difference. In truth, the "real Christianity" that Matthews credited to race literature was defined as much by its ability to counter white supremacy—and correct a racist literary and political record—as it was by any specific doctrinal orthodoxy.

Among the first to both theorize and practice race literature, Matthews was certainly a singular figure. Yet she was in good company with a group of other black elites who were engaged in a larger effort to launch a New Negro movement. She was also at the forefront of a group of activists who were both writing and organizing to secure full citizenship for women. Together, these commitments made Matthews part of an even smaller group of black women, like Frances Ellen Watkins Harper, Ida B. Wells, and Fannie Barrier Williams, who moved across these overlapping movements to champion the cause of "Afro-American womanhood." Agitating against racial and gender oppression, each of these women played a key role in forming the organizations—like the Congress of Colored Women—that provided Matthews with the platform to deliver her speech on race literature in 1895.[33] At the same time, the grand ambitions that she harbored, as both a writer and an activist, were enlivened by a wider set of cultural, political, and religious aspirations—indeed, a utopian impulse—that animated much of American liberal culture and thought during the Gilded Age.[34]

When Matthews argued that "greatness, true heroism and real Christianity" would distinguish race literature, she pointed to the Czech musician Antonin Leopold Dvořák as a model—eight years before Du Bois would do the same in the final chapter of *The Souls of Black Folk*. When composing his New World Symphony Dvořák found inspiration in Negro Spirituals, crediting them as "the folk songs of America." Just as Dvořák drew upon the Spirituals for his distinctively American composition, Matthews claimed that race literature would similarly transform "the scenes of our ordinary existence" into a "universal literature."[35] The Spirituals, along with being a novel American folk form, were an early touchstone in a nascent African American tradition of cultural expression that spoke simultaneously to spiritual and social concerns. Moreover, the Spirituals developed alongside the slave narratives during a historical moment and under a racial regime that, in fact, required a blurring of the line—obfuscation and indirection as mode and means of survival—between these two spheres on the part of black people, enslaved and free. By invoking the Spirituals (via Dvořák), Matthews made a bold claim for the broader significance of black life—and black ways of being in the world—even as she in effect channeled a young nation's desire to transcend the parochialism of its relatively short past (compared to Europe and the East) and take a place of prominence on the international stage.

Pluralism and the Problem of Racial Difference at the First World's Parliament of Religions

The end of the nineteenth century was a time of intense ferment and transformation within a variety of American religious traditions and communities. On one end of the spectrum, the literary and reasoning rules of catechism had given rise to a set of mainline denominations and a Protestant establishment which occupied a proximity to political power and largely set the social terms of what counted as "good" or "true" religion. Liberal Protestantism, by all accounts, constituted the norms of high culture in American Christianity. At the other end, the popular fervors of revivalist Christianity had continued to spread. The conflict between these positions—between "rational" liberal Protestantism and "emotional" embodied evangelicalism, and racially between white and black America—was evident at one of the century's most important events. For seventeen days in September 1893 representatives from around the world met in Chicago for the first World's Parliament of Religions. As part of a much larger World's Fair—the Columbian Exposition celebrating the four-hundredth year since the "discovery" of the New World—the Parliament was the culminating event in a series of gatherings sponsored by an organization known as the Congress of Religion. With participants from over forty denominations (Protestant, Catholic, and Jewish), these meetings focused on a range of pressing topics, including Zionism, a growing Fundamentalist movement, the role of women, and the rise of Jim Crow. All of the conversations together aimed to discern the future of religion in modern America.

Within the context of the World's Fair, as historian Richard Seager has shown, the Parliament's organizers understood their event as "the most noble expression" of the Columbian Exposition.[36] While the organizers of the Fair may not have shared the Parliament's estimation of itself, with regard to race (and specifically the place of black Americans in the festivities) the two entities were like-minded in their practices of exclusion. By all accounts, African American participation in planning, staging, and speaking at the World's Fair was extremely low. Accordingly, a primary point of debate within black communities at the time was whether it was wiser to accept the very few invitations to participate that were extended or to actively protest the Columbian Exposition as a whole. Several black newspapers dubbed the affair "simon-pure and lily-white" and "the white American's World's Fair."[37]

Foremost among those who endorsed a position of protest was Ida B. Wells, the prominent journalist and antilynching activist. Wells, for one, objected to the proposed idea of a "Colored People's Day"—a day dedicated to recognize black Americans.[38] She attempted to organize a demonstration and authored the pamphlet *The Reason Why the Colored American Is Not in the World's Columbian Exposition* to galvanize opposition to the Fair. She found support from a number of black leaders, including author, former abolitionist, and statesman Frederick Douglass. By then an international celebrity who was serving as the U.S. ambassador to Haiti, Douglass was one of the only nonwhite speakers at the event, although he was an impromptu addition to the program who was there in his official capacity to represent Haiti at the Exposition. Despite his participation, Douglass was openly critical of the Exposition's exclusionary practices, penning the introduction to Wells's pamphlet. But like the Fair itself, *The Reason Why* became a point of contention among members of the black press, from whom Wells sought funding. Though many in the black press were critical of the Columbian Exposition, they were also unsupportive of her efforts. Nevertheless, Wells planned to distribute *The Reason Why* at the Fair, in part, to shame the event's planning committee as well as the host nation. After all, it was President Benjamin Harrison who had appointed an all-white Board of National Commissioners to oversee the World's Fair, setting a precedent that all of the Fair's subsequent selection practices followed.

Indicative of Wells's ambition, and with the foreign audience of Fair attendees in mind, the pamphlet's preface was printed in English, French, German, and Spanish. Yet even with its prestigious roster of contributors, *The Reason Why* had fundraising challenges that stymied Wells's plans. Ultimately, it was not published until August 30, 1893, several months after the Exposition opened and shortly before the start of the Parliament. Albeit delayed, and arguably ineffective in achieving Wells's immediate goals, the pamphlet was a powerful and persuasive piece of literature. In addition to contributions by Douglass and Wells herself, it featured writing by I. Garland Penn, an educator and journalist as well as a lay leader in the Methodist Episcopal Church, and Wells's husband, the journalist and lawyer Ferdinand Lee Barnett.[39] Echoing coverage of the Fair in the black press, Barnett's closing essay played off of the Exposition's neoclassical and Beaux Arts–inspired architectural design. "Theoretically open to all Americans," he wrote, "the Exposition practically is, literally and figuratively, a 'White City'"—the nickname often used to refer to the fairgrounds.[40]

In truth, *The Reason Why* was as much, if not more, concerned with detailing the racial (anti-black, really) violence of post-Reconstruction America as it was with exposing the particular racial politics of the Exposition. Only Douglass's and Barnett's contributions focused squarely on the Fair's racial exclusions. In his introduction, Douglass offered a rather simple rationale: "[T]he answer is slavery. . . . The life of a negro slave was never held sacred." And in the present moment, he observed, "a new determination is born to keep him down."[41] By contrast, Barnett offered a much more granular account, detailing how, why, and by whom "the Negro" had been excluded. As the pamphlet's final chapter, titled simply "The Reason Why," Barnett's essay proceeded as a litany of the decisions that were made by the Exposition's organizers to exclude "the colored American" at every turn.[42]

In between the bookends provided by Douglass and Barnett, three chapters authored by Wells and one by Penn were the pamphlet's core. Together they captured the central contradictions of the period in which the Columbian Exposition took place. On one hand, Penn chronicled racial progress during the previous three decades, highlighting the range of post-Emancipation black achievement across the spheres of the arts, education, and religion. To recall, the 1890s were a decade in which many heralded the birth of a New Negro. On the other hand, Wells documented the steady tide of white backlash that greeted every effort of "the colored American" to secure full citizenship in the wake of Emancipation. If America's pre-Emancipation culture and identity were defined by the entanglement of slavery and freedom, then the fundamental paradox of the postbellum United States was one of unforeseen achievement on the part of the formerly enslaved in the face of rampant legal and political repression enforced by a culture of violence and organized white supremacy in the form of Black Codes, disenfranchisement, Jim Crow legislation, and groups like the Ku Klux Klan. This truth crystallized all the more in the summer of 1893, as a series of lynchings made national headlines during the same months that the Columbian Exposition took place.[43]

Ultimately for Wells and her collaborators, the Fair's racial exclusions were evidence of a more significant social problem. And this was precisely their point. Negligible participation was nothing to ignore, but the pageantry obscured a more insidious, and distinctively American, irony. Lynch laws put the lie to the nation's hopes, expressed in the form of the Fair, to present itself as "highly liberal and civilized" to the rest of world.[44] In this view, if slavery was the country's original sin, the Columbian Exposition was most certainly an act of bad faith. As Douglass put it in his introduction, the World's Fair was a performance by "men who are perjured before God and man."[45] *The Reason Why* helped ensure that the ambitious event, as a form of bearing false witness, would not stand unquestioned.

While Wells led the charge in protesting the 1893 World's Fair, a small contingent of "Colored Americans" were invited to participate in some form. Unsurprisingly, given her stature at the time, Matthews was among this select group, one of only six black women authors whose work was included in the Fair. Reprinted in stand-alone form, her "Aunt Lindy" story was featured in the library of the Exposition's Women's Building.[46] Despite her Christian bona fides, Matthews did not participate in the World's Parliament of Religions, although it's not clear whether or not she was invited to do so. Though her theological commitments were neither veiled nor subtle, Matthews's writing and activism were organized primarily by the racial and gender paradigms of the day even as they were commonly rendered in a religious register.

In contrast to the nation's racial order of black and white, the principal concern of the 1893 World's Parliament of Religions was facilitating an encounter between East and West.[47] However, similar to Douglass's observation in his introduction to *The Reason Why*, the Parliament's inclusion of representatives from nations around the world worked "to shame the Negro." The African contingent present, in Douglass's estimation, was intended all the more—by way of contrast—to "exhibit the (American) Negro as a repulsive savage."[48] The Parliament's comparative model—which helped lay the framework for the study of "world religions"[49]—made an awkward fit for "the colored American." Despite largely embracing the nation's dominant religious tradition, namely Protestant Christianity, Afro-Protestantism continued to be imagined as something of a different order, a tradition somehow outside both East and West even as it was undeniably American. Betwixt and between, within yet outside, in this way the World's Parliament of Religions captured black people's fraught relationship to modernity, and specifically to the United States as the presumed beacon of modern democracy.

Such apparent contradictions did not prevent a few black Americans from accepting invitations to speak. Only two—one man and one woman—were official participants in the first Parliament, which met at the Art Institute of Chicago on September 11–27. This peculiar racial delegation comprised Fannie Barrier Williams, the Unitarian educator and women's rights activist, and the Right Reverend Benjamin Arnett, an educator, elected official, and bishop in the oldest independent black denomination, the AME Church. Both Barnett and Barrier Williams delivered formal speeches, addressing the Parliament on consecutive days. They spoke, by default, on behalf of "the colored American," to use the phrase from Wells's pamphlet. This designation meant that they were the only participants on the program who were not identified with either a discrete religious tradition or a specific (non-American) national/ethnic identity. Their primary identification was racial, not religious. They were there to represent "the race."

Arnett's and Barrier Williams's remarks weren't especially original or novel. Much of what they said was in keeping with the religious—which is to say, Afro-Protestant—vision cast by Matthews that same decade. They both advanced variations on what was by then a familiar theme: white Christians continued to reveal themselves as decisively un-Christian in light of their inhumane treatment of African Americans. The two speakers' lines of argumentation, however, were quite distinct.

Arnett turned to history to make his case, countering the standing narrative of Western Christianity as ostensibly white. He began his address, "Christianity and the Negro," by congratulating the delegates from "all nations of the earth." He celebrated the World's Parliament of Religions as a "triumph of human freedom" and a testament to humanity as the "greatest mystery of creation." At the same time, he offered a theological reading of history in which the Parliament held the promise of redeeming humanity's past sins. In this vein, Arnett invoked the story of the Tower of Babel in the book of Genesis, in which the people's ambitions to build a tower that ascended to the heavens are frustrated by a God who intervened and "confused their language."[50] Describing the biblical scene as "the Parliament in Shinar" (another name for Babylonia), where the people "plotted treason against the divine command," Arnett placed the burden of redemption on the present gathering. "In fact," he declared, "this is the adjourned meeting, from Shinar to Chicago." If the original event was defined by "disloyalty to God" and ended in confusion, then the 1893 Parliament would lead to "the future prosperity of our race and country." Arnett continued in language that echoed the New Testament story of Pentecost: "The evolution in the religious thought of the world has enabled us to assemble in one place and on one accord."[51]

Having established both the historical and religious significance of the 1893 World's Parliament on biblical terms, Arnett then turned to the heart of his address: an account of Africa's place in the propagation of Christian faith. "The negro is older than Christianity, as old as man," Arnettt declared, adding, "No history of the past is complete without some reference to the negro or his home, Africa." He lauded Africa as a long-standing site of intellectual, military, and political accomplishment—"the home of scholars, of philosophers, of theologians, of statesmen, and of soldiers." Africa, the AME bishop proclaimed, was "the cradle of art and science" which "contributed more than its proportion" to Christianity's early years. From gospel writers and early Christian teachers to Simon the Cyrenian, who "became the cross-bearer of the Son God," Arnett outlined a short list of African founders of the faith. To be sure, he sought to leverage the authority associated with the relatively novel idea of historical objectivity. Church history could not be told if one ignored Africa's role. Yet Arnett did not pretend to be either disinterested or dispassionate. His African reading of Christian history was most certainly presentist, intended to provide the audience with a "usable past."[52]

Arnett's revisionist history buttressed his hopes for the 1893 Parliament, and for racial equality in general. Given the African contributions to early Christianity, Arnett reasoned, the American Negro was entitled to "enjoy the blessings purchased with so much sorrow, suffering and tears." He aimed to hold his audience accountable to such a vision. Accordingly, he exhorted the World's Parliament to "start a wave of influences that will change some of the Christians of this land and the brotherhood of man." His ambitions were clear. "Treat us as American citizens, as Christian men and women," Arnett implored. A fuller account of history, in this view, ought to help make the way for the Negro to receive "the rights and privileges that belong to every citizen of a Christian commonwealth." In sum, Bishop Arnett appealed to history in order to redraw a familiar theological line that cast true Christianity in opposition to slavery and recast the Negro as a rightful American citizen. His was a call to conscience for (white) American Christians before the World's Parliament's international audience. In so doing, Arnett affirmed racial equality not just as the Negro's birthright, an American ideal, or a Christian concept. It was a universal sacred tenet: one of "the fundamental truths of each of our religions."[53]

If Bishop Arnett attempted to leverage the long arc of history in the Negro's favor, Fannie Barrier Williams began by naming the contemporary political stakes more directly. Barrier Williams addressed the World's Parliament one day after the AME preacher. She did so on what would seem to be less exclusively Christian terms, as one might expect given her Unitarian commitments. The title of her address, "What Can Religion Further Do to Advance the Condition of the American Negro?," signaled as much forthrightly, while also foregrounding her practical concerns. Counterintuitively, however, Barrier Williams quickly focused her attention on Christianity specifically. In her estimation, black people were an entirely Christian species. They had been "treated, estimated, and gauged by what are called Christian ideas of right and wrong." The Negro "was entirely the product of Christian influences" and "is by every mark, impulse and aspiration an American Christian." Such insistence that "colored people in this country" were created by and assessed according to a set of Christian concepts and categories did not, for Barrier Williams, signify an endorsement of Christianity. Instead, her claims were intended to lead listeners to the conclusion that the Negro's rightful home was America, not Africa. With emigration and colonization debates as one horizon against which the Parliament was situated, she insisted, "The fetiches and crudities of the Dark Continent had long since ceased to be a part of his [the Negro's] life and character."[54]

In some ways, Barrier Williams picked up right where Arnett left off the previous day. Arnett had opened with early Christianity and followed a loose chronology forward to make a claim on the American present. Barrier Williams began with the role of Christianity in the bowels of American slavery. The wonder, for her, was that "black Christians" had "any religious sense of the purities of Christianity" at all, given "the false, pernicious, and demoralizing gospel" that was their first introduction to the faith. Such circumstances were to blame for any religious shortcomings in black social life rather than anything inherent in the nature of Africa and its descendants, as was asserted in the era's racial science and popular culture.[55] In fact, the contrary was the case. Despite the "false teachings and vicious examples" that were the rule under the "old dispensation of the slave Bible," black people had distinguished themselves with a tradition of "religious heroism and self-respect."[56]

This record was first witnessed during the Civil War, Barrier Williams averred, when the enslaved continued to care for the homes and families of Confederate soldiers rather than seek immediate retribution. Such an example of "moral fortitude" could be found "nowhere else in Christendom." Furthermore, "in spite of his lack of real religious instruction," the educator and club woman continued, "the colored American" created his own Christian institution. Celebrating "the African Methodist Episcopal Church, with its million members, vast property in churches, schools, academies, publications, and learned men and women," Barrier Williams did what Arnett perhaps could not do the previous day—lest he seem overly biased—as a bishop in that very church. In fact, the independent black denomination that she lauded was an example of heroism that was readily accessible to the audience, as the AME Church was then in the midst of holding a denominational congress at the Parliament.[57]

Barrier Williams proceeded to highlight an evolution in thought that had become apparent in white American churches, she claimed, during the final decades of the nineteenth century. She praised a new "philanthropic impulse" that underwrote the "all-important work of building schools and churches" in the South. And, having expressed gratitude for this "significant change," she restated her central query to the Parliament: "[W]hat can religion further do for the colored people?" "More religion and less church" was her answer. All of her address to this point slyly slipped back and forth between Christianity and religion, almost conflating the two terms. Now the Unitarian lay leader drew a line, hard and fast. "Less theology and more of human brotherhood, less declamation and more common sense and love for truth," she proclaimed. "Creeds and doctrine . . . obscure religion," she argued, hinder "moral progress." Barrier Williams called instead for "practical religion that can make pure and sacred every relationship it touches of man, woman and child."[58] Such remarks aligned well with the noncredal orthodoxies and religious naturalism associated with Unitarianism, to be sure.

Bringing together her dual work as a race leader and club woman, Barrier Williams called for a religion that taught (and sought to protect for all) the virtues of "marriage, motherhood and family . . . those domestic virtues, moral impulses and standards of family and social life that alone are badges to responsibility." She pointed to what she took to be the "higher and purifying influences of religion." Yet she also insisted that no single religious tradition was the sole source of such influence. Even those who "profess no religion" had a role to play—a radical claim by any metric at the time.[59] Indeed, by her criteria, those who fell in the latter category were "often the most religious." Bringing the racial norms that guided her practical vision of religion into full view, Barrier Williams explained:

> It is a shameful thing to say of the Christian religion as practiced in one part of our country that a young colored man susceptible of spiritual enlightenment will find a readier welcome in a saloon or any other plan than he will in any evangelical church. . . . [T]he Golden

Rule of fellowship taught in the Christian Bible becomes in practice the iron rule of race hatred.[60]

Appealing to a term of modern industry, Barrier Williams called for a "code of ethics" that, if embraced, might help to correct "the irreligious conduct of white American Christians." And she concluded by putting the fate of the Negro's future squarely in the hands of the very people who had organized the World's Parliament of Religions. "The hope of the Negro and other dark races in America," she declared, "depends upon how far the white Christians can assimilate their own religion."[61]

The vision that Barrier Williams put forward in her address to the Parliament—of a practically oriented faith and commonsense theology that prioritized racial justice—reflected the teachings of the Unitarian Church, the liberal Protestant denomination she had joined as an adult. It also squared well with the tradition of Afro-Protestantism instantiated over a century earlier in the slave narratives. Notably, a number of early abolitionists, like Barrier Williams, were inspired by Unitarian teachings.[62] Indeed, her call for an ethical compass that assessed Christianity according to its treatment of "the Negro and other dark races" was an established norm in Afro-Protestantism by the 1890s. Arnett's speech on the previous day had, unsurprisingly, evinced a similar logic, given his position as a Bishop in the oldest independent black denomination. And the line that Barrier Williams drew between "false teachings" and "something higher and better in the Christian religion" was quite similar to the distinction that Douglass had made decades earlier between the "Christianity of this land" and the "Christianity of Christ."[63]

Though Barrier Williams and Arnett were the only official black participants on the program, one other "colored American" did grace the stage of the 1893 World's Parliament of Religions. As noted earlier, Douglass was extended an impromptu invitation to the Parliament's platform. He began his brief and unscripted remarks by playing on the legacy of anti-Catholic sentiment in the United States—and perhaps signaling the significant Catholic presence in Chicago. "I take it that it would be very dangerous in this meeting to pitch into the Roman Catholics," he joked. He then pivoted and praised the Catholic Church as a model for the gathering: "For we are all Catholics, ready to strike hands with all manner of man, from all nations of the earth."[64] He may also have been riffing off the address given by the Rev. J. R. Slattery that same day. Slattery, a pioneer in advocating for black priests, had declared, "In the eyes of the Catholic Church the negro is a man." Slattery further affirmed that "there can be no slave, save him who is in bondage to sin. . . . Our Christian advantage flows from our spiritual birth and adoption into the family of God."[65] Also drawing on metaphors of spiritual kinship, Douglass proclaimed that anyone who possessed "the spirit of liberty" was one of his "brothers beloved." He then proceeded to praise the Parliament's ambitions even as he fashioned himself an outsider at the affair. After all, the one-time licensed lay preacher and longtime member of the AME Church demurred, his life had been defined by "studying the great question of human rights instead of human religions."[66] Nevertheless, he lauded the effort to assemble "men of all varieties of opinion, as well as complexion" for the purposes of "bringing them all into unity." Returning to a more familiar arena of activism, Douglass ultimately called attention to "the race problem—the negro problem," only to recast it as "[t]he great problem that confronts the American people to-day."

Together, the speeches given by Douglass, Barrier Williams, and Arnett were consistent with the Parliament's desire to discern in the world's disparate religious traditions a shared modern sensibility that could be in service to a vision of human brotherhood—"brothers beloved," to use Douglass's phrase—that transcended the lines of religious difference. At the same time, albeit by different methods and modes of argumentation, Arnett, Barrier Williams, and Douglass each positioned the question of racial difference—and, more precisely, "the Negro problem"—as *the* great question for the international body that gathered in 1893 for the first World's Parliament of Religions. Even if not acknowledged as such by the event's organizers, this problem was most certainly recognized as such by the host nation, which had spent the previous three decades violently struggling to come to terms with the meaning of black freedom.

Pentecostalism and the Problem of the Color Line

Organized by Protestantism's liberal vanguard, the Parliament was a particular species of American internationalism that took the form of a Christian engagement with religious difference. However, in appealing primarily to a range of religious traditions outside the borders of a still fragile United States (and especially those from the East), the organizers largely overlooked and obscured the problem that "the colored American" took to be most important. Just a few years later, and fueled by decades of restorationist and revivalist fervor, a dramatically different group of Christians assembled in 1906 to worship in Los Angeles. Refusing the racial logics of segregation (which had become the law of the land in 1896) and the dominant dispensational rules of liberal Protestantism at once, this unlettered band of black and white believers began to speak in tongues. Claiming the New Testament gift of the Holy Spirit for the twentieth century, what came to be known as the Azusa Street Revival signaled an auspicious—and interracial— birth for the modern Pentecostal movement.[67]

Pentecostalism, at least in part, grew out of a desire to reclaim the gifts associated with the Holy Spirit, as recorded in the New Testament book of Acts, on the Day of Pentecost, from which the movement gained its name. Given the heterogeneous racial composition of early participants and the theological vision of racial transcendence associated with the Azusa Street Revival, early Pentecostalism can (and should) also be understood—much like the Parliament—as a novel response to the politics of racial and religious difference that ordered a fragile and fractured United States in the final years of the nineteenth century. William J. Seymour, the legally blind Negro preacher at the center of the Azusa Street Revival, is central to any account of the genesis of American Pentecostalism and its interracial Christian vision. After observing the events at Azusa, including Seymour's charismatic presence, one white Pentecostal preacher declared, "The 'color line' had been washed away in the blood."[68] Yet this notion—that the shedding of Jesus's blood on the cross superseded the Supreme Court's decision in *Plessy v. Ferguson* (1896)—by no means achieved a consensus at Azusa or across the nascent Pentecostal movement more broadly.

As the numbers of Pentecostals grew in the years that followed the famed revival, the social habit of racial segregation would have its way with these distinctly modern Protestants, too. The interracial congregations on display during the earliest years of American Pentecostalism evolved rather rapidly in ways that adhered to the prevailing racial logics of Jim Crow. Indeed, in the years that followed the Azusa Street Revival black and white Pentecostals would pursue their newfound spiritual gifts within the confines of separate, racially homogeneous denominations.[69] The question of what sense to make of "the color line" was a central preoccupation for Pentecostals, as it was for most Americans at the time. As was the case a little over a decade earlier, at the 1893 World's Parliament, the early years of this new religious movement revealed a set of contradictions endemic to a moment in which a range of outsized spiritual ambitions was frustrated by the structures of a racial (and now legal) order that would persist for at least another seven decades. In this way, Protestant appeals to the biblical story of Pentecost—wherein the Spirit descends and overcomes linguistic and cultural difference—to underwrite a new kind of Christian community were entangled with what many described as the birth of a New Negro (and the interracial literary and political circles that announced it) at the beginning of the twentieth century.

William Seymour rightly occupies a position of singular importance in the history of American Pentecostalism. However, he was by no means the only black preacher who played a major role during the movement's early years. In fact, what would become known as the first black Pentecostal denomination had been founded nine years before the Los Angeles revival started. When two Baptist preachers in Mississippi, Charles Harrison Mason and Charles Price (C. P.) Jones, embraced Holiness teachings concerning a "second baptism," they found themselves on the outs with their church communities. Together, in 1897, Mason and Jones started the Church of God in Christ (COGIC). Ten years later, and with at least ten congregations from three states in their fellowship, they incorporated the young denomination in Memphis, Tennessee. The Azusa Street revivals played a key role in COGIC's founding, as it was there that Mason was "baptized in the Holy Spirit" and began to speak in tongues. Azusa also proved to be the breaking point in Mason's partnership with Jones, who rejected the revival and subsequently founded a separate denomination, the Church of Christ (Holiness) USA.[70]

In agreement concerning the doctrine of sanctification yet at odds over the practice of glossolalia (speaking in tongues), Mason and Jones together (and then on their own respective paths) helped to inaugurate a new form of Afro-Protestantism, with roots in nineteenth-century Holiness revivalism, a tradition now recognizable under the shared rubrics of Afro-Pentecostalism.[71] Their Afro-Protestant predecessors (i.e., AMEs and African Baptists) had long since split from white denominations over the experience of their unequal terms of inclusion, which is to say the experience of white supremacy as it constrained institutional church life. By contrast, the origins of Afro-Pentecostalism were primarily defined by a series of doctrinal disputes rather than by "the race problem," to borrow Douglass's term. Both Mason and Jones, however, were most certainly race men. Moreover, both men held on to a heterodox set of beliefs and practices even as they founded denominations that were typically understood as theologically conservative. And both men also maintained, albeit in different ways, deep ties to Africa—like many other "colored Americans" at the time—contrary to what Barrier Williams argued in her speech to the Parliament. For instance, Mason was known to harbor a special fascination with "roots," the name for a kind of talisman associated with the African American spiritual tradition known as Conjure or Hoodoo. Indicative of the ways in which Christianity and Conjure were often entangled in black life, as hinted at in Matthews's "Aunt Lindy's Tale," Mason was known to refer to these roots as "wonders of God."[72]

Jones also forged a vision of Afro-Pentecostalism that appealed to the significance of Africa, yet he did so in ways that are more readily recognizable alongside the literature and politics of the New Negro movement. Jones sought to develop a theology of holiness that addressed concerns that are often neatly bracketed into the separate categories of religion and race. As David Daniels has argued, Jones extended "the holiness message of freedom from different forms of captivity, such as immorality and denominationalism, to racism." Where Mason held together new commitments to the "Baptism in the Holy

Ghost" with Hoodoo, for Jones race politics and Holiness piety were necessarily entangled. At the same time that he was establishing a new denomination with roots in nineteenth-century Restorationist and revivalist movements, Jones was actively engaged in debates about colonization, emigration, and pan-Africanism.[73] In addition to his preaching, he elaborated on these topics in writing, including in a book he published in 1902. A collection of Jones's poems and prose, *An Appeal to the Sons of Africa* spanned a wide variety of topics that illustrate the range of the preacher's commitments. In it, he offers religious instruction, especially to black youth, and inspiration concerning the virtues of education and right living. Jones's *Appeal* is also animated by the ideology of racial uplift that was prominent at the time among black leaders.

Part race literature, part religious propaganda, *An Appeal to the Sons of Africa* is by all accounts a complicated text. This is quickly made clear, as Jones dedicated the book to "Him Whose I am and Whom I serve *and* to the Noble Youth of the African Race" (italics added for emphasis). His intended audience was both "Youth of African blood" and "all classes of readers and lovers of redeemed humanity." Even with its Pentecostal difference, Jones's *Appeal* squares well with other models of literature and leadership within Afro-Protestantism and race politics—and visions of Afro-modernity more generally—at the turn of the century. Jones applauded the advent of modern technologies in recent years, such as "the telegraph, printing press, and locomotive." He also gave voice to lofty social visions more commonly associated with liberal Protestantism or with leaders of the independent black denominations, such as the AME bishop Henry McNeal Turner or the Baptist preacher Sutton Griggs. Tapping into what was then the central issue in black political organizing, Jones noted that his book was not inspired by the doctrinal/theological disputes that left him alienated from his black Baptist colleagues in Mississippi. Rather, it was "the lynching of two colored men in the Middle West" that prompted Jones to pen his *Appeal*.[74] Indeed, the very ironies that defined black life, irrespective of religious affiliation or theological orientation, at the onset of Jim Crow—a moment in which "race literature" flourished alongside the rule of the lynch mob—were, unsurprisingly, formative to this foundational text in the history of Afro-Pentecostalism.

The emergence of Afro-Pentecostalism at the turn of the twentieth century, from one perspective, signaled a break from the independent black church movement—the Afro-Protestant institutional norm—that began over a century earlier. Similarly, black Pentecostal writers, such as Jones, are not typically considered alongside the cohort of New Negro writers and activists who were, by all accounts, his contemporaries in the field of race literature and politics. And though the revivals at Azusa Street took place thirteen years after the first World's Parliament of Religions, it is fair to assume that neither Jones nor Mason would have been invited to participate—not that either man would have cared to attend. Indeed, Afro-Pentecostalism's dispensational politics and theological exclusivism, even if in service to a vision of black freedom, was an affront to liberal Protestantism's modernist vision of interreligious unity. Even still, the way early black Pentecostals braided together the discourses of race and religion—in breaking away from black Baptists, in refusing racial segregation, and in subsequently forming their own black denominations—was in step with the longer history of Afro-Protestantism, a tradition defined more by contestation than consensus, and its long-standing literary and political aspirations.

The title of Jones's book, *An Appeal to the Sons of Africa*, echoed earlier calls for black people to rise up, including David Walker's *Appeal to the Coloured Citizens of the World* (1829), Lydia Maria Child's *An Appeal in Favor of That Class of Americans Called Africans* (1833), and Henry Highland Garnet's *An Address to the Slaves of the United States* (1843)—all of which made black people's freedom and full citizenship a matter of Christian duty. Jones never gained the currency or platform of these other orators, who occupy privileged positions within the history of Afro-Protestantism (and black studies, for that matter!). Still, with slavery now in the past tense, in its push for spiritual freedom Jones's *Appeal* reflected an awareness that Emancipation had not quite provided freedom, never mind full citizenship, for the nation's colored citizens. To be sure, Jones held much in common with other Afro-Protestant clergy at the turn of the twentieth century. Yet *An Appeal to the Sons of Africa* was distinctive in the degree to which Jones both engaged with and reimagined the standing racial discourses of the day through the emerging ortho-doxies of Pentecostalism. In this regard, the new religious movement wove an additional set of doctrinal commitments into an already conservative ideology of racial uplift. His exhortation "Live by faith, and leave inequalities to God" reads like a theological concession to the social logic of Jim Crow. Of course, Jones was by no means the only black leader to articulate an accommodationist position of this sort. However, insofar as he submitted modes of social engage-ment to a model of Christian piety, his *Appeal* followed a peculiarly Pentecostal logic that asserted "the color line" was overcome—or, on eschatological terms, would be overcome—by the salvific work that Jesus's death and resurrection and the baptism in the Holy Spirit ac-complished for all "redeemed humanity."[75]

Unlike the independent black church movement (of AME and African Baptist churches), which began when black Christians parted ways with their white denominational counterparts over the matter of racial inequality, the story of Pentecostalism's earliest years is often narrated as though the movement was defined solely by questions of doctrine, devoid of social or political concerns. Yet, in choosing to worship together with white Christians on Azusa Street, the religious movement enacted a corporate practice that refused racial segregation. In doing so, albeit in the form of an in-terracial revival, they suggested that racial difference—better yet, white supremacy—was in fact a religious doctrine. The tensions that defined, and divided, early Pentecostalism—between a theo-logical claim for racial equality and the separate, racially homoge-neous Pentecostal denominations that developed in the aftermath of the Azusa Street revivals—was constitutive of the heterodox his-tory of Afro-Protestantism writ large. It was also part and parcel of the emergence of what might be identified as Afro-Protestant modernity—an important iteration of a wide-ranging set of efforts to wrestle with the "problem of the color line" on religious terms— which created the conditions of possibility for a distinctly black take on modernism in subsequent decades.

W. E. B. Du Bois and the Disciplinary Terms of
Afro-(Protestant) Modernity

The Souls of Black Folk is often, in hindsight, identified as a founding text that helped set a trajectory for what has become the interdisciplinary mode of scholarly inquiry now known as black studies. To be sure, *Souls* is best understood, on less presentist terms, as a product of its own moment in time and place. Even still, that Du Bois had already demonstrated a mastery of multiple disciplines is well established. Indeed, he was moving within and across disciplinary lines at the very moment that such distinctions were being demarcated (as discrete academic disciplines) and professionalized in North America.[76] Trained as a historian at Harvard, Du Bois turned his dissertation, "The Suppression of the African Slave Trade to the United States, 1638–1870," into his first book when it was issued in 1896 as the first volume in the Harvard Historical Monograph Series. While pursuing a doctorate in history, Du Bois also studied in Germany with the pioneering sociologist Max Weber. Shortly after graduating from Harvard, Du Bois worked as a research assistant at the University of Pennsylvania. While there he conducted expansive fieldwork in the city of Philadelphia that eventually led to *The Philadelphia Negro: A Social Study*, Du Bois's account of one of the oldest black communities in the urban North. Published in 1899, *The Philadelphia Negro* helped to set an agenda for the nascent field of sociology in the United States, although the book is only recently beginning to gain recognition as such.[77]

Alongside his early contributions to the emerging fields of history and sociology, as several scholars have noted in recent years, Du Bois also played an instrumental role in setting a course for the study of African American (and thus American) religion.[78] Fewer than thirty of the more than five hundred pages in *The Philadelphia Negro* were devoted to discussing "the Negro church." However, four years later Du Bois published a comprehensive account of the institution in what was the eighth of twenty studies that appeared in the Atlanta University publication series, seventeen of which Du Bois edited between 1897 and 1914.[79] *The Negro Church* (1903) would remain the most systematic scholarly inquiry into Afro-Protestantism for decades to come. Alongside his formal academic work on the Atlanta University series, perhaps Du Bois's most instructive treatment of religion is his first—and still most famous—book written for a popular audience. Not insignificantly, *The Souls of Black Folk* was released in 1903, the same year as *The Negro Church*.

In *Souls* Du Bois does more than insightfully analyze the role that the church played in mediating black people's passage to and place within North America. His engagement with and investment in Afro-Protestantism both haunts and structures the entire text. Indeed, just as with the black men and women who participated in the first World's Parliament of Religions and the early Pentecostal movement, Du Bois's writing in *Souls* illustrated the complexities and contradictions—including the grand liberal, American spiritual ambitions—that animated black social life at the time of its publication. With that in mind, a rereading of *Souls* helps to reveal just how much the author's own normative religious commitments are being worked out within the book's pages. Indeed, in *Souls* Du Bois synthesizes a set of debates about the constitutive ideas and practices that had thus far defined Afro-Protestantism's heterodox history. The book beautifully navigates, and synthesizes, the animating tensions between literary catechesis and conversion, revivalism and reason, emotional expressiveness and ethical reflection, African influences and American conditions. Du Bois also advances a vision and models a method for structuring the relationships between these competing impulses in the context of black modern life. Indeed, his claim to "dwell above the Veil" reveals much about the entangled racial and religious logics that underpin Afro-modernity. More precisely, with *Souls* Du Bois both calls for and enacts a set of disciplinary logics that have worked to order Afro-modernity on decidedly Protestant terms.

Primarily a collection of previously published essays, *Souls* is most commonly associated with Du Bois's claim in the book's forethought: "[T]he problem of the Twentieth Century is the problem of the color-line."[80] In addition to drawing on what might now be called an "interdisciplinary" methodology, the book moves swiftly across multiple genres. A blend of autobiography, social analysis, and practical recommendations, the entire text is rightly understood as a meditation on—better still, a theory of—the meaning of race in modern America. Though his primary audience was domestic, at the start of the book's second chapter Du Bois clarifies his broader conceptual framework. *Souls*'s central concern is "the relation of the darker to the lighter races of men in Asia and Africa, in America and the islands of the sea." The American color line, in this view, was a particular iteration of a set of global asymmetries—in Du Bois's words, "a phase of this problem."[81]

The international history and scope of colonial relations, for Du Bois, was important for grasping the particular challenges faced by the United States in the aftermath of slavery. Indeed, the promise of a multiracial democracy associated with Reconstruction, and its subsequent demise, provided the book's historical context. Chapters 2 through 9—all of which were previously published elsewhere—read as a series of topical essays or as position papers on different dimensions of "the problem of the color line." From Emancipation, education, and leadership to colonialism and industrial capitalism, in each chapter Du Bois documents one of the many interlocking challenges that "the Negro" (and thus, the nation and the world) faced as racial segregation was codified in *Plessy v. Ferguson*. With this decision, the Supreme Court had confirmed for black people the closure of a certain window of opportunity and clarified a new set of challenges.

The book's title has contributed to the special status that "soul" still maintains in interpretations of black life. However, "spirit" is the primary term that Du Bois used in the book to describe the ongoing struggles of "the freedmen's sons." There are many ways to read how these two terms, "spirit" and "soul," work together in the book to help frame a set of cohering claims out of what were previously a disparate set of essays. If "soul" affirmed the interiority of a people whose humanity had been systematically denied, then "spirit" called attention to their human activities and collective endeavors in the social world.[82] By attending in detailed fashion to their "spiritual strivings" across a variety of spheres, Du Bois offered a compelling and complicated portrait of "the Negro people"—frustrated at every end but pressing forward—for a white liberal reading public whom he invited to peer within "the Veil."[83] Yet along with being a story of a people, as Robert Gooding-Williams argues, *Souls* is a "carefully wrought and subtly argued political theoretical [response] to the now defunct system of American racial apartheid." Importantly, for Gooding-Williams, "a spiritual identity" is at the center of the vision of black politics that Du Bois advances therein.[84]

Along with the spiritual grammar that Du Bois draws upon to frame the book as a whole, two sections attend to religion most obviously. In the mode of description and historical analysis, chapter 10 offers a sustained treatment of the history of "negro religion." Underscoring the centrality of religion to the work that Du Bois did to convert several independently written essays into a single book, Jonathan Kahn has called attention to the fact that all of the never-before-published chapters (11–14) in *Souls* are rife with religious themes. In this view, religion is the framework that provides *Souls* with its conceptual coherence, the proverbial glue that holds the book together.[85]

Neither a valorization of religion writ large nor a wholesale critique, the book engages in a reasoned discussion of the multiple ways that religion animates and informs modern black life. Borrowing again from Gooding-Williams's reading of the book as political theory, *Souls* can be read as a response to the question: What kind(s) of religion, if any, will play a role in helping black people rise to meet the "constitutive norms of modernity"?[86] Chapter 10 and what follows provide, if nothing else, a provisional theory of religion in and for Afro-modernity. However, by taking on a religious form (i.e., a prayer) in "Afterthought," Du Bois blurs any facile distinction between theory and practice, description and prescription. Addressed to "O God the Reader," *Souls* comes to a close with a sermonic quality.

What is just as interesting is that the newly written chapters, which afforded *Souls* its shared fabric, follow the one chapter that is entirely devoted to the subject of "Negro religion." Chapter 10, "Of the Faith of the Fathers" (which was previously published elsewhere), figures in the text as a transition from the old to the new writing. However, the new chapters that follow it also follow a logic that is mapped out within that transitional chapter. Chapter 10, an interpretation of what might be called "old-time religion," offers a literal and figurative bridge, or segue, into a discussion (and performance) of a different kind of religion. It beckons toward, in Du Bois's words, "a new religious ideal."[87] That is, chapters 11 through 14 of *Souls* are structured in such a way as to model the disciplined and differentiated version of modern black life that Du Bois imagines and calls for throughout the book. Taken as a unit, chapters 10 through 14 bring together his larger argument and evidence most forcefully. The substance of these chapters is amplified all the more as the book ends with an "afterthought" that is a prayer, which is simultaneously a benediction and an invitation to a new beginning. Accordingly, *Souls* might be read as both an elegy for and an invocation of Afro-Protestant modernity.

"Of the Faith of Our Fathers" was first published as "The Religion of the American Negro" in December 1900 in what was the final issue of *The New World: A Quarterly Review of Religion, Ethics and Theology*. Du Bois begins the chapter with a discussion of the emotional fervor of a "southern Negro revival" and ends with an analysis of the "ethical tendencies" that oriented black religious life. In doing so, he synthesizes two trajectories that had long defined the history of Afro-Protestantism: the rational rules of literary catechism and the embodied, emotionally expressive aesthetics of revivalism. At the time Du Bois was writing *Souls*, these two trajectories were best represented by the poles of liberal Protestantism, as seen in the 1893 World's Parliament of Religions, and a nascent Pentecostalism, which would be best exemplified by Azusa Street in 1906—both of which are, again, responses to the problem of religious and racial difference. Rather than mutually exclusive movements, Du Bois rightly observes that, within the context of "Negro religion," they represented constitutive, if competing, ideas and practices that were vigorously contested.

At the center of chapter 10 of *Souls* Du Bois situates "the Negro church" as the primary place in which such contests took place. "The Negro church" was "the social centre of Negro life in the United States," he explains; it was also "the most characteristic expression of African character." In this view, the church was both a black American public sphere and evidence of an African cultural inheritance. The narrative structure of the chapter, which moves from the register of affect to that of reason, also suggests a clear historical teleology. To understand the church, Du Bois argues, one has to chart "its gradual changes from the heathenism of the Gold Coast to the institutional Negro church of Chicago."[88] Here the church is figured as a transitional space, a site where debates about theology, aesthetics, and politics are being worked out. Afro-Protestantism, as such, functions as an institutional bridge from the African past to the American present. Although the church is a site in which the two remain entangled, "Of the Faith of the Fathers" and subsequent chapters direct readers toward a specific end.

En route to that end, Du Bois identifies three constitutive entities that define "the religion of the slave": "the Preacher, the Music, and the Frenzy." Although he locates these three entities initially in the era of slavery, his tone and tense shift subtly as he moves through a description of each. The preacher's gifts achieved for him a certain "preeminence" and, he asserts, continue to "help him *maintain* it." Under the strains of the decades that followed Emancipation, the music "*became* the one true expression of a people's sorrow, despair, and hope." For Du Bois, the first two elements evolve over time but continue to be a significant resource. By contrast, he situates the frenzy—"the last essential of the Negro religion and the one more devoutly believed in than all the rest"—more squarely in the past. "So firm a hold *did* it have on the Negro," he explained, "that many generations *believed* that without this visible manifestation of the God there could be no true communion with the Invisible." (All italics are added for emphasis.) In doing so, Du Bois asserted a trajectory in which the powers of the preacher and the music persist even as they are refined. At the same time, the "pythian madness"—that is, the passionate frenzy acknowledged as previously being the seat of deepest black devotion—is described as in decline.[89]

Following the historical shifts that Du Bois suggests are underway to "the Preacher, the Music and the Frenzy," each of these entities receives a more sustained discussion in the four chapters that follow. Chapter 12 utilizes a portrait of the Episcopal clergyman Alexander Crummell to continue a discussion of the figure of "the Preacher." Chapter 14, "The Sorrow Songs" (Du Bois's interpretation of the Spirituals), analyzes the meaning in and of "the Music." Notably, in devoting discrete chapters to "the Preacher" and "the Music," Du Bois extends his discussion of Negro religion to follow the quintessentially modern distinction between ethics (i.e., in the figure of the preacher) and aesthetics (i.e., in the form of the music). Meanwhile, "the Frenzy" figures as especially central to the unfolding of the plot of chapter 13, "Of the Coming of John." The one piece of fiction in *Souls*, "Of the Coming of John" brings together many of the themes taken up in previous chapters, including education, leadership, and religion. Yet it does so by narrating the story of one young Negro boy, John. It offers a portrait of his passage into manhood, as well as the challenges and setbacks he faces in pursuit of education and his ambition to be a leader to his people. The chapter has been read both as an extension of the Crummell chapter and as semi-autobiographical with regard to Du Bois's own ambitions for racial leadership.[90] "Of the Coming of John" is not so much about "the Frenzy," at least on forthright terms. However, "the Frenzy" emerges at the precise moment when John's dreams are undone, as he stands before the church community that had supported his educational aspirations and that now are unable to understand him.

Prior to John's failed speech, Du Bois cues his readers regarding what to expect. "The meeting of welcome at the Baptist Church was a failure," he begins the scene. The church is "crowded to overflowing" with expectant members of the community, ready to hear from the son who has returned home. Three preachers—a Methodist, a Presbyterian, and a Baptist, in that order—precede John in addressing the gathered crowd. All three fall short of eliciting anything more than "faint enthusiasm." Finally, John rises to reply to the three preachers, beginning his remarks with a call for "new ideas." Strikingly, the substance of John's fictional remarks is quite similar to those delivered by the black leaders who spoke, just a decade earlier, at the 1893 World's Parliament of Religions: an appeal to "broader ideas of human brotherhood and destiny"; calls for a greater concern with "unity" and less investment in "religious and denominational bickering"; "[m]ore religion and less church," as Barrier Williams had put it.[91] John asks the congregation, "What difference does it make whether a man be baptized in river or wash-bowl, or not at all?" Then he offers his own reply: "Let's leave all that littleness, and look higher."[92]

John's speech is met by a "painful hush," silence signaling the failure of his words to resonate with the crowd. John has proclaimed the "new religious ideal," which Du Bois called for (and claimed black folk were "seeking") at the end of "Of the Faith of the Fathers." But it is as though John has spoken in an "unknown tongue."[93] A collective silence greets him as he returns to his seat. In its wake, an "old bent man" whose "voice and hands shook as with a palsy" and who had the "intense rapt look of a religious fanatic," rose to stand behind the pulpit. Whereas John's address was reasoned and deliberate, this old-time and unlettered lay preacher "quivered, swayed and bent; then rose aloft in perfect majesty." Accordingly, the congregation responds to the elder in an abundance that matches the power of his sermon. As Du Bois narrates, "the people moaned and wept, wailed and shouted." And, recalling the revival he described in chapter 10, "a wild shrieking arose from the corners where all the pent-up feeling of the hour gathered itself and rushed into the air." While John has disregarded his people's "one true Religion" and devalued what "this little world held sacred," the old man affirms the faith of the community and makes space for them to join in, which they confirm by the shared experience of what Du Bois decries as "the Frenzy."[94] An abiding desire for and ongoing commitment to "the Frenzy"—"the last essential of Negro religion, and the one more devoutly believed in than all the rest"—emerges at the end of "Of the Coming of John," frustrating John's appeal to a "new religious ideal." John's failure to elicit a frenzy is, in fact. his undoing.

Du Bois's historical diagnosis in "Of the Faith of the Fathers" suggested that the devout commitment to "the Frenzy" evident under slavery no longer held as much sway by the time *Souls* was published. Yet his fictional portrait in "Of the Coming of John" implied something quite different. "The Frenzy" emerged as the foil to John's racial ambitions, overshadowing and undermining his welcome home and his claim to leadership. The dissonance between presumed historical fact (chapter 10) and fiction (chapter 13) in *Souls* illumines Du Bois's ambivalence about "the Frenzy" and clarifies the degree to which his discussion of Negro religion was governed by prescriptive concerns perhaps more than dispassionate description. In this reading, the constitutive elements of "the Preacher, the Music, and the Frenzy" are seen to proceed into the three separate chapters on ethics (chapter 12), aesthetics (chapter 14), and emotional excess (chapter 13). Fittingly, "the Frenzy" is not bound to its appearance in the climactic scene in "Of the Coming of John." In fact, what Du Bois identified as the "last essential of Negro religion" haunts and structures all five of the final chapters of *Souls*.

"The Frenzy"—as a religious sign of an excessive black difference in "Of the Faith of the Fathers"—figures as central to the denouement of chapter 13, but it is also present, even if unnamed as such, in Du Bois's discussions of both Crummell and the Spirituals. In the former, it is signaled by the affective "temptations" (i.e., hate, despair, and

doubt) that constrain Crummell's ability to fulfill his religious vocation. As for the latter, though "the sorrow songs" are a true expression
of "sorrow, despair and hope," they still needed to be "cleared of evident dross"—that excess associated with the black masses who created
the Spirituals—for their "singular spiritual heritage" to be claimed. In
their current form, Du Bois writes, these songs were "naturally veiled
and half articulate."[95] In both instances, Du Bois figures "the Frenzy"
as a form of blackness that is tied to the past and exceeds the norms
of the present day. More important, for Du Bois, this excess must be
disciplined in order for either black ethical or aesthetic formations—
ultimately, for black people—to realize their rightful place in modern
America.

In his discussion of Negro religion across the five final chapters of
Souls, Du Bois makes a claim for and models an ideal of Negro religion
for Afro-modernity in which "the Frenzy" is effectively disciplined
but has not fully disappeared. For Du Bois, "the Frenzy" is regarded
as a relic of a primitive African past. Yet it also represents, in his view,
the frustrated manifestation of an unrealized desire to transcend the
constraints of Jim Crow—that set of structural arrangements that limited the possibilities for black flourishing at the turn of the twentieth
century. By this logic, it would seem that a need for "the Frenzy" would
subside once the impediment of "the color line" was removed, with
black people being granted social inclusion and, accordingly, appropriate outlets for their "spiritual strivings." Du Bois, however, follows
an inverse logic. As part of an argument for the end of Jim Crow, he
suggests that Negro religion was already relinquishing its attachment
to "the Frenzy." That is, he asserts that black people are shedding their
commitment to "the Frenzy," and thus being reformed as modern
subjects. This assertion, to be clear, was not borne out when *Souls* was
published in 1903, three years before the Asuza Street Revival. The
persistence of this excess was, however, very much a preoccupation of
black and white leaders at the time.[96] In this regard, *Souls* was illustrative of a broader set of efforts to re-present "the Negro" as new—as
modern and reasoning rather than religious and overly emotional.

Here, more precisely, *Souls* might be read as making a case for the
disciplining of Afro-Protestantism into the differentiated spheres of
ethics and aesthetics. In *Souls* Du Bois put forward a religious vision of

Afro-modernity—or, as he termed it, "a new religious ideal"—in which the affective excesses of "the Frenzy," taken to be definitive of "the religion of the American Negro," have been disciplined by a distinctly modern (read: ethical and reasoning) version of Afro-Protestantism. Otherwise put, Du Bois actively drew a line—as both theory and practice—between the ethical and aesthetic dimensions of "Negro religion" as a means for harnessing the creative, expressive energies of "the Frenzy" in support of a vision of Afro-Protestant modernity that is consonant with Enlightenment reason and racial democracy. Only through an appropriate alignment of ethics and aesthetics might "Negro religion" be reborn with its excess repurposed as resource for and expression of modern black devotion. As a response to a classical philosophical question, in *Souls* ethics precedes aesthetics.

This theme of rebirth and reform (recalling Gronniosaw and the slave narratives; see chapter 1) invites a final turn to the one chapter yet to be discussed. The shortest chapter in *The Souls of Black Folk* is, by far, the most deeply personal one. Chapter 11, "Of the Passing of the First-Born," is the book's most overtly autobiographical writing, with Du Bois narrating his experience of the death of his firstborn son, Burghardt. Readers are made witness to the depth of the author's loss even as the chapter might also be read, more generally, as probing the challenges of raising a black child in Jim Crow America. Du Bois describes his young son's death, with a certain measure of ambivalence, as that of an "awful gladness." In view of the oppressive regime of racial segregation, Du Bois wonders if perhaps his son was "[n]ot dead, not dead, but escaped; not bond, but free."[97] A record of a grieving father's fleeting search for consolation, chapter 11 of *Souls* can and should be read, literally, as a memorial for Du Bois's dead son. It is, first and foremost, a mourning song that attempts to make sense of profound and absurd loss while also seeking to elicit empathy from white readers. After all, what kind of inhuman creatures would not empathize with a parent grieving the sudden death of their child?

At the same time, however, one might ask: What is to be made of Du Bois's decision to place "Of the Passing of the First-Born" immediately after chapter 10, "Of the Faith of the Fathers," which enlists the idea of fatherhood to entirely different ends? In what ways does "the faith of the fathers" speak to and through the despair of one black father at the turn of the twentieth century? In this view, Du Bois's dirge—the author's own "sorrow song"—for his firstborn son might also be read metaphorically as an elegy for another kind of firstborn: the first independent black institution, the Negro church. Keeping in mind that Du Bois's discussion of "Negro religion" in chapter 10 is both a historical account and a contemporary appeal for a "new religious ideal," chapter 11 can be read, more figuratively, as an elegy for a particular iteration of "Negro religion."

Recall that in "Of the Faith of the Fathers," Du Bois observes the decline of a version of institutional Afro-Protestantism in which "the Frenzy" prevailed "above all the rest." For Du Bois, "Negro religion"—in its earliest iteration—was a "pagan" form of "Voodooism." However, he observes further, at the same time that formerly enslaved Africans became American, "the Negro church became Christian."[98] In one narrative sweep, Du Bois both positions the emergence of Afro-Protestantism as an American institution and posits the steady passing away of that "last essential of Negro religion and the one believed in more devoutly than all the rest." As such, "Of the Passing of the First-Born"—much like "The Afterthought"—can also be read both as a benediction for what was and an invocation of what could be. Just imagine what The Negro Church—and black institutions in general—might be without the impediments of Jim Crow! The passing of the firstborn institution, as such, provides the very condition of possibility necessary for the formation and flourishing of Afro-Protestant modernity. Published the same year as his seminal study *The Negro Church*, *The Souls of Black Folk* can be read—first and foremost—as a strident call for a "new religious ideal" and a modern, disciplined and reasoning, aesthetically rich but ethically driven "Negro church."

Summary

During the final years of the nineteenth century, liberal Protestantism's international, interracial, and interreligious aspirations converged with the artistic and political ambitions of a New Negro movement to shape a vision of and for an Afro-Protestant modernism—a "new religious ideal"—that would, hopefully, serve black people well in confronting "the problem of the color line." Black writers from Matthews to Du Bois affirmed that their efforts to enunciate a race literature were concerned with more than just negotiating the apparently competing ends of expressive freedom and political progress. Race literature, in Matthews's formulation, would both provide "an outlet for the unnaturally suppressed inner lives which our people have been compelled to lead" and "rightly interpret our unappreciated contribution to Christianity."[99] As such, the work of New Negro writers provided a shared cultural terrain through which to interpret and organize an increasingly heterodox black religious experience in the face of the novel, if familiar, racial hierarchy that was Jim Crow.

At the dawn of the twentieth century, when race literature first emerged as an idea, America witnessed an entangled set of spiritual aspirations and religious ambitions take the shape of several novel social formations. These entanglements took on a variety of corporate forms, ranging from the convening of the 1893 World's Parliament of Religions to the Azusa Street Revival that took place, more spontaneously, starting in 1906. Across this spectrum, a clearly heterodox Afro-Protestantism was animated by concerns that would continue to enliven debates about the politics of black culture in the ensuing decades. In this way, race literature inherited and reconfigured various tensions that existed within Afro-Protestantism for some time (as seen in the slave narratives), such as between catechism and conversion or literary mastery and embodied expressiveness. Race literature at its very inception was understood to carry religious significance, animated as it was by a concern with orienting the "spiritual strivings" of black folk in a society that often denied them the possession of souls.

In her 1895 speech to the First Congress of Colored Women of the United States, Matthews argued that race literature would facilitate a convergence of "true heroism and real Christianity."[100] Seven years later, in *An Appeal to the Sons of Africa* (1902), Jones's poetry, prose, and preaching similarly venerated education to a level that would seem to grant it a sacred status. In this way, Jones's *Appeal* was in line with Du Bois's observation concerning post-Emancipation black life in *The Souls of Black Folk* (1903) just one year later. Therein Du Bois noted that the desire to acquire "book learning" and to "know and test the powers of the cabalistic letters of the white man" had become an almost "mystical" pursuit for black people.[101] To be sure, Afro-Pentecostalism's embrace of glossolalia (which Jones himself rejected) and its privileging of ecstatic forms of worship—much like Du Bois's notion of "the Frenzy"—ran afoul of much of the normative vision for black life advanced by a New Negro movement at the dawn of the new century. Yet Jones's preaching career and literary pursuits—and Pentecostalism's early interracial practice—were in keeping with and contributed to the Afro-Protestant terms of modern black cultural and political life at the turn of the twentieth century.

Afro-Pentecostalism's apparent privileging of a form of religious excess that Du Bois insisted—or, more accurately, hoped—was in decline would push religious leaders like Jones to the margins of race leadership and literature at once. The new religious movement's doctrinal commitments would also seem to be more exclusively Protestant than either Matthews's literary vision or the religious ambitions articulated by Barrier Williams, Arnett, and Douglass at the first World's Parliament of Religions. Even still, Jones (along with Mason and others in the early Afro-Pentecostal movement) was among a group of black writers and leaders grappling in novel ways with questions of cultural, racial, and religious difference at the precise moment that Du Bois declared that "the problem of the color line" was *the* problem of the twentieth century. At the same time, he was just as ensconced in the religious questions of the day. Indeed, an abiding concern with religion, and with Afro-Protestantism specifically, is at the heart of Du Bois's best known book.

As much as Du Bois was preoccupied by "the color line," *The Souls of Black Folk* is perhaps even better understood as a meditation on the meaning of religion in the modern world. Otherwise put, the question of religion's place in the modern world—and of "Negro religion" specifically—was arguably the central question guiding Du Bois's early efforts to both theorize and counter the color line. To be sure, "Of the Faith of the Fathers," in its singling out of the "the Preacher, the Music, and the Frenzy," remains a seminal social scientific interpretation of the role that religion played in the making of black life in the so-called New World. Yet Du Bois's reasoned, scholarly account of "Negro religion" was just as much a constructive enterprise skewed by the young race man's desire for an Afro-modernity that synthesized and resolved abiding tensions in black life and effectively disciplined "the Frenzy." In this regard, *Souls* stands as a distinctly Protestant theory and practice of Afro-modernity—dare I say, a performance and enactment of an Afro-Protestant modernity that not only disciplined black excess but also, and even more, sought to direct this excess toward an undoing of "the color line."

In keeping with Afro-Protestantism's heterodox history, insofar as *Souls* revealed his desire for a "new religious ideal" at the dawn of the new century, Du Bois found himself in the company of black writers, leaders, and preachers who were all pursuing a form of religion that would orient the black masses and make a claim on the larger society. This new religious form, if realized, might then help black folks, and the nation, move together "toward the Goal, out of the Valley of the Shadow of Death" that was Jim Crow. In doing so, Du Bois also helped to set the theoretical terms and disciplinary limits through which African American religion would be imagined and analyzed for decades to come.

3
Afro-Protestantism and the Politics of Studying Black Life

With the publication of *The Souls of Black Folk* in 1903, W. E. B. Du Bois established himself as a leading theorist of "the problem of the color line." As was argued in chapter 2, *Souls* also revealed Du Bois's intellectual preoccupation with religion—and "Negro religion" specifically— as one of the central phenomena shaping black people's prospects for achieving some measure of equality in modern society. In this regard, *Souls* offered a complicated account of the role that religion had played in the making of Afro-modernity, but it also enacted a performance of Afro-Protestant modernity, evidenced in Du Bois's call for (and modeling of) a "new religious ideal," as he phrased it, in *Souls*. Along with the larger Atlanta University publication series that led to "The Negro Church," at the turn of the twentieth century Du Bois brought together a set of descriptive and prescriptive commitments that helped to set the theoretical terms and disciplinary limits through which "The Religion of the American Negro"—and modern black life more generally— would be imagined and analyzed for decades to come.

As this chapter will show, the period from the 1920s through the 1940s saw race literature and religious practice broaden beyond an Afro-Protestant paradigm of the sort seen in the writing of Victoria Earle Matthews and Charles Price Jones or in the speeches delivered by Benjamin Arnett, Fannie Barrier Williams, and Frederick Douglass at the 1893 World's Parliament of Religions. To be sure, as the New Negro movement grew into the Negro Renaissance during the roaring twenties, African American activists, artists, and intellectuals wrote in ways that reflected the novel intraracial pluralism and religious difference(s) that developed in northern cities as black people migrated from around the diaspora. New black gods were born in Chicago, Detroit, New York City, and elsewhere; accordingly, black cultural,

Black is a Church. Josef Sorett, Oxford University Press. © Oxford University Press 2023.
DOI: 10.1093/oso/9780190615130.003.0004

political, and intellectual life bore witness to all that was taking shape in these metropoles, and to the vital exchanges maintained between the various places from which black people came.

Nevertheless, a similar politics of religion, and a particular vision of Afro-Protestant modernity, influenced the academic and activist pursuits of a new generation of black scholars in powerful ways. Not incidentally, many of these intellectuals also happened to be the children of preachers, active church members, or even ordained clergy. As it were, a specific kind of religious orthodoxy and a politics of racial authenticity coalesced to set the terms for the study of "The Negro Church" and black religion more broadly. In doing so, black scholars tended to privilege a liberal Afro-Protestantism as the normative object of study and as the most respectable form of religious practice in African American life. In turn, what might be described as a politics of (academic) respectability often made black scholars reluctant to engage with what were perceived to be less legitimate kinds of religious practice, be they Christian or otherwise. Similar to how Jones did not receive the same kind of platform as Arnett and Barrier Williams in the 1890s, during the 1940s Pentecostalism and non-Christian forms of black religion began to garner more interest but were still, more often than not, rendered marginal by the scholarly gaze. Having followed the literary emergence of Afro-Protestantism (chapter 1) as a form of subjectivity and social life worked out in the slave narratives, and then (in chapter 2) foregrounded the social movements and political struggles, and the attendant literatures, in which this tradition found purpose at the turn of the twentieth century, chapter 3 explores how a set of Afro-Protestant logics informed the scholarly pursuits of black intellectuals in the decades that followed.

To understand this blend of continuity and change, this chapter first follows the small but significant black scholarly elite that emerged during the first half of the twentieth century and the pioneering research they conducted during the 1920s, 1930s, and 1940s on religion in the context of black life. Carter G. Woodson's *The History of the Negro Church* (1927), Benjamin E. Mays and Joseph Nicholson's *The Negro's Church* (1934), Mays's *The Negro's God as Reflected in His Literature* (1938), Zora Neale Hurston's folklore writings, and Arthur Huff Fauset's *Black Gods of the Metropolis* (1944) are among the most substantial writings on the subject. All of these works provided readers with a rich and nuanced set of accounts, including a sense of the variety, of black religious life even as they generally reaffirmed an Afro-Protestant norm. After outlining the emergence of this new generation of black scholars, chapter 3 examines some of the dominant discursive logics that animated their research on religion, and then follows Du Bois's return to academic life via the founding of *Phylon: An Atlanta University Journal of Race and Culture* during the 1940s. *Phylon's* early years, in this view, offer a case study in how race politics and academic ambitions, against the backdrop of Jim Crow, converged to privilege a familiar form of Afro-Protestantism as the true site, source, and object of the study of black religion even as it was encoded as the normative logic guiding interpretations of and expectations for black culture more generally.

Black Scholars and the Burgeoning Study of African American Religion

In the years that followed the publication of *The Souls of Black Folk*, Du Bois moved from his academic post at Atlanta University to the front lines of race politics. In the first decade of the twentieth century, he was a leader in the 1906 Niagara movement and helped to found the NAACP in 1909. He then took on a leadership position at the NAACP and became the editor of the fledgling civil rights organization's journal, *The Crisis*. Serving in this capacity until 1933, Du Bois played a singular role in helping to advance a platform of scholarship, journalism, and literature that would counter the racial logics and deathly violence that maintained legal segregation.

During these decades he continued to give sustained attention to the topic of religion, researching and writing in a range of genres and weighing in from a number of perspectives. For instance, he wrote essays for *The Crisis* that were highly critical of both black ("The Negro Church," 1912) and white ("The White Christ," 1915) Christians. Following "The Afterthought" in *Souls*, Du Bois continued to author prayers that enacted the norms of the "new religious ideal" he still hoped to see realized. As in "The Coming of John," religion also continued to figure as a prominent theme in his fiction, with such short stories as "The Gospel According to Mary Brown" (1919) and "Jesus Christ in Texas" (1920). By the mid-1920s, as the New Negro Renaissance was getting underway, Du Bois seemed to be reconsidering some of the arguments he had first made at the turn of the century.

In the final chapter of *The Gift of Black Folk* (1925), Du Bois rehashed some of the history lessons he first provided in "Of the Faith of the Fathers," highlighting the church as a bridge between Africa and America. However, in "The Gift of the Spirit," he more explicitly valorized "the peculiar spiritual quality, which the Negro has injected into American life and civilization." This, Du Bois averred, was a testament to "an unbreakable set of world-old beliefs, manners, morals, superstitions, and religious observances." Although he stopped short of endorsing "the religion of Africa," he now framed it less as the stubborn persistence of something primitive and premodern and more as an abiding social fact—what results when humans are forced to live "in districts where death and danger are everyday affairs."[1] He no longer posited that this "world-old" religiosity was on the decline, as he had in *Souls*. Now, instead of asserting that progress was impending, he doubled down on the current racial situation (which he claimed fomented "fetishism"), as well as the fundamental ethical quandary it occasioned. "Until the day comes when color caste falls before reason and economic opportunity," he prophesied, "the black American will stand as the last and terrible test of the ethics of Jesus Christ."[2] While he appeared less sanguine about the prospects of "the Frenzy" subsiding and a "new religious ideal" being realized, he reaffirmed that real (i.e., reasoning and ethical) Christianity was aligned with racial progress and opposed to white supremacy in any ideological or institutional form.

In 1903, when Du Bois published *The Souls of Black Folk* and *The Negro Church*, he was just eight years beyond making history as the first Negro to earn a PhD from Harvard University. In the intervening years, a small group of black students followed Du Bois into doctoral programs at the nation's elite (white) universities. In 1912, Carter G. Woodson followed in Du Bois's footsteps as the second black person to earn a PhD in history at Harvard. A year after he founded Negro History Week in 1926, Woodson authored a pioneering historical study of black churches. Best known as the "dean" of the Harlem

Renaissance, Alain Locke received his PhD in philosophy from Harvard in 1918, but this was after he had already graduated from the college with honors, was elected to Phi Beta Kappa, and was selected as the first black Rhodes Scholar. Like Du Bois, George Edmund Haynes graduated from the historically black Fisk College in Nashville. He then earned a master's degree from Yale and became the first black person to earn a PhD from Columbia University, where he studied sociology. Haynes wrote a dissertation on black labor, helped found the organization that later became the National Urban League, and established a career working for racial equality in the economic sphere. Haynes, however, went on to spend the lion's share of his professional life working with churches, leading the Department of Race Relations of the Federal Council of Churches. Although on different terms, both Locke and Haynes interpreted the black cultural flourishing in 1920s Harlem as a "spiritual" phenomenon.[3]

One of the literary stars of the Harlem Renaissance, Zora Neale Hurston spent two years as a doctoral student in Columbia's Anthropology Department. It was in this capacity that she conducted the bulk of the ethnographic and folklore research that informed her popular novels of the 1930s, including *Jonah's Gourd Vine* (1934) and *Their Eyes Were Watching God* (1937). The daughter of a Baptist preacher, Hurston wrote both fiction and nonfiction that wrestled with the powers of religion in black life in the southern United States and the Caribbean. Arthur Huff Fauset, son of an AME preacher and a white Jewish woman, earned BA, MA, and PhD degrees from the University of Pennsylvania. Like Hurston, Fauset also had an interest in religion and folklore in the black South, although his most popular book, *Black Gods of the Metropolis*, would explore such topics in the context of the urban North. By no means a complete list, a new cohort of black scholars now equipped with advanced degrees from Ivy League institutions would effectively change the face of scholarship on race (and other subjects) in modern America.[4] Most important here, they also played a key role in shaping the study of black religion.

Of course, not everyone in this generation of black intellectuals focused their research on "the Negro." Nor did they all position their scholarship to confront "the problem of the color line." However, like Hurston and Fauset, for the majority who did, religion emerged as the key focal point in their efforts to understand and chronicle modern black life. In this regard, Du Bois's early work in *The Negro Church* and *The Souls of Black Folk*, as well as his writing on religion in the intervening years, cast a long shadow. In many respects, new academic writing on "the religion of the American Negro," as Du Bois termed it, both confirmed and complicated his early arguments from the turn of the century. And these individuals played a role in defining the shape of scholarship on African American religion and culture for years to come. Although several of these studies directed attention beyond black churches, the scholarship of this period played a key role in reinscribing the preeminent place of Afro-Protestantism in modern black life.

From *The Negro's God* to *Black Gods of the Metropolis*: Constructing the Study of Black Religion

Two years before he assumed the presidency of Morehouse College, Benjamin Elijah Mays's second book, *The Negro's God as Reflected in His Literature* (1938), went to press. As the first work to offer a religious history of African Americans through literature, *The Negro's God* charted new terrain for the study of religion more generally.[5] The book still stands as a unique accomplishment, both in terms of the materials it engaged and the methods it deployed.[6] In the years since its initial publication, *The Negro's God* has been reissued twice: first, in 1968 at the height of a Black Arts movement that understood itself as a spiritual extension of Black Power politics, and once again in 2010, just months after a nationwide debate about the alleged death of "The Black Church." Both its initial publication and subsequent reissues came in the wake of what scholars have identified as pivotal moments in the history of African American literary and cultural expression.[7]

Completing his PhD at the University of Chicago's Divinity School in 1934, Mays submitted a shorter version of *The Negro's God* as a doctoral thesis titled "The Development of the Idea of God in Contemporary Negro Literature."[8] The aim of any dissertation is to make an original contribution. Mays accomplished this, and more. Though it was certainly a novel academic direction, Mays filed his dissertation in Hyde

Park around the same time that T. S. Eliot was writing his now classic essay, "Religion and Literature."[9] And it was several years before the Divinity School would help to found a new field of study under a similar rubric (i.e., literature and theology and, later, religion and literature), albeit with aims quite different from those of Eliot or Mays. Most academic work in this vein did not begin to reach an audience until the 1940s and 1950s.[10] In this regard, not only was Mays ahead of the curve in his literary approach to studying African American religion; he very well might be identified—even as he is largely unacknowledged in this regard—as helping to forge a new mode of literary inquiry within the study of religion.

As both a race man and a scholar of religion, part of Mays's academic intervention was his interdisciplinary method, long before the term was in vogue. *The Negro's God* synthesized the sociohistorical method, then popular at the University of Chicago's Divinity School, with the burgeoning field of race relations being advanced by social scientists at the university. In fact, a decade earlier Robert Park—one of the most prominent sociologists associated with the Chicago School— published an essay titled "Negro Race Consciousness as Reflected in Race Literature" (1923).[11] Roughly around the time that Mays first arrived in Chicago, Park observed that "the Negro" had been producing poetry since first arriving in the Americas. Although this verse was of uneven aesthetic quality, in his estimation, "it has always been a faithful reflection of [the Negro's] inner life."[12] To be sure, Park's primary interest was not religion. Still, he noted that it was through "religious songs" that enslaved blacks first gained "a consciousness of [their] race," if not a full-fledged "race consciousness." With the air of academic authority, the Chicago School of Sociology helped set the terms under which "the Negro" came to be seen as innately religious. Here Park made a simple observation, not at odds with Du Bois's earlier arguments in *The Souls of Black Folk*, regarding the historical role of religion in cultivating racial identity.[13] If nothing else, Park's 1923 essay suggested the need for a more substantial study of black literature, like the one Mays conducted leading to *The Negro's God*.

During the years that Mays researched and wrote his dissertation and then revised it for publication, he could not have anticipated its reception. With the generous attention afforded black literature and culture vis-à-vis the Harlem Renaissance in the preceding years, there was perhaps cause for some optimism. *The Negro's God* was generally well received, but any notice it garnered paled in comparison to the attention that was being given to research on black churches, the traditional locus for the study of African American religion.[14] Very few people seemed concerned with the role of religion in black writing at the time, even if so much of black literature was animated by religious aspirations, ideas, and idioms. And while his analytical focus was on black literature, Mays's primary concern was actually with fomenting a more radical political vision in black churches.

Fortunately for Mays, he was very much at the center of black church life as well. As much as his reading of religion in Negro literature was an academic innovation, he was more invested in the book's implications for race relations and the future of black churches. Unsurprisingly, Mays's research questions were aligned with contemporary discussions of churches, as institutional Protestantism (and its clerical class) was the primary subject of most studies of religion in America, irrespective of race, at the time. Revisions for the book involved some additional research, but Mays also penned a new introduction that clarified what he understood to be the stakes of his arguments. While he may have borrowed from Park's methods, Mays intended for *The Negro's God* to counter the caricatured racial representations of hyper-religious Negroes that Park had propagated. In keeping with the legacy of minstrelsy, images of natural Negro religiosity were a prominent feature of American popular culture (e.g., *The Green Pastures*), and now these ideas found academic backing in the claims of social scientists.[15]

While still in graduate school, Mays received a grant from the Rockefeller-funded Institute for Social and Religious Research to conduct a national survey of black churches. From this research Mays (and coauthor Joseph Nicholson) produced *The Negro's Church* (1933), which was then one of the most substantial sociological accounts of black churches. The book was greeted accordingly, with a positive reception and reviews from such prominent figures as Howard Thurman, an ordained minister, theologian, and then dean of Howard University's Rankin Chapel, and the writer and race leader Walter White, who was helming the NAACP at the time.[16] To date, the only comparable studies of African American religion were Woodson's

The History of the Negro Church (1921) and, of course, Du Bois's *The Negro Church* (1903).[17] Together these three texts helped solidify the idea of "the Negro Church"—namely, black mainline Protestants such as Baptists and Methodists—as the normative site of (and source for scholarly inquiry into) African American religious life. Following *The Souls of Black Folk*, these texts also confirmed the political stakes, which assessed religious institutions in light of their perceived ability to address what Du Bois termed "Negro problems." By the middle of the 1930s, a political reading of Afro-Protestantism—with the social backdrop of Jim Crow—had been instantiated as the proxy for black religion writ large.

Though *The Negro's Church* affirmed the Christian norm, Mays's turn to literature in *The Negro's God* was not the only effort to examine religion in black life outside of institutional Afro-Protestantism. During the 1930s, a new generation of anthropologists, Zora Neale Hurston foremost among them, turned a wider scholarly eye to the religious worlds of black Americans, especially in the rural South. As an ethnographer and collector of folklore, Hurston recognized that black churches did not develop in isolation from the broader set of ideas and cultural practices that preceded, as well as the material conditions and structural arrangements that both sustained and constrained, black life in the Jim Crow era. Her research reflected an effort to reprioritize the descriptive over the prescriptive in studying black life. In this regard, her work signaled a critique of the normative concern with race politics—apparent in Mays's writing on both churches and literature—that often governed black literary aspirations and writing on race in general.

Indeed, Hurston had made a name for herself by refusing the imposition of such "racial" expectations on her novels.[18] Additionally, her ethnographic and folkloric research on black cultures in the American South and Caribbean opened up to an international analysis that did not adhere to a teleology of progress oriented toward the Christian West or inclusion in American democracy. From Hurston's perspective, the religious practices nurtured within black churches could not be understood in isolation or within an isolated national framework. Afro-Protestantism, in the present, was part of a larger cultural geography, as well as it bore the marks of a longer temporal frame. For Hurston, the spiritual vitality apparent in black culture—whether attributed to the cultural worlds of the American South or West Africa—ought not be reduced to the racial and political metrics of what Du Bois had deemed "the problem of the color line."

At the same time that scholars like Hurston traveled the South in search of American folkways and African retentions, the early years of what came to be known as "the Great Migration" had fostered a novel cultural pluralism within burgeoning black communities in northern cities like Chicago and New York. New religious communities grew out of an urban black pluralism in the North, which contributed to a host of anxieties about the city—and about what black people were doing within them. In the academic parlance of the day, these new social formations—known both for their charismatic leaders and "unorthodox" theologies—were typically identified as "sects" and "cults." Such nomenclature marked such groups as distinctly non-Christian, departures from the established norm: namely, institutional Afro-Protestantism.[19]

To be sure, fascination with non-Protestant religious formations during this period was not an exclusively black phenomenon. For instance, the radical activist and writer V. F. Calverton wrote *Where Angels Dare to Tread* (1941), which was described in *The New Yorker* as a "social history of more or less Utopian colonies in the United States."[20] Yet several popular interpretations of black life at the time—including *Harlem: Negro Metropolis* (1940) by the poet and novelist Claude McKay and journalist Roi Ottley's *New World A-Coming: Inside Black America* (1943)—devoted significant attention to the enigmatic figures who fronted the new religions that emerged in the urban North. More than the journalistic accounts offered by McKay and Ottley, Fauset's book *Black Gods of the Metropolis: Negro Religious Cults in the Urban North* (1944) was paradigmatic. And *Black Gods of the Metropolis* is still recognized as a—if not *the*—pioneering scholarly contribution to the study of black religion outside the context of "The Negro Church."

Trained in anthropology at the University of Pennsylvania, Fauset deployed "cult" as an operative category, again signaling a departure from a normative Afro-Protestantism. He used this term to refer to Afro-Pentecostal congregations (e.g., the Holy Church of America and the United House of Prayer for All People), as well as several more explicitly heterodox religious bodies, including Father Divine's International Peace Mission Movement and Noble Drew Ali's Moorish Science Temple, a forerunner of the Nation of Islam. Fauset's analysis credited both urban pluralism and racial exclusion with spawning these newly formed communities. Even if they were not to be considered entirely Christian (i.e., they exceeded the theological and political orthodoxies of a normative Afro-Protestantism), he nonetheless acknowledged their respective merits in addressing the social conditions that black people encountered in the modern city. Fauset's book helped to put these new religious groups on the intellectual map. Yet his rendering of them as "cults" (read: not church) worked to reinscribe the idea of a disciplined and doctrinally orthodox "Negro church" as the normative script for African American religion.[21]

Mays's *The Negro's God* similarly did not depart entirely from existing academic conventions. This may be the case, at least in part, because of Mays's own Christian commitments, which are evident throughout the pages of *The Negro's God*. He was concerned, in particular, that many black writers, such as those of the Harlem Renaissance, displayed an ambivalence, if not outright hostility, toward Christianity. Yet this did not prevent Mays from utilizing Christian categories and language to make sense of their literary musings. *The Negro's God* outlined three primary trajectories in black literature: (1) ideas of God that adhered to "traditional, compensatory patterns," (2) interpretations of God that supported a "growing consciousness of social and psychological adjustment," and (3) views that threatened "to abandon the idea of God as a 'useful instrument.'" In addition to being organized around competing conceptions of a Christian God, each of these positions revealed the author's concern with assessing religion *and* literature in light of their perceived social utility. As an unabashed "race man," Mays measured the merits of both according to their perceived ability to bring about social change on behalf of "the race."[22] Ultimately, his engagement with black literature reflected his goal of carrying forward a vision of Afro-Protestantism that countered the laws and logics of Jim Crow.

The Negro's God appeared at the end of a New Negro movement that dated back to the turn of the century and reached its apex in the 1920s amid a black literary flourishing that several critics described as a secularizing force.[23] In 1925, years before writing about utopianism in *Where Angels Dare to Tread*, as editor of *Modern Quarterly* V. F. Calverton announced the arrival of a "newer spirit" in American literature, which undoubtedly influenced New Negro writers.[24] Given the acclaim and attention afforded writers such as Langston Hughes at the time, Mays was motivated, at least in part, by a desire to defend Christianity—and black churches in particular—against Marxist and modernist critiques alike. Mays observed a nascent secularism in black letters, as he identified a "growing tendency or threat to abandon the idea of God" in the literature of the Negro Renaissance. For these writers, he observed, religion was viewed as outdated at best and harmful at worst.[25]

Accordingly, Mays warned that "liberal prophetic religion" would have to take more aggressive action, or atheism and a potentially violent militancy might take root within black communities. In the years to come, Mays heeded his own counsel as he went on to become one of the most prominent representatives of black liberal Protestantism of the twentieth century.[26] Occupying a series of important leadership posts as dean of Howard University's School of Divinity and president of Morehouse College, Mays spread his vision of interracial cooperation, racial equality, and "prophetic religion." And he mentored a generation of black clergy who followed suit. In fact, Mays's prominence within standard histories of "The Black Church" may be second only to his most celebrated mentee, Martin Luther King Jr., who remains today the most iconic representative of Afro-Protestantism in service to civil rights the world over.[27]

The Negro's God was published on the heels of a moment of cultural flourishing that had petered out by the early 1930s, as opportunities for artists, black and white, diminished in the shadows of the Great Depression. Amid the economic crisis, Mays and other black Christian leaders feared that Communism was poised to usurp the influence that black communities traditionally ascribed to Christian churches.[28] The year before Mays's book was published, Dorothy West's leftist journal, *New Challenge*, printed Richard Wright's now classic essay, "Blueprint for Negro Writing" (1937). Mays may very well have read Wright's essay not long before he put the finishing touches on *The Negro's God*.[29] Perhaps, as a preacher, Mays was provoked by Wright's insistence that "the Negro writer" ought to assume the "moral authority" once wielded by black clergy. If Wright was correct that "Negro middle class leadership"—with preaching as arguably the most prominent professional role—had been sedated by its relative privilege, then Mays would be compelled to sound the alarm to awaken a renewed commitment to "liberal prophetic religion."[30]

Though he made no explicit mention of Wright or his "Blueprint" essay, it is clear that Mays hoped to invite a broad audience of readers to reexamine what they thought they knew about black religion. In the introduction to *The Negro's God*, Mays singled out the then-popular play *The Green Pastures*, which won the Pulitzer Prize for Drama in 1930, enjoyed an extended Broadway run, and was turned into a film in 1936. According to Mays, alongside a history of minstrelsy, shows like *The Green Pastures* reinforced the image of black religious life as entirely "otherworldly," overly emotional, and devoid of any ethical compass. Marc Connelly's play put forward the idea that African American culture was defined more by backward superstitions than by "true" religion. Upon seeing *The Green Pastures*, audience members might reasonably conclude that "the Negro" was out of step and ill-suited to contribute to modern society.[31] Such images, Mays averred, served as justification for the continuance of racial subordination in the segregation era.[32] As a counter to these popular logics, his argument privileged ethics and politics over aesthetics and metaphysics. Ideas about God apparent in black literature were not important because they cultivated an appreciation for "the beautiful," or even because they accurately mapped the order of the universe. To the contrary, literary representations were significant for Mays because they demonstrated the political salience of Afro-Protestantism in the here and now. That is, they suggested a stage—contrary to *The Green Pastures*—for the sort of forward-thinking church work in which Mays was thoroughly ensconced.

In 1934, the same year that Mays submitted his dissertation and took over as dean at Howard University's School of Religion, a group of black clergy gathered to form what became the Fraternal Council of Negro Churches. The FCNC was a first effort to harness the energies of black churches across denominational lines on a national scale. Reverdy Ransom, an A.M.E. bishop who called for the meeting, announced that the newly formed group would offer "an authoritative voice for us to speak on social, economic, industrial and political questions."[33] Although records don't show that Mays participated in the formation of the FCNC, its vision of providing an organizing base for black Americans via an ecumenical institutional Afro-Protestantism was certainly consistent with his call for a "liberal prophetic religion" in the introduction to *The Negro's God*. As a national body guided by similar ideas, the FCNC was born out of an effort by black clergy to harness the collective resources of "The Negro's Church"—published that very year—to address the social demands of the Great Migration and the economic challenges posed by the Great Depression.

As a scholarly corollary to the FCNC, Mays researched and wrote *The Negro's God* in response to recent developments in the realm of culture. The evolution of American literature during the roaring twenties also presented a challenge to the legitimacy of Christian churches.[34] More precisely, for Mays the nascent atheism that he observed in a new generation of black writers seemed to hold the potential to unseat the cultural authority traditionally assigned to Afro-Protestantism and Christian clergy such as himself. As much as Mays focused on the work of black writers, the periodization (i.e., 1760–1865, 1865–1914, after 1914) that he adopted signaled broader concerns. For Mays, the first Great War and the subsequent Communist Revolution altered the trajectory of African American literature, which now bore witness to the inroads that Marxism had made within black communities.

The catastrophic levels of death occasioned by the war, along with the formation of the Soviet Union, called into question the viability of Mays's distinctly American brand of "liberal prophetic religion." Not only did the categories of Christian theology inform his inquiry into black literature, but the exigencies of international politics—and anxieties about Christianity's role therein—further delimited his literary line of reasoning.[35] Such an approach, overdetermined by a political binary (i.e., otherworldly vs. this-worldly), also limited the possibilities for imagining the contributions of religion (really, Protestant Christianity) to race literature. Though Mays was concerned with the problem of racial representations in the 1930s, the narrative arc of his chronology proceeded toward (and anticipated) a coming confrontation between Christianity and Communism. Mays's anxieties about

Communism would be affirmed by the rise of "Red Scare" politics in subsequent years, including especially Senator Joseph McCarthy's hearings on "anti-American activities" in the 1950s.[36] However, had Mays followed the evolution of the New Negro from its genesis in the final decade of the nineteenth century, *The Negro's God* might have noted the movement's underlying, and abiding, Protestant aspirations.

The Negro's God was, at least in part, a product of the ambitions of the era in which it appeared. In other ways it proved to be prescient, anticipating the convergence of several methods (i.e., theology, religious studies, literature, and history) in the formation of a new field (i.e., religion and literature). Park's 1923 essay on race literature and Calverton's 1925 book, *The Newer Spirit: A Sociological Criticism of Literature*, may have provided viable models and methods of literary criticism. Yet Mays had his specific motivations, and he offered his own interpretations. Where Park contributed to a romantic racialist discourse on black culture specifically, Calverton celebrated the triumph of scientific rationalism over religion in general. In contrast, Mays argued that "the Negro" was not naturally religious, nor was black religion divorced from social realities or at odds with modern social science. Rather than reinforcing the status quo or being oriented by "otherworldly" concerns, the theology/ies apparent in Negro literature, according to Mays, adhered to a race politics rooted in a deeper commitment to ecumenical activism within churches, nonviolent protest, and the struggle for social equality through the courts.[37]

At that time there were several efforts, supported with ample evidence, to independently narrate the religious and literary histories of African Americans. Yet Mays attempted to hold these narratives together against the developing orthodoxies of American literary studies and the academic study of religion.[38] In addition to providing an expansive catalogue of theological themes and assessing their social significance, his arguments illumined the degree to which both African American religion and literature—black culture more generally—were each, more often than not, evaluated according to their perceived social and political utility.[39] Though Mays advanced a novel historical argument about African American religion—evidenced in literary sources—he also shared Park and Calverton's sociological lens, which assessed both religion and literature through a set of instrumentalist concerns. In this way, Mays carried forward a way of narrating African American history in which an ethical and reasoning Christianity—"liberal prophetic religion," as he called it—both stood at the center and shaped the terms and boundaries of the story.[40]

As was noted both earlier in this chapter and in chapter 2, the earliest studies of African American religion figured a vision of "The Negro Church" that was informed by the urgency of race politics even as it took for granted a Protestant object and conceptual approach to the source materials. By this logic, "the religion of the American Negro" and "The Negro Church" were one and the same. However, the political weight assigned to Afro-Protestantism was never exclusively a religious burden, something borne solely by what is now referred to as "The Black Church." As Mays's *The Negro's God* confirmed, instrumentalist appraisals of black churches that dominated during the Migration era (and which persist in many quarters today) also prevailed in accounts of African American literature and culture more broadly.[41] In the 1930s, Mays was one of the first to scrutinize this literary history for its theological sensibilities even as he reinscribed the instrumentalist terms of the debate. However, in attempting to counter racial stereotypes and shore up a renewed role for "prophetic" Protestantism, Mays inadvertently tapped into the tradition's lifeblood.

When the formal idea of race literature first developed in the wake of Reconstruction's demise, its origins, sources, and aims were as much attributable to religious ambitions as they were to race politics. By this time, as was seen in chapters 1 and 2 of this book, American religious norms had been entangled with forms of literary reasoning for well over a century. And race politics—then under the name of abolitionism—had long provided a set of criteria for discerning the difference between what was "real" religion and what was not. We saw in chapter 2 that at the turn of the twentieth century, the writings of both Victoria Earl Matthews and Du Bois similarly assessed the prospects of religion according to its capacity to address "the problem of the color line." Around the same time, an Afro-Pentecostal movement—as seen in C. P. Jones's *Appeal to the Sons of Africa*—cultivated a religious vision that resisted the dominant logics of racial segregation. And when Douglass, Barrier Williams, and Arnett addressed the first World's Parliament of Religions in 1893, they each called for a modern religious sensibility capacious enough to embrace and overcome the inequalities attached to racial difference. Decades before that, in the genre of the slave narrative one can observe a way of imagining, enlisting, and performing religion—a literary and reasoning Afro-Protestant subject—in service to the cause of emancipation.

Both *The Negro's Church* and *The Negro's God* linked Mays to this tradition. Now, in the 1930s, his vision of and for religion privileged an ethical and reasoning Protestantism to underwrite a form of race politics that pursued black civil rights and countered Jim Crow. Mays's own stated Christian commitments, as an ordained Baptist clergyman, were the thread that wove a particular religious orthodoxy together, once again, with a normative vision of black identity and culture. Yet one need not be Christian clergy to harbor religious ambitions or to imagine religion on Afro-Protestant terms. Afro-Protestantism, in ways that were both obvious and at times more subtle, was by this time thoroughly stitched into the fabric of black social life in ways that disciplined bodies and minds without demanding or requiring church membership. This was as true for "regular" black folk as it was for the intellectual "elite." Even as a number of scholars were beginning to examine African American religion on more expansive terms, the kind of normative Afro-Protestantism that Du Bois both theorized and performed in *The Souls of Black Folk* (1903) continued to set the disciplinary terms for the study—the theory and the practice—of black religion and culture in the years after *The Negro's God* was published.

Du Bois was Mays's senior by twenty-six years. At the same time that Mays was stepping into the overlapping spotlights of liberal Protestantism and race politics, Du Bois was increasingly on the outs with the civil rights establishment. In 1934 Mays completed his dissertation and moved to Washington, D.C., to serve as dean of the School of Divinity at Howard University. That same year Du Bois resigned from his longtime post as editor of the NAACP's magazine *The Crisis* and rejoined the faculty of Atlanta University, where he had begun his academic career in the 1890s. Mays made his way to Atlanta just a few years later, in 1940, when he became the president of Morehouse College. Although they were in close physical proximity for only four years, as Du Bois was forced into retirement in 1944, the two men's academic careers had been entangled for some time. As president of

Morehouse College, Mays had secured a prime stage from which to enunciate (and recruit others to) his vision of "prophetic religion." Meanwhile, back at his old academic home, Du Bois continued to propagate an updated version of the "new religious ideal" that he first called for in *The Souls of Black Folk*—in ways that were perhaps less overt, but no less Protestant, than Mays's approach.

Afro-Protestantism and the Politics of Religion at *Phylon*

When Du Bois returned to Atlanta University in 1933, he had spent more than two decades on the front lines of race politics and civil rights activism through his work with the NAACP. In this regard, Du Bois was in the vanguard of a group of writers engaged in what the historian David Levering Lewis has referred to as an effort to achieve "civil rights by copyright."[42] Indeed, before finding himself at odds with the NAACP's new president, Walter White, in the 1930s, Du Bois employed *The Crisis* as his primary vehicle for waging war against "the color line." Now the seasoned scholar, author, and activist returned to the academic institution where he had launched his career in the 1890s, when he published a series of major studies of black life.[43]

Several years after settling into his new role as chair of Atlanta University's Sociology Department, and at the age of seventy-two, Du Bois launched yet another new project. *Phylon: The Atlanta University Review of Race and Culture* printed its first issue in 1940. With his hopes for an encyclopedia Africana gradually unraveling before northern philanthropic boards, *Phylon* provided Du Bois with a new outlet for his energies.[44] If anyone was inclined to view his return to academia as a retreat from the battlefield of race politics, the journal's first number disabused readers of any such notion. His international vision, anticolonial analysis, and commitment to engaging America's race problem were readily apparent in the journal's leadership, as well as in the contributions to its inaugural issue. In addition to original scholarship on everything from the "social conditions" of the South to "architectural acoustics," visual art and poetry, and bibliographical resources, the journal's first edition provided a contemporary "chronicle of race relations." *Phylon*'s intellectual ambitions included the artistic, social, and political lives of race in the modern world.

In assembling an editorial board, Du Bois gathered a team of scholars impressive for their academic pedigrees and cosmopolitanism. The journal's managing editor was Ira De A. Reid, the son of a Baptist preacher. As an adult Reid joined the Society of Friends and was the first black faculty member to be tenured at Haverford College. Joining Reid in a supporting role, William H. Dean Jr. was also a minister's son. One of the nation's first black economists, he earned his PhD from Harvard and later joined the staff of the soon-to-form United Nations. The first issue of *Phylon* identified Dean simply as a "sometime Harvard fellow." W. Mercer Cook, a Roman Catholic, was a professor of French at Atlanta University. He was also a diplomat who would later serve in ambassadorial posts in Senegal, the Gambia, and Niger. The team of editors also included the British-born feudal historian Rushton Coulborn, an Atlanta University professor who was a "former Vice-Principal of Sussex House" in London. Oran W. Eagleson, a professor of psychology and longtime dean at Spelman College (and later Peace Corps consultant), was also enlisted. Finally, the poet and anthologist William Stanley Braithwaite, who was generally considered to be the first Negro literary critic, rounded out the editorial committee.

Phylon's advisors included Atlanta University's current president, Rufus Clement. The journal also acknowledged two renowned historians as contributing editors: Horace Mann Bond and Rayford Logan. Bond was then president of Fort Valley State University in Georgia and would shortly take the helm at Lincoln University in Pennsylvania. And Logan, a Harvard graduate and longtime Howard University professor, was a member of President Franklin D. Roosevelt's "Black Cabinet," a capacity in which, just a few years later, he would draft FDR's executive order to end the exclusion of black people from military service in World War II.[45] *Phylon*'s masthead was nothing short of a list of the leading black intellectuals—and, more precisely, race men—of the day.[46]

Though Du Bois most likely penned it on his own, the editorial team is credited with a three-page "Apology" that made the case for the value of the "new venture." *Phylon* was to offer a "new view of the social sciences," they explained, one that "emphasize[d] the use and place of human differences as tool and method of progress." In doing so, the journal would provide a "new orientation and duty" to intellectual inquiry that extended beyond "the internal study of race groups" to a "general view of that progress of human beings." The "Apology" explained further that *Phylon* would "proceed from the point of view and the experience of the black folk where we live and work, to the wider world."[47] Otherwise put, for *Phylon*'s editors, an analysis of African American life was necessarily significant to the global stage and human progress. Even as a human rights discourse was emerging as a topic of global significance during the 1940s, *Phylon* would continue to center the black struggle for civil rights and legal equality in North America. In this regard, the journal's approach was indicative of a historical moment in which black American intellectuals were increasingly aware of their importance on both the national and international stage, and they understood the latter to be incomprehensible without consideration of the former. Accordingly, *Phylon* staked a claim about the universality of the particular experience of "black folk" in the United States.[48]

The growth of this global black perspective, with its attending aspirations, became apparent in commercial culture, radio and print media, and political organizing.[49] Within the United States, for instance, the Double Victory campaign linked American efforts to dismantle fascism in Europe with domestic struggles to end racial segregation.[50] In its own way, *Phylon* announced a new era in black intellectual life, providing an academic base from which to mount claims consistent with the international view of the Double V platform, with support from the authority of modern (social) science. Along with the print publication, Du Bois organized the Phylon Institute, which hosted a series of convenings at Atlanta University that aimed to "utilize science in the solution of Negro problems."[51] Questions associated with race and cultural difference were, obviously, *Phylon*'s primary focus. Yet the journal was also animated by a religious impulse that was evident, if not explicitly articulated, in the "Apology." To be sure, a general liberal optimism underwrote much of black ambition and fueled interracial efforts to dismantle segregation during this time. However, *Phylon*'s editorial vision was informed by and emblematic of a religious liberalism that was enunciated anew in American culture more broadly during World War II.[52]

Phylon's liberal religious vision, first of all, was grounded in an awareness of the nation's racial history and the desire to rectify past wrongs. As the "Apology" explained, the journal was committed to debunking the idea that "the industrial organization of the nineteenth century"—that is, the plantation economy of racial slavery—"was permanent and sacred." By 1940 slavery had been abolished for almost eighty years even as the racial apartheid of Jim Crow prevailed. Now, in the aftermath of the Great Depression, the task was to "abolish the present economic illiteracy" as a step toward ending material deprivation. In this view, race (i.e., slavery) and class (i.e., poverty) were cast along a historical continuum, as well as across an international horizon. Notably, the editors' language highlighted how these entangled social orders—what is now often referred to by the shorthand "racial capitalism"—had been granted the authority of divine sanction.[53] As a counter, *Phylon* set its sights on publishing social science research, racial and cultural commentary, and cultural expression in the form of literary and visual arts that would address "the problem of abolishing poverty as a first step toward real freedom, democracy and art among men."[54] Though deeply rooted in the domestic, *Phylon*'s religious vision was both interdisciplinary and international.

Though oriented by the secular ethos of the social sciences, *Phylon*'s appeal to "freedom, democracy and art" was entirely consistent with a distinctly modernist brand of Christianity. This strand of religious liberalism harkened back to the 1893 World's Parliament of Religions, bearing witness especially to a tradition of outward-facing liberal Protestantism. However, at the time of its founding in 1940, *Phylon*'s perspective was informed by new encounters with racial and cultural difference facilitated by two world wars and a new era of international air travel.[55] Moreover, the history of asymmetrical "international" encounters now led to a figuring of cultural difference—the racial and religious "other"—as an entity to include and embrace, and of social inequality as a goal to be overcome.

These uneven occasions of cultural contact, in this view, provided a mandate to spread the culture and values of Western democracy and, in doing so, extend the boundaries of the human community.

Promulgating cultural pluralism was, in short, envisioned as a pathway toward world peace. It was, otherwise put, a missionary endeavor woven together with the metrics of modern social science.[56] The tributaries of such liberal religious ambitions would be most evident, for instance, in novel political projects of the 1940s such as the United Nations (1945) and the utopian vision articulated in the Universal Declaration of Human Rights (1948).[57] With the aid of social scientific methods, echoing the Hebrew prophet Isaiah, *Phylon* would help "make straight the path to a common world humanity through the development of cultural gifts to their highest possibilities."[58]

Phylon's grand vision of the international significance of race squared well with the entangled projects of religious and cultural pluralism that gained in prominence at the time. A number of black leaders both invested and actively participated in this pluralist effort to extend democracy, and the "American Way," to the world.[59] At the same time, as subjects still on the underside of Jim Crow, they also drew upon pluralism to make a claim for an end to segregation, arguing for black people's full inclusion within American democracy and as equal members of a "common world humanity." Yet pluralism was not simply a neutral ideology. Nor was it naturally aligned with racial equality or with expanding democracy. Rather, pluralism provided a set of discursive legal and social practices that aligned with a particular idea of religion (i.e., ethical and reasoning) even as it policed those forms of religion (i.e., emotional and embodied) that failed to adhere to its norms. To be sure, *Phylon* mobilized novel theories of pluralism to help its readers rethink racial and cultural difference, to educate a broader public on such matters, and to pose solutions to "Negro problems." Nevertheless, the scope of the journal's engagement with religion was also constrained by pluralism's prescriptive powers, which took cues from and reinscribed an ethical and reasoning Afro-Protestantism as the site, source, and object of inquiry.[60]

In this way, *Phylon*'s early years offer a compelling case study of an instance in which political, racial, and religious histories were at stake in the study of black life. Though typically understood within the registers of war-time politics—and race politics, more precisely—the journal's proceedings offer a revealing inroad into the longer history of religion in America, and of Afro-Protestantism more specifically. As a "review of race and culture," *Phylon* waged a full-scale intellectual attack on the dominant racial science of the day, which abounded with narratives of black pathology and hyperreligiosity at once. Even better, excessive religiosity was often pointed to as evidence of black deviance from and deprivation of the values and practices that befit modern democratic subjects.[61] Scholarly and popular accounts alike at the time imagined an abundance of undisciplined religiosity, and an absence of reason, to be definitive of black life. In response to this predicament, then, through *Phylon* Du Bois and a cohort of scholars and writers forged a field of presumably secular inquiry as a form of political critique. In doing so, the journal engaged with and conceived of religion in ways that adhered to a normative "Negro church" as the embodiment of all that black culture was not, at least according to the dominant social science of the day. In this view, the idea of an ethically driven, politically engaged, and disciplined institutional Afro-Protestantism—that is, the black church as a site for and example of the practice of democracy—came to define the study of black religion. *Phylon* was no exception to this rule.

Reading the "Apology"—*Phylon*'s raison d'être—in its first issue helps to highlight some of the journal's primary commitments. The way the editorial board cast its vision was emblematic of the tensions attendant on a scholarly publication that both subscribed to the objective airs and secularizing norms of social science and sought to intervene concretely in race politics—that is, to "solve Negro problems." *Phylon*'s delicate dance between its academic and activist commitments was informed by the emerging discourse of pluralism in the United States, which had its own distinctive (liberal) religious genealogy.[62] As such, an examination of *Phylon*'s early years helps to illuminate how race politics and religion—really, a privileged Afro-Protestantism—converged yet again to set the terms for the interpretation and practice of African American culture. In keeping with a longer tradition, the norms of black equality and freedom were the measure of true Christianity. Conversely, a certain Christian orthodoxy was encoded within the interpretive logics used to analyze modern black social life.

Phylon's editorial vision was in keeping with this normative script. Indeed, it exemplified what Barbara Dianne Savage has described as "*the* politics of black religion" (italics mine) as it took shape during the 1940s—what William Hart has called "the standard narrative of black religion."[63] As part of these developments, the journal published some pioneering work on black religious life, but it also participated in the construction of a particular kind of "black religion" as *the* norm. Although it was not an explicitly stated aim of the journal, *Phylon* helped to valorize Afro-Protestantism as the exemplar for the study of (and as the authentic form of practicing) black religion. *Phylon* both reinforced and gave new language to this long-standing tradition—from literary and reasoning to, now, liberal and democratic—against a broader array of ideas, practices, and social arrangements that comprised black religious and cultural life at the time. As such, *Phylon* exemplified one response to the question of (and thus played a key role in defining) what constituted "good religion" in the context of modern black life, which at the moment reflected a broader set of debates about cultural difference, Western democracy, and the United States' place in the world during and after World War II.[64]

Indeed, as *Phylon*'s early proceedings confirm, religion was a key site of contestation in debates over the significance of race in general, and the place of black people specifically, in modern America. In this regard, Edward Nelson Palmer's "The Religious Acculturation of the Negro," Effie Lee Newsome's "Early Figures in Haitian Methodism," and René Maran's interview with Bishop Joseph Kiwanuka illustrate how the journal's particular vision of race and politics set the parameters for the kind of religion that would be privileged, and how religion would be presented, for *Phylon*'s readership. As just a few examples from the journal's early years, all three essays reveal how a set of ideas, practices, and values associated with liberal Protestantism and American democracy were both evident in as well as mapped onto black religious practices in the context of the United States, the Caribbean, and Africa, respectively. Together, these articles show *Phylon* to have given religion detailed consideration even as the journal participated in the privileging of a reasonable, democratic Afro-Protestantism as constitutive of and paradigmatic for modern black life.

Edward Nelson Palmer and the Christianizing of the Negro

Phylon contributor Edward Nelson Palmer pursued doctoral studies under the renowned sociologist Guy Johnson at the University of Michigan in the early 1940s. As historian Jamil Drake has shown, Johnson himself played an outsized role in shaping perceptions of black religion and culture at this time.[65] Before earning his PhD in 1945, and as an assistant to Johnson, Palmer authored an essay on black secret societies for Gunnar Myrdal's classic study of race in the United States, *An American Dilemma: The Negro Problem and Modern Democracy* (1944).[66] However, prior to establishing himself as a scholar of black fraternal organizations, Palmer had written a master's thesis on the prominent black preacher and radio broadcaster Elder Solomon Lightfoot Michaux. He classified Michaux's church as an unorthodox "religious sect" that amounted to little more than "institutionalized dancing crowds."[67] Recent discoveries by historian Lerone Martin show that Elder Michaux's ministry wielded a great deal of political power and was anything but marginal, which is how Palmer then described him.[68] Even still, Palmer's deployment of the term "sect" was consistent with Fauset's use of "cult" in *Black Gods of the Metropolis*. Both worked to draw a clear line between mainline Afro-Protestantism and other kinds of black Christians.

While he devoted his thesis to Michaux, Palmer was no less interested in what was generally considered the mainstream of black religious life. During the early 1940s he published an essay that positioned "the religious life of the Negro" as part and parcel of the making of American history. When Palmer's essay "The Religious Acculturation of the Negro" appeared in *Phylon* in 1944, he had not yet completed his PhD. He had, however, already joined the sociology faculty at Fisk University, which was then chaired by the noted black sociologist Charles S. Johnson. Palmer's basic argument in the essay asserts that an effective way to measure how well black people were adapting to American society was to examine the degree to which they had embraced Christianity. Best described as a work of historical sociology, his narrative was organized into three major periods. As a whole, the article might otherwise have been titled "The Christianization of the Negro."

The first period that Palmer examined was that prior to the American Revolution. Here he focused attention on the familiar eighteenth-century debate over whether slaves who embraced Christianity would be emancipated. The question, otherwise put, was whether or not conversion necessitated manumission. In Palmer's telling, this moment was to be understood as the age of Anglican catechesis. He noted that few among the enslaved converted under these terms, although those who did were "thorough[ly] grounded in the fundamentals of Christian faith."[69] The next period under discussion spanned from 1740 until the end of U.S. chattel slavery. Most important for Palmer, this era included both the First and Second Great Awakening. Here, he explained, a faith promulgated through the mastery of certain sacred texts gave way to the rise (and triumph) of an evangelical experientialism. Put another way, the Anglicans had been outdone by the Baptists and Methodists. Under these terms, the number of slaves who converted to Christianity dramatically increased. However, a shift in emphasis from catechesis to personal experience meant that a quantitative advance, in Palmer's estimation, came at the expense of a qualitative decline. Christian salvation, he argued, was no longer indicative of acculturation in the same way that it was under the literary rules of catechism.

Palmer's third and final period began when slavery ended, following black religious life from emancipation until the contemporary moment in which he penned his essay. He posited, in this instance, that black Christian experience had begun to take on greater institutional form. Palmer offered the spread of independent black churches—primarily black Baptist and Methodist denominations—as evidence that Christianity had become "a normal function of Negro life." This, for him, was a sign that the goal of acculturation was not lost, because "these denominations are conventional in every respect." By this Palmer meant that black denominations displayed no substantive differences from their white Baptist and Methodist counterparts. Ultimately, Palmer advanced the idea that the growth of Afro-Protestant institutions facilitated the cultivation of shared American civic virtues even as black and white Christian churches remained divided by the dictates of Jim Crow. The numerical and institutional growth of black Christianity was indicative of an embrace of American culture despite the fact that white Americans, Christian or otherwise, refused to embrace their fellow citizens across "the color line."

While black denominations showed signs of flourishing, Palmer noted, African Americans continued to lag behind in "other phases of religious life." He pointed to "excessive emotionalism," "frequent schisms," and the "lack of an adequately trained ministry" as examples of such underdevelopment.[70] In this regard, his critique of black denominational churches was similar to his diagnosis of Elder Michaux's congregation. Palmer acknowledged that emotionalism, schisms, and lack of education were key attributes of the long history of American Christianity, in general. And, contrary to Melville Herskovits's recently published work on African cultural "retentions" in the Americas, Palmer insisted that these qualities did not testify to a "peculiar negro temperament or to a survival of African customs." Instead, Palmer took pains to clarify that such issues were evidence of "incomplete acculturation." These were the "usual marks of a developing social institution," he explained, which could also be observed in an "earlier phase in the religious behavior of white Americans."[71] Ultimately for Palmer, Christianization was synonymous with Americanization—even if the nation failed to recognize black churches as fully American or truly Christian. Acculturation was the desired goal. And, at least in 1944 when his essay appeared in *Phylon*, the Christianizing process was not yet complete for the Negro.

Effie Lee Newsome and the Making of an Afro-Protestant Caribbean Nation

If Palmer's essay used Afro-Protestantism as a lens through which to assess the Americanization of black people in the United States, then Effie Lee Newsome's contribution, "Early Figures in Haitian Methodism," was a celebration of missionaries, martyrs, and the making of black Methodism in the Caribbean. While in the pages of *Phylon* she appears as a hagiographer of Afro-Protestant pioneers, Newsome is better known within the context of the Harlem Renaissance. With degrees from Wilberforce, Oberlin, the Pennsylvania Academy of Fine Arts, and the University of Pennsylvania, she built a literary career as both a writer and an editor. Newsome published over one hundred poems in *The Crisis* over two decades, when Du Bois was at its helm, and edited a column during the 1920s.[72] Additionally, she illustrated children's literature and edited a children's column in *Opportunity*, the National Urban League publication. Newsome was the daughter of the Rev. Benjamin Franklin Lee, a bishop in the AME Church, and she wed a preacher from the same denomination, the Rev. Henry Nesby Newsome, in 1920.[73] After some time in Birmingham, Alabama, the couple eventually moved to Ohio, where she found work as a librarian. Across these multiple contexts, Newsome spent much of her life in service to the AME Church.

Palmer's account of Afro-Protestantism presented a sociology of "culture contact," in which matters of theology appear inconsequential. Christianity, instead, is positioned as a proxy for citizenship and democracy. By contrast, Newsome's article offered an example of history in service to a claim for "good religion"—a historical theology, of sorts.[74] Her narrative of religious life in the Republic of Haiti was also, at least in part, a lay discourse on toleration and religious freedom.[75] In this view, the first independent black nation in the Western hemisphere was an early experiment in religious diversity. Embedded within her portrait of Haiti, Newsome provided a strident critique of how pluralism was practiced in the former French colony. In her estimation, toleration was a virtue that Catholics publicly claimed but one by which Methodists actually abided. Newsome's real story, then, was about Methodist faithfulness in the face of Catholic (and state) persecution.

Haiti's religious history provided Newsome with a platform on which to stage a familiar drama of the cosmic struggle between good and bad religion—Methodism and Catholicism, respectively. In this rendition, an embattled minority of Protestant believers who were "consecrated solely to God" fought off the "surrounding practices" of "a region in which worship meant ceremony." The Methodists on the island during the early nineteenth century were a "creed-bound people" struggling in a nation where imprisonment, stonings, and "sectarian surveillance" were social rituals that maintained the order of a "Catholic world." Even still, hope was not lost for Newsome's pioneering Haitian Methodists. Hers was a tale of triumph for those who proclaimed "the gospel that the true shrine is the heart." Though Catholicism presently occupied the center, due to its proximity to state power in Haiti, Newsome imagined a time "when those idols are taken away and the gospel [is] preached in its purity." Until then, she explained, "[p]ersecutions from man and compassion from God formed the daily portion of these forerunners of the faith."[76]

In this vein, Newsome enumerated the deeds of the black fathers of a Haitian pan-Methodist alliance, including Scipio Beans, "the first representative of Negro Methodism to die on foreign soil."[77] Along the way, she subtly wove together a larger set of debates about toleration and pluralism, which also revealed a strain of anti-Catholicism. In doing so, Newsome offered a telling illustration of how Afro-Protestantism—in her case, black Methodism—once again set the normative terms of black religion in the modern world. *Phylon*'s social scientific and historical engagements with religion, as seen in the work of Newsome and Palmer, elevated one particular strand of Protestantism, which privileged an autonomous and reasoning black subject for whom religion was an ethical disposition and/or an interior condition of right belief. Institutional Afro-Protestantism, along with individual believers, was figured favorably in contrast to the emotion, ritualism, and oppressive excesses associated with American revivalism and Haitian Catholicism. Moreover, in both articles, religion was conceived of in terms that were consonant with and provided a pathway for modern democracy, both in the United States and around the world.

René Maran and the Contours of a Catholic Black Imaginary

As much as both of their essays were concerned with the making of black religious life in the Americas, Newsome and Palmer attended to different geographic contexts and were guided by differing disciplinary conventions. On the one hand, Palmer decried sectarianism and denied Africanisms at a time when cutting-edge research was shedding new light on both the African influences and (what were then perceived to be) the heterodox fringes of black faith in the United

States. Herskovits's *The Myth of the Negro Past* and Fauset's *Black Gods of the Metropolis* (1944), respectively, were exemplary in this regard. Newsome's article, on the other hand, offered a polemic against "popery" at the precise moment that black Americans, on the heels of urban migration, were joining the Catholic Church in greater numbers than ever before. In this regard, both essays appeared to be out of step with an era that witnessed the development of more ecumenical notions of a shared Judeo-Christian fabric facilitated by domestic demographic shifts, international military contests, and cultural connections around the globe.[78]

Rather than simply a crude anti-Catholicism or a crass Americanism, both authors' claims suggested a broader argument that aligned black religious life with "The Negro Church." And this singular proposition, as shorthand for an otherwise unwieldy array of Afro-Protestant churches, was cast as an institution made in the image of American (read: white) Christianity and democracy writ large.[79] This liberal religious vision even made allowances for the inclusion of Catholics as part of the growing Judeo-Christian sensibility. Yet this was true only insofar as Catholicism could be presented as consistent with values and practices associated with Protestantism and American democracy. Such logics were seemingly apparent in African American religious life and could accordingly be found in the pages of *Phylon*. In fact, the journal's inaugural issue also featured an extended essay by René Maran in which an image and story of African Catholicism—in the likeness of global democracy—took center stage.

Translated from French to English by romance language scholar and *Phylon* editorial board member W. Mercer Cook, "Rene Maran Looks at the Negro in France" is perhaps best classified as a work of travel literature.[80] Maran was a renowned Francophone novelist from Martinique. In 1921 he was given France's most prestigious literary award, the Goncourt Prize, for his novel *Batouala: A True Black Novel*. By 1940, Maran had authored a biography of the nineteenth-century explorer, abolitionist, and Congregationalist missionary to Africa, David Livingstone. He had also served as a colonial officer to Ubangi-Shari (now the Central African Republic).[81] His *Phylon* essay began with general observations about black life in France at the beginning of the 1940s. It ended with Maran's reflections on an interview he conducted with the Most Reverend Joseph Kiwanuka, who had recently become the first native-born African prelate in the Roman Catholic Church. With his consecration as bishop, Kiwanuka quickly became the most prominent black son of the Catholic Order of the White Fathers, which had long been involved in missionary work on the continent.

As has already been noted, what *Phylon* published concerning religion at this time tended to take for granted, or even actively privilege, a Protestant norm. Still, the journal's first number prominently featured an account of black Catholicism, including a full-page photo of Bishop Kiwanuka. Maran's rather celebratory essay on the "Vicar Apostolic of Masaka, Uganda" was indicative of how interpretations of black American culture and African Catholicism were animated by a patriotic commitment to freedom, democracy, and religious pluralism at once. Such arguments reflected a specific set of domestic and international concerns occasioned by World War II—to wit, the Double V campaign's pinpointing of segregation and fascism—even as they evinced a larger and longer set of Christian logics that reimagined religion under the sign of the modern.[82]

Maran's narration of his initial arrival at the bishop's quarters in France was consonant with standing caricatures of both African culture and ethnic Catholicism. Upon entrance to the rectory in Porte d'Orléans, Maran found a "little museum of Negro art," which he described in ways that faintly echoed the esteemed founder of French sociology, Émile Durkheim. The room was filled with "the rarest and strangest amulets, all undeniable and authentic."[83] In his obvious ambivalence, Maran marked these objects as simultaneously other and real. Indeed, it was their alterity that verified their authenticity. These were artifacts of African material culture, decidedly primitive remnants of the localized rituals of premodern "folk" cultures. Yet now they had been made safe by virtue of their extraction from the rhythms of real time and place. Ironically, putting them on display in a "little museum," which was actually a rectory (i.e., a Catholic bishop's quarters), effectively secured their secularized status. By moving them from the realm of religion and reclassifying them under the rubric of the arts (even within an overtly religious setting), he remade these relics as modern.[84]

Maran's overall tone, in presenting his time with the bishop, was sober yet celebratory. He praised the Catholic Church for its recent consecration of four "colored" bishops: two Indian and two African, including Kiwanuka. He interpreted this act as evidence of a tradition of racial egalitarianism within the Church and as representative of the best and truest form of Catholicism. According to Maran, the Church's commitment to racial equality—as confirmed by the presence these new bishops—also helped to explain anti-Catholic sentiments in Nazi Germany. "Hitler attacks the Church so bitterly in *Mein Kampf*," he explained, "for 'preaching the evangelical doctrine successfully to Hottentots and Kaffirs.'"[85] Here the author's arguments would have struck a familiar chord with *Phylon*'s largely American readership, as the Double V campaign framed fascism in general through a racial lens. In this view, the Third Reich joined Jim Crow segregation in the United States in maintaining an unjust social order. Both were enemies of true democracy. That Maran made a clear connection between "the ravings of Hitlerism and the excesses of *racists*" perhaps helps to explain why *Phylon*'s editorial team—which otherwise seemed much more interested in Protestant churches and their leaders—opted to include the essay in the journal's inaugural edition.[86] In this regard, Bishop Kiwanuka was a prime example of how an institution could move concretely toward racial equality. And this was at a time when racial tensions flared between black Americans and ethnic Catholics, often turning violent, as the Great Migration brought them into close contact in cities across the United States.[87]

In addition to connecting the dots between fascism and segregation, Maran took the occasion of his interview with Bishop Kiwanuka to make a larger claim concerning the Catholic Church in particular and Christianity writ large. First, he praised Pope Pius XI for his leadership in developing and establishing the encyclical *Rerum Ecclesiae*, which in 1926 made the "building up of a native clergy" a Catholic priority.[88] Although the encyclical had addressed the issue of "Catholic missions" in general, it also laid the groundwork within the Catholic Church for Pope Pius XII to consecrate Kiwanuka as the first African bishop thirteen years later.[89] Such Catholic advances—calling for clergy across the lines of color, caste, and colonialism—were part of "the great work of Christian colonization and of spiritual civilization." According to

Maran, the consecration of these first four colored bishops was "consistent with the great and true Christian tradition." Bishop Kiwanuka was, as such, the embodiment of "the most important spiritual victory of modern times."[90]

Maran's presentation of Catholicism exemplified a long-standing tradition of reading religion more generally through the measures of race politics. The Catholic Church was figured as significant insofar as it was a model of an institutional Christianity committed to racial equality. Indeed, the idea that a multiracial democracy was the test of "true Christianity" continued to appear on the pages of *Phylon* well beyond its first issue, as seen in the essays by Newsome, Palmer, and others. Celebrating the Most Reverend Joseph Kiwanuka's ascent in the Church's hierarchy was consistent with the broader aims and aspirations of black intellectuals during the early 1940s. Significantly, Kiwanuka's Catholicism—in contrast to *Phylon*'s Anglo and Protestant orthodoxy—highlighted the form of Christianity shared by the growing Negritude movement of black artists and leaders, such as Maran, across the Francophone African diaspora.[91] At the same time, the idea of locating a democratic commitment within the Roman Catholic Church coalesced well with American interests abroad, which helped facilitate the forging of a Judeo-Christian identity and alliance during the war. Ultimately, presenting such an image to *Phylon*'s largely American readership helped connect the dots and posited a shared spiritual sensibility for a growing black internationalism.

Protestantism, Politics, and Poetics in *Phylon*

If Maran's profile of Bishop Kiwanuka (and his portrait of "the church") suggested a role for Christianity in the struggle for racial equality, then William Stanley Braithwaite carried this vision of a democratic faith into the realm of the arts. A member of the journal's editorial board and a professor at Atlanta University, by 1940 Braithwaite was one of the most esteemed black literary figures in the world. In 1918 he had won the NAACP's Spingarn Medal and was a regular contributor to leading publications like the *New York Times*, *Atlantic Monthly*, and *New Republic*. His writing had also been included in most of the premier black anthologies of the preceding decades, including James Weldon Johnson's *The Book of American Negro Poetry* (1922), Alain Locke's *The New Negro* (1925), and, most recently, *The Negro Caravan* (1940), edited by Sterling Brown, Ulysses Lee, and Arthur Davis. While raised in Boston, the poet's heritage reflected the class and regional differences of the black diaspora. Braithwaite's maternal grandmother had been a slave in North Carolina. On his father's side, he was a descendant of a wealthy family from the Caribbean nation of what was then British Guiana.[92]

One of Braithwaite's poems appeared in the first issue of *Phylon*, just one page before the photograph of Bishop Kiwanuka. To recall, in his portrait of Kiwanuka, Maran subtly invoked the primary site of the art world—that is, the museum—to (re)present artifacts of what are now called African traditional religions.[93] In contrast to Kiwanuka's Afro-Catholicism (and Maran's own French Martinican strand of the same), Braithwaite's literary vision was no doubt shaped by the Anglicanism that prevailed in his father's country of origin. The poem "Ascension" epitomized the sort of aestheticized (and secularized) religiosity that garnered a significant degree of spiritual authority in the decades after World War I occasioned a crisis of meaning for institutional Christianity in the West. Like Maran and many other writers of the period, Brathwaite refigured religious phenomena on aesthetic terms, and thus as distinctly modern.[94]

Braithwaite's first poem for *Phylon*, "Ascension" celebrated universal virtues even as it asked the timeless question of which one was most important. "Wisdom or Beauty, Power or Grace?," the poet queried. In this view, the arts were granted the air of a certain catholicity alongside other essential human values. The poem's title illustrated how well an undefined idea of spiritual ascent resonated with an uplift ideology that had long underwritten, and delimited, black cultural and political aspirations.[95] In their "Apology," *Phylon*'s editors neatly wove together the arts and sciences by lauding "the scientific value of the creative impulse."[96] "Ascension" offered a literary example that was well aligned with such sentiments. To the point, it was an occasion where poetry was lent in service to the authority of reason and science. Better yet, Braithwaite's verse suggested a rapprochement between beauty and wisdom on spiritual terms: "O Beauty, in whose spirit lives/

The majestic triumphs Wisdom gives."[97] The poet positioned wisdom and beauty as sites of veneration. Science and art were akin to "mystic searchings"—recalling a formulation put forward by Du Bois in the first chapter of *The Souls of Black Folk*.[98] Accordingly, Brathwaite wove together, in verse, the modern values of beauty, science, and "spirit" through the ancient archetype of divine wisdom.

Braithwaite's verse specifically appealed to the idea of "apocryphal" status to note movement from "mystic searchings" to scientific knowledge. In this way, the poem located within modern black life a teleology of historical progress from religion to reason. *Phylon*, for that matter, was not simply an academic exercise in racial uplift, be it on sacred or secular terms. As a review of race and culture, the journal published social science research directed to addressing race problems, as well as literature and criticism that was guided by a normative concern with the (spiritual) maturation of black culture. In this way, the journal's vision of race and religion was marked by the tensions between descriptive and prescriptive concerns that animated the novel theories of cultural pluralism in which it participated. That is, pluralism allowed for, even valorized cultural difference even as it remained clear about which forms of culture were most desirable.

Summary

The politics of religion at *Phylon* in general were consistent with how a liberal religious sensibility—that is, a modernist Christianity—reimagined traditional theology in light of the novel authorities of the arts and modern (social) sciences.[99] As seen in articles by Newsome and Palmer, for the journal's primarily American audience this often took the form of privileging an institutional and ethical (Afro-)Protestantism imagined in the image of democracy. Whether studying evangelicalism in the United States or Methodism (and anti-Catholicism) in the Caribbean, the argument was the same. This distinctly modern view of religion was constrained by a normative masculinist, North American Protestantism even as it was conceived through the prism of an increasingly international political order. On occasion, it was capacious enough to abide Roman Catholicism (i.e.,

Maran on Kiwanuka), the key provision being that being Catholic was understood as consistent with the aims and ends of American democracy. Taken together, the politics of religion displayed on *Phylon*'s pages embraced and enunciated an ecumenical vision for making "straight the path to a common world humanity" that simultaneously adhered to and maintained the boundaries of a very familiar and well-established tradition of Afro-Protestantism. Ultimately, *Phylon*'s brand of racial science was animated by religious ambitions, which shaped the scholarly interventions, political critiques, and aesthetic performances that the journal published when it was first founded, but also in the years to come.

In many respects, even beyond the pages of *Phylon*, the study of what Du Bois once called "the religion of the American Negro" reached a point of critical maturity during the 1930s and early 1940s as a small yet critical mass of black scholars launched their academic careers. The pioneering studies of religion in the context of black life published during these decades—from Mays's *The Negro's God* and Hurston's folklore writings to Fauset's *Black Gods of the Metropolis*—both deepened and broadened the field of inquiry within and outside the bounds of the Negro church. At the same time, the vision of an Afro-Protestant modernity that Du Bois first theorized and enacted in *The Souls of Black Folk*, and which he seemed no less committed to four decades later, continued to have sway. To put the matter another way, the logics of religious liberalism—a familiar ethical and reasoning Protestantism—continued to shape the practice of race politics, as well as the politics of studying religion, well into the middle of the twentieth century. More than an academic exercise, the prescriptive Afro-Protestantism on display in *Phylon* would continue to order the content and scope of black scholarship, politics, and literature as well as to shape the forms of black subjectivity and social life for decades to come.

4

The Afterlives of Afro-Protestantism

Chapters 1, 2, and 3 attempted to show how, over the course of American history, the logics of racial authenticity and religious orthodoxy have been entangled in all sorts of surprising ways. These logics have shifted across time and space. They have converged to produce surprising alliances, peculiar yet compelling performances, and complicated and at times seemingly contradictory ideas. What has remained constant in this genealogy is the way religion (Christianity, really) has been encoded within the presumably secular rubrics of race—that is, blackness. More precisely, in literature, in politics, and in scholarship, Afro-Protestantism has been made and has remained constitutive of black subjectivity and social life in North America. Put another way, Afro-Protestantism has constituted the core of a tradition of theorizing and practicing blackness. To restate a claim asserted by the book's title, also put forward in the introduction, *Black is a church!*

First, in the literary form of slave narratives (chapter 1), we witnessed the working out of a particular performance—what some considered a pretense—of Afro-Protestantism. As readers will recall, a demonstration of literary and reasoning Christianity, an early Afro-Protestant orthodoxy, emerged to authorize and articulate a form of black subjectivity in service to the cause of freedom. This orthodoxy was made possible through disciplining and obscuring a range of other religious ideas and practices, from African pantheism, indigenous deities, and the creolized forms of Conjure/Hoodoo to the emotional, expressive practices of Christianity (i.e., evangelical revivalism). Subsequently, in the convergence of literature, politics and religion at the end of the nineteenth century (chapter 2), Afro-Protestantism—as heterodox as ever—once again played a key role in giving rise to new forms of (political, religious, and cultural) social movements. Among these developments were the rise of a New Negro movement and the emerging genre of "race literature," the practice of religious pluralism on

Black is a Church. Josef Sorett, Oxford University Press. © Oxford University Press 2023.
DOI: 10.1093/oso/9780190615130.003.0005

display at the first World's Parliament of Religion, and the novel forms of Christianity associated with the Azusa Street revivals that then gave rise to a tradition of Afro-Pentecostalism.

Ultimately, Afro-Protestantism provided a set of frameworks and resources (but also some challenges) for these distinctive and diverging visions of American democracy as the United States settled into the racial regime of segregation that followed the 1896 Supreme Court ruling in *Plessy v. Ferguson*. Each of these movements also modernized and mobilized religious practice in ways that directly responded to "the problem of the color line," as W. E. B. Du Bois diagnosed it in *The Souls of Black Folk*. Ultimately, like Du Bois, each of these movements participated in the making of an Afro-Protestant modernity. Several decades later, in the set of academic conversations that took shape during the 1920s, 1930s, and 1940s (chapter 3), Du Bois and a number of other black intellectuals contributed to the development of a set of ideas about African American culture in ways that, once again, positioned Afro-Protestantism as constitutive of and normative for the black experience even as they broadened black religion's interpretive frame to the pluralistic lens associated with the burgeoning social sciences.

Across time and space and in different media, social contexts, and institutional settings, Afro-Protestantism both produced and persisted in defining the contours of, to paraphrase Fred Moten, "the practice of blackness."[1] The long-standing practice and performance of a rather heterodox Afro-Protestantism (which some still consider a pretense) provided "the" lens through which to understand, and the logic through which black people envisioned, enunciated, enacted, and— dare I say—theorized, "the black." And this Afro-Protestant formation persists in all three of the genres around which each chapter was organized: in literature, politics, and scholarship. Chapter 4 explores three more contemporary examples of what I have called Afro-Protestant modernity—from the 1980s, 1990s, and the 2010s—bringing the book to a close by approaching more closely the present. Staying true to the episodic form of the history this book provides, each of these more recent episodes serves to illustrate, in shorter form, one of the many afterlives of Afro-Protestantism. In sum, this chapter tracks the robust forms of life (scholarly, literary, political, and more) in which Afro-Protestant modernity continues with great vitality.

We begin with scholarship (via black religious studies) circa 1980. By this time scholars had been trying for several decades to trouble the practice of making Afro-Protestantism—that is, "The Black Church"— a proxy for the wider black religious experience and of taking it as normative for black social life in general. We then move to literature (via black cultural criticism, circa 1990) and follow artists and critics working across genres and media to complicate notions of blackness (at the nexus of class, gender, and sexuality) under the guise of a "New Black" that still, if more subtly, bore the markings of Afro-Protestant modernity. Finally, we follow the persisting religious and racial logics that animated the resurgence of black protest politics during the 2010s by way of the entangled practices of black writing and politics during this decade. In doing so, one can discern in the rise (and the reception) of #BlackLivesMatter, or the Movement for Black Lives, a desire to de-center the church as the perceived primary mode of organizing and the institutional context for black politics and culture. All the while, many members of this new generation continued to gather resources from and collaborate with "The Black Church" even as others drew upon a variety of other religious ideas and practices to guide their activism. Accordingly, what might be observed as either a new form of (religious) pluralism or secularism in black protest and political activism during the 2010s both resembled and renewed the long and heterodox history of Afro-Protestantism.

In moving across scholarship, literature, and politics—three spheres that have remained interwoven across the story that *Black is a Church* has tried to tell—this final chapter also provides an occasion to revisit the respective foci of chapters 1, 2, and 3 (in a slightly different order) while bringing home one of the book's central claims: that attempts to decenter Afro-Protestantism, descriptive accounts of its decline, and polemics about its demise have often served as the very conditions of possibility—or provided the pretense—for its reinvention and persistence. In fact, one way one might read *Black is a Church* is as an extended meditation on the persistence of an argument about the decline and decentering of black churches as a social and institutional force in African American life. Yet such claims, as should now be clear, about the death and decline of black churches seemed to have produced precisely the opposite result. To put the matter another way, *Black is a*

Church follows a prevailing set of arguments wherein claims about the declining relevance of religion—and "The Black Church" specifically—in modern black life have functioned, often by design, to make a claim for a renewed, if reimagined role for religion (and often black churches specifically) in the present moment. To return to a phrase from a forum responding to an online elegy for Afro-Protestantism that figured in the introduction to this book: "The Black Church Is Dead—Long Live the Black Church."[2]

Scholarship: Black (Religious) Studies, circa 1980

On October 22, 1980, the historian of religion Charles Long delivered a "state of the field" address at the annual meeting of the Society for the Study of Black Religion (SSBR), an organization he had helped found only a decade earlier. The occasion for Long's lecture was, in fact, a celebration of the Society's tenth anniversary. Given the persistence of white supremacy in the modern academy, SSBR had been founded both to clarify and to further academic questions related to the study of religion in the African diaspora. The Society was also created to provide important existential and professional support to its all-black membership, most of whom were an overwhelming minority within academic institutions that were inhospitable and, often, overtly hostile to their presence.[3]

In this way, SSBR served as a mediating organization that operated alongside and within the American Academy of Religion (AAR), the primary professional association for scholars of religion and theology, by providing an intellectual community for black faculty working in religious studies, in theological education, and in service to "the church." Significantly, just three years after helping to found SSBR, Long was elected president of the AAR, making him the first African American to serve in this capacity. Three years later, in 1976, the Christian ethicist Preston Williams—the first black professor tenured at Harvard Divinity School—became the second African American to hold the post. A decade later Nathan Scott, a scholar who helped form the subfield of religion and literature, followed Long and Williams as the AAR's third black president.[4] Notably, both Scott and Williams were also ordained Protestant clergy. In contrast to the prominence of these select few (men, notably), black scholars of theology and religion remained a statistically small minority, as they did in the professoriate generally, when Long addressed the SSBR in 1980.

Long focused his lecture on what he took to be the primary scholarly challenges facing members of the young organization. More specifically, he called attention to what would years later be described—in academic terms—as the problem of "Christian hegemony" as it informed the study of black life.[5] To be sure, Long's assessment that the black religious academy was overdetermined by Christian categories and questions was neither exceptional nor anomalous. After all, the AAR was then itself a relatively new entity. When Long was elected its president in 1973, just ten years had passed since the National Association of Biblical Instructors renamed itself, under the more ecumenical (and ostensibly secular) rubric of religious studies, as the American Academy of Religion. Thus, Long's critique of the centrality of Christian traditions and theological methods within SSBR was part of a growing conversation within the academic study of religion. Both organizations aimed to broaden scholarly inquiry beyond the field's Protestant, Christian, and theological genealogies, and to account for the material conditions of slavery and colonialism in which such ideas took on historical and institutional form. For obvious reasons, such concerns mattered all the more for black scholars in general and for SSBR specifically.[6]

In his address, Long gave special attention to how theories of secularization, although not named directly as such, were circulating within the study of black religion to maintain a Christian hegemony. Long had been a central presence in SSBR since its inception. Yet his core claims largely remained at the margins of the intellectual agenda advanced by most of the association's members, many of whom were trained as theologians and ethicists, taught at seminaries and divinity schools, and, for that matter, were ordained as Christian clergy.[7] From the moment of the organization's founding, Long was a minority voice insisting that churches not be viewed as the exclusive or primary site for studying religion within the context of African American communities. Black religion, he insisted, was not to be conflated with what took place within Christian churches. Christianity did not account for the full diversity and breadth of the black religious experience. In both the SSBR and the AAR, Long's was an uphill battle in a field that had inherited its key questions, analytical categories, and methods (as well as its primary institutional support) from a decidedly Christian, and colonial, genealogy.[8]

Long's concern with the predominance of churches (as sources, subjects, and sites of inquiry) and Christian theology (as method of inquiry) in the study of African American religion had preoccupied him for some time. As was discussed in the introduction, nine years prior to his address at the 1980 SSBR meeting, he penned a now classic essay that proposed a new course for the study of African American religion that would not privilege Christianity, methodologically or substantively. In that essay Long argued, first, that "The Black Church" should be decentered. Second, he insisted that scholars ought to employ what he called "extra-church" sources (i.e., non-Christian literature, folklore, and music) in interpreting black life. This shift was necessary, according to Long, if scholars were going to grasp the "true situation" of black communities in North America.[9] In his 1980 SSBR address, Long connected his standing critique of the privileged narrative of "The Black Church" to a series of debates about the place of religion, then presumed to be on the decline, in modern society.

Toward the start of his address, Long summarized the situation, with regard to the study of black religion, as follows:

> One of the themes running through a great deal of the interpretations of Black Theology and Black Religion is the assertion that the Black community did not and does not make distinctions between the secular and the sacred and that it follows from this assertion that the Black church is and has been the locus of the Black community. If this is so, then it means that the church is the locus of the expression of Black cultural life.[10]

To state the matter more pointedly, Long argued that assertions of a certain sacred/secular fluidity in the context of black life served to underwrite the singular authority of "The Black Church." His lecture, more generally, troubled scholarly interpretations that suggested black communities were somehow immune to the technological, rationalizing, and disciplinary—that is, the secularizing—forces of Western modernity. In doing so, he countered a normative narrative of modern progress, in which black and brown folk figured as the hyper-religious foils to what was otherwise observed as a rapidly secularizing world, a development that was hailed as triumphant in the decades that preceded his SSBR address.[11]

To be clear, history has since shown the secularization thesis to be more myth than fact. However, even before social scientists and humanists were diagnosing the "return of religion" or theorizing the secular, African Americans were imagined as the religious excep-tion to a secularizing rule.[12] If an increasingly secular telos declared that the West had effectively cordoned off its "premodern" religious pasts, then black people confirmed that modernity's racial subjects were not so easily restrained.[13] More precisely, if secularism pur-ported to be an ordering logic that disciplined modern difference, then the frenzied excess associated with African American religion and culture proved that black difference was not readily contained. In this telling, the prospects for a black secular were slim to none. That "the black" was fundamentally religious was a foregone conclusion.[14]

Long suspected a more specific logic at play in such claims, espe-cially as it concerned his SSBR colleagues. The interpretive claim that "the Black community did not and does not make distinctions be-tween the secular and the sacred," he argued, served the interest of a specific theological position. It functioned as a claim, he averred, for the social, political, and cultural centrality of "The Black Church." In this view, assertions that sacred/secular distinctions did not hold in black communities authorized claims for the abiding significance of Christianity in modern black life and underwrote the idea of a dis-tinctive black culture rooted in black churches. For Long, such claims subtly advanced the position, vis-à-vis Melville Herskovits, that so-called African retentions persisted in the "New World," providing an enduring ethos for black culture in North America. At the same time, he noted, assertions of black sacred/secular fluidity also often attrib-uted this cultural distinctiveness, in institutional form, to "The Black Church." Recall that Du Bois made a similar argument in the tenth chapter of *The Souls of Black Folk* (see chapter 2) when he identified the

Negro church as a bridge between an African past and an American present. Long observed that positing, in descriptive terms, that African Americans did not recognize sacred/secular distinctions also served, prescriptively, to blur the lines between black churches and the entirety of black social life. Moreover, he asserted, these logics worked to reinscribe the authority of the former (i.e., black churches) over the latter (i.e., black social life).[15]

Long alleged, in effect, that a form of Christian apologetics—better yet, a set of Afro-Protestant commitments—was often cloaked within the idea that black people were unsusceptible to the modern forces of secularization. In this way, his 1980 address crystallized a long-standing set of ideas and practices in which religious (i.e., Christian) orthodoxy and racial (i.e., black) authenticity were entangled in ways that often obscured each other. Long called into question a set of Christian commitments that continued to exercise undue influence on the field. In doing so, he set the stage for a nascent black religious pluralism and secularism at once—even as the norm of Afro-Protestant modernity did not abate.

Long's argument went further than simply decentering churches in interpretations of black life or creating analytical space to account for the diversity of black religious practices. Instead, by asserting that "extra-church" sources were more exemplary of the *"true situation"* (italics added) in which African Americans found themselves, he advanced an "extra-church" vision of black identity and culture as normative. By this count, "true" blackness was necessarily to be found outside of, or even in opposition to, Christianity. That which was truly black was contrary to the long and heterodox history in which Afro-Protestantism had been made constitutive of black subjectivity and social life—and in which black freedom had become the litmus test of "true Christianity." Instead, on Long's insistence, "true" blackness was necessarily "extra-church." In this view, Christian orthodoxy was naturally antagonistic to authentic blackness.

Even if one rejected Long's assertion of the "extra-church" as the site of "the true situation of the black community," his provocation illumined a particular analytical configuration. In this view, secular and non-Christian forms of religious practice—that is, atheism (and a variety of idioms of presumed unbelief) and African-derived religious practices (e.g., Conjure, Santería, and Vodun)—were conjoined in opposition to the normative position of "The Black Church."[16] In short, the secular conceived as such encompassed all that was "extra-church" even as his appeal to the "extra-church" required and reinscribed the church as the normative (or categorical) center of African American religious life.

To put the matter another way, in Long's formulation racial authenticity (i.e., blackness) and religious orthodoxy (i.e., Christianity) were fundamentally at odds with one another. In this way, his 1980 SSBR address captured the entanglement of racial and religious discourses in ways that raised as many questions as it answered. For one, Long neglected to identify any specific sources to substantiate his assertion that an Afro-Protestant hegemony was underwriting ideas about black sacred/secular fluidity. Additionally, his lecture offered little, if any, evidentiary support for what he diagnosed as a Christian account of black cultural distinctiveness. Nor did he unpack the precise details of what amounted to a theory of African-Christian syncretism, a phenomenon that he observed and critiqued at once. Perhaps as a clue, Long highlighted several recent works in (presumably "secular") African American history as models for his colleagues in theological and religious studies.[17]

The veracity of Long's claim regarding "the true situation of the black community" remains an open question and, as such, is perhaps better understood in the interrogative—as a provocation and question rather than a definitive conclusion. To his credit, Long now appears prescient on several fronts. He both anticipated and invited a more specific inquiry into the relationships between blackness and secularism decades before the latter topic became an expansive interdisciplinary field unto itself. Focusing his inquiry specifically for an SSBR audience, Long called attention to African American religion and culture, which remains an underexamined area in the field of secularism studies. In the decades since Long's 1980 address, scholars have attended to a range of more subtle distinctions, parsing what is meant by the secular, secularisms, and the "post-secular."[18] Secularism studies, however, are just beginning to interrogate race and to analyze black culture specifically.

Conversely, while Long appealed to then burgeoning historical and literary approaches to African American culture to advance his theory of black religion, the field of black studies outside of religious studies has rarely responded in kind or interrogated the ways in which religion animates the field's assumptions. To the contrary, also during the 1980s leading theorists and critics of black literature and culture tacitly embraced a secular and secularizing norm for black studies that largely remains unquestioned to this day.[19] Though an interest in secularism has experienced steady growth across a range of fields and disciplines, black studies has largely left the subject of secularism (which is to say, religion) underexamined and untheorized. Moreover, blackness itself is often granted sacred status and anti-blackness attributed metaphysical significance, even as a secular orthodoxy continues to order the day.

Literature: Black Cultural Criticism, circa 1990s

On October 10, 1994, the author, choreographer, dancer, and director Bill T. Jones graced the cover of *Time* magazine with the headline "Black Renaissance: African-American Artists Are Truly Free at Last." Otherwise a typical issue of the popular American news publication, the caption lauded contemporary black art even as it harkened back to a previous era by invoking the final words of Martin Luther King Jr.'s famous "dream" speech on the Mall at the 1963 March on Washington: "Free at last, free at last, Great God a-mighty, we are free at last." In an eight-page story, "The Beauty of Black Art," former *Time* staff writer Jack E. White enumerated a "who's who" of black creatives across the fields of dance, literature, music, drama, and film. Positioned against a backdrop of "crime, broken families, failing schools, abject hopeless[ness]," White hailed a "new black cultural renaissance" as emerging in stark contrast to "the bleak circumstances that envelop so much of the African American community" during the 1990s. Approaching hyperbole, White declared, "Never before . . . have black artists produced so much first-rate writing, music, painting and dance."[20] A seasoned journalist with over twenty-nine years of experience at *Time*, White was the magazine's first black staff writer, bureau chief, and editor. He'd left *Time* in 1992 but returned to the company in 1995 to spearhead Time Inc.'s efforts to recruit minority journalists across all of its publications.[21]

With expertise and experience reporting on ethnic politics and domestic news, White was well positioned to report, for a general audience, on black art and culture. Even still, his article was followed directly by a shorter piece penned by a leading scholar of African American literature, Henry Louis Gates Jr., who added intellectual authority to White's observations. Then chair of Harvard's Afro-American Studies Department, Gates located contemporary developments within the longer history of African American artistic expression. He also hedged a bit on White's optimistic assessment. Titled "Black Creativity: On the Cutting Edge," Gates's essay suggested that the "latest flowering *may* be the most promising of all" (italics mine). His argument also had a distinct emphasis that was as much about black creativity as it was about the relationship between black artists, their public accolades, and their place in the American cultural marketplace. "It's not that there are black artists and intellectuals who matter," Gates explained, "it's that so many of the artists and intellectuals who matter are black."[22] In addition to noting that contemporary black artists found "themselves in an era of creativity unrivaled in American history," Gates broadened White's scope to make a place for black intellectuals and critics such as himself. He also highlighted the importance of "economic developments," which produced a heightened class divide. In the decades since the 1960s, the United States simultaneously gave rise to "the largest black middle class and the largest black underclass." For Gates, these growing divisions facilitated a platform and a consuming public, as well as a pronounced sense of precarity, for the newest generation of black creatives.[23]

In many ways, Gates's pairing of promise and peril to frame his analysis of black art during the 1990s echoed how scholars (including Gates himself) often described an earlier moment in the longer history of black creativity that his piece in *Time* chronicled. In fact, Gates opened his essay with an account of what is generally considered the first "renaissance" in African American letters: the New Negro movement that took shape during the final years of the nineteenth century.

Then named the " 'negroid' renaissance" by the literary critic William Stanley Braithwaite, this moment of black cultural flourishing took place against a spike in the rule of the lynch mob, alongside the legal codification of racial segregation in *Plessy v. Ferguson* and the onset of Jim Crow.[24] Elsewhere, in a more academic venue, Gates himself described the mythic qualities of the discourse that surrounded black writers and the degree to which appeals to a "New Negro" obscured the dire social conditions in which most black folks lived and labored in the 1890s.[25] In doing so, Gates pointed to a history of contesting racial inequality through a politics of representation in which the black elite, across a variety of fields, sought to re-present black life in ways that countered racist stereotypes and offered a more complex account of "the race" in general. Whether "renaissance" was the best descriptor of black cultural production during the 1990s, and whether or not it would amount to "the renaissance to end all renaissances," as Gates suggested might happen, the decade was indeed one in which black artists and critics garnered a popular hearing (and viewing) as never before.

Just a few months after Bill T. Jones appeared on the cover of *Time*, *The Atlantic Monthly* featured a cover story by Robert Boynton, "The New Intellectuals," which hailed the rise of a generation of public intellectuals—all of whom were African American and many of whom were university professors—like Gates, whom Boynton mentions by name. During the 1980s and 1990s, these scholars and critics—whose presentation styles often blurred the false divide between critical and creative work—seized the national stage with television appearances, packed lecture halls, lucrative book deals, and prestigious awards. In addition to Gates, Boynton named Kimberlé Crenshaw and Stanley Crouch, bell hooks and Houston Baker, Robert Gooding-Williams and Lani Guinier, June Jordan and Jerry Watts, Michele Wallace and Cornel West, among several others. Just a few years after West insisted that "the black intellectual" was forced to inhabit an "isolated and insulated world" defined by "self-imposed marginality," Boynton noted that the celebrity these thinkers achieved was extraordinary, "especially considering the marginal role of the intellectual in America." As this new cohort of intellectuals gained prominence across a variety of academic fields, many of them also turned to cultural criticism—and the complex and oft-contradictory terrain of popular culture—as a form of intellectual engagement and political struggle.

Indeed, the ironies of marginality and mainstream acclaim would abound all the more in the first years of the twenty-first century, as the United States would experience eight years with the nation's highest office occupied by a black man. And while President Barack Obama was often criticized for being too "professorial" (read: dispassionate, reasoned), an even newer cadre of black professors, many of whom were in graduate school during the ascendency of Boynton's "new intellectuals," launched to new heights in various dimensions of the public sphere, readily embracing the opportunities available to black elites made possible by an Obama administration. During the 1990s, Boynton observed the following:

> In addition to their individual achievements and talent, a number of external factors have helped give them prominence: four are particularly important: They have unprecedented access to the mass-circulation print media. They have been sought out by the electronic media, and shows like Nightline, Today, and the Oprah Winfrey Show give them extraordinary visibility. Those who are professors—and most are—have used their prestigious university positions to extend their influence beyond the academy. And, finally, they have benefited from America's current concern about race, serving as experts on everything from the L.A. riots and affirmative action to the nominations of Clarence Thomas and Lani Guinier, and anything having to do with Louis Farrakhan.[26]

The signal novelty of these new intellectuals was, at least in part, a result of what the novelist and music critic Nelson George identified as "post-Soul access," a position occasioned by the civil rights gains of the 1960s that brought an end to legal segregation. That is, they capitalized effectively on access to the institutions that brokered academic prestige, media platforms, and economic opportunities in American society, all of which was inconceivable for earlier generations of black intellectuals—and black professionals generally. Boynton also identified two important qualities as distinguishing these African American intellectuals. First, "new intellectuals" were willing to interrogate the hybrid nature ("both sides of the hyphen") of the "African-American" experience. And, second, they possessed an anti-elitist view of culture as "the complex world we live in, encompassing everything and everyone from T. S. Eliot to Ice-T."[27] In the process (and perhaps as a by-product) of this cultural turn, black intellectual life itself became a key component of American popular culture, and with it the black public intellectual emerged as an iconic, and almost cultic, figure.

While the tone of Boynton's essay veered toward the celebratory, the ascent of this new cohort of black public intellectuals also met with no small measure of criticism. Perhaps the most strident critique came from Adolph Reed, who himself was among those named in *The Atlantic Monthly* piece. Just a month after Boynton's essay was published, in a *Village Voice* article titled "What Are the Drums Saying Booker? The Current Crisis of the Black Intellectual," Reed pointed to the fact of their celebrity as indicative of a problem, which he detailed in a long litany of complaints. "In this arena," he explained, "the prominence of author counts more than weight of utterance."[28] However, at the heart of Reed's critique, which included a substantial yet abridged account of black intellectual history, was a rejection of what he diagnosed as "black intellectuals' insistence on defining politics centered in the exercise of state power as inauthentic, which in turn underwrites all the Aesopian interpretive twaddle in black cultural studies."[29] What Reed seemed to decry was a perceived move away from the orthodoxies of Marxist/Leftist materialism (i.e., political economy) toward a version of black authenticity (be it analyzed or performed) that centered culture—and religion specifically—as a valid site of political activism.[30] In fact, the only scholarly work that Reed cited was a 1993 *Journal of American History* article in which Robin D. G. Kelley exhorts historians to take seriously "a connection between the spirit and spiritual world of African Americans and political struggle."[31] In this regard, Reed's diagnosis of an intellectual crisis betrayed his broader (and deeper) concern that a familiar religious mythos, which often delimited black politics, was also having its way with black scholars.[32]

The substantive merits of Reed's critique notwithstanding, cultural criticism had taken center-stage, both in black studies and in the public work of black intellectuals. No event better captured this trajectory than the Black Popular Culture Conference, which took place in 1991.

That fall Michele Wallace, then a professor at City College, convened a group of scholars and critics for a three-day gathering in New York City. The conference was hosted uptown at the Studio Museum in Harlem, as well as at the downtown Dia Center for the Arts, the latter of which published the proceedings the following year with Bay Press. These two institutional locations—one black, one white—illustrated the hyphenated context that Boynton had noted. The conference featured a "who's who" of black artists, critics, and intellectuals, including many of the folks mentioned by Gates and Boynton but also Hazel Carby, Stuart Hall, Marlon Riggs, Tricia Rose, Valerie Smith, and Greg Tate.

Wallace had established herself in the 1970s as a scholarly and public presence and as a leading black feminist critic with her first book, *Black Macho and the Myth of the Superwoman* (1978). On this occasion, Wallace called for speakers and attendees to grapple with "the growing presence of politicized popular culture and to explore debates on participation by black communities in the creation and critique of popular culture." More concisely, she sought to "nurture critical practice among African American intellectuals."[33] Aware of the shifting tensions between art and politics that had long animated black cultural expression and criticism, conference participants examined the relationship between criticism, popular culture, and contemporary political struggles. At the Black Popular Culture Conference, blackness was a site of inquiry and a space of contestation. It was a formation that suggested heterogeneity and difference rather than consensus. Blackness, in short, was the question—which is precisely the cue that Stuart Hall followed in his keynote address (and the volume's opening essay) by asking "What is this 'Black' in Black Popular Culture?"[34]

A year after the conference came an anthology. Edited by Gina Dent, then a PhD student at Columbia University, it contained twenty-nine essays and five thematic discussions, which were first staged as presentations at the Black Popular Culture Conference. Contributions explored a variety of media, including film, music, and pornography, and tackled such topics as multiculturalism, gender and sexuality, nationalism, and corporate capitalism. *Black Popular Culture* garnered a broad reading. It was widely reviewed and was selected as a book of the year by the *Village Voice*.[35] Wallace's closing essay, titled "Why Are There No Great Black Artists? The Problem of Visuality in

African-American Culture," captured well the ambitions of the conference and the volume. She began by highlighting the recent public confrontation between Anita Hill and Clarence Thomas (during the latter's confirmation hearing for the Supreme Court) and ended by analyzing the public response (or lack thereof) to the HIV/AIDS crisis of the 1980s. In doing so, Wallace opened a discussion about gender and sexual politics and thus clarified the real-world—life-and-death—stakes that were the political context for black cultural criticism. The framing of the AIDS epidemic, which was then ravaging black communities, confirmed how black subjectivity was often rendered, according to Wallace, both "invisible and impossible."[36]

Together Wallace's two examples—Hill versus Thomas and HIV/AIDS—underscored her gender critique. The pairing also revealed her expansive view of the visual arts—everything from advertising and conceptual art to fashion and architecture—as contested political space. And it clarified her commitment to challenging how the "institutionalization of visual regimes" erased black aesthetic traditions and constrained black identity and social life.[37] Standing visual regimes, Wallace argued, undermined artistic and critical work and effected a "crisis of mind" in black people generally.[38] Accordingly, she insisted that popular culture representations, but also cultural criticism, were of great consequence for black people. Her essay, along with the volume as a whole, captured efforts at the time to reconsider (and recast) black identity and experience as fundamentally heterogeneous, always fragmented by the realities of gender, class, and sexual orientation and any number of other variables. Her analysis also highlighted how "mainstream" art institutions, despite the rise of multiculturalism during the 1980s, continued to undervalue and render invisible black artists and critics. In response to the problem she'd named, Wallace called for more resources to be devoted to black artists and critics to take up this work.

The 1991 Black Popular Culture Conference took place at the height of a moment in which the idea of a monolithic blackness, at the level of theory and criticism, was being fundamentally challenged. That same year bell hooks referred to this idea of black subjectivity and social life as necessarily heterodox most concisely as "Postmodern Blackness."[39] In this way, the conference and subsequent anthology both documented and contributed to the articulation of a racial sensibility that was self-critically engaged with the "New World" (i.e., Western, American, white) context in which it emerged. Rather than oppositional or antagonistic, in cultural terms black and white were here understood as entangled and mutually informing even as the political asymmetries of racial inequality continued to define life around the globe. The Black Popular Culture Conference, then, was organized and understood as both an academic event and a public intervention. It performed the very idea of black popular culture—as a heterogeneous and contradictory space and as a site of political contestation—that Wallace and the conference participants were theorizing. In this regard, the conference also countered a "visual regime" that had historically rendered black artists and critics as marginal. Instead, it called attention to and created a shared stage for a community of black scholars, artists, and critics who were then capturing national attention.

This new generation of black artists and critics, many of whom were not academics, were participants in a moment of black cultural flourishing that had begun to pick up steam as an industry developed around the discourse of multiculturalism during the 1980s. Indeed, a shared commitment to simultaneously straddling the cultural hyphen and blurring the line between high and low, which both Gates and Boynton noted in the mid-1990s, had been identified as a "New Black" sensibility at least a decade earlier. While an undergraduate at Stanford, Trey Ellis began working on an essay that eventually was published as "The New Black Aesthetic" in the black literary journal *Callaloo*.[40] Then a debut novelist, he coined the term "cultural mulatto" to push back against essentialized ideas of blackness associated with the art and politics of Black Power.[41] Signifying on Du Bois's notion of "double-consciousness" and the Afro hairstyle popularized during the 1960s, Ellis declared, "Today, there are enough young blacks torn between the two worlds to finally go out and create our own. The New Black Aesthetic says you just have to *be* natural, you don't necessarily have to *wear* one."[42] Whereas in 1903 Du Bois had described the tensions attached to being "Negro and American" as being nearly irreconcilable, Ellis employed parody both to refuse racial authenticity and to valorize cultural heterogeneity as a new orthodoxy for black artists and critics.

During the years that Ellis was revising his midterm paper into a creative manifesto, a conversation about "the rise of a New Black Culture" had begun on the pages of the popular New York City publication *Village Voice*. What the 1991 Black Popular Culture Conference represented for higher education, the *Village Voice* had been doing for popular writing throughout the 1980s (and before). The *Voice* was publishing work by and about black artists and critics, including the likes of Hilton Als, Thulani Davis, Lisa Jones, Joan Morgan, and Joe Wood, to name just a few. Foremost among the *Voice's* recurring black voices was Greg Tate, a New York–based writer who, in addition to his work as a journalist and critic, helped found the Black Rock Coalition with Vernon Reid of the rock band Living Colour in 1985.[43]

Tate's 1986 essay "Cult-Nats Meet Freaky-Deke" appeared on the front page of the *Voice Literary Supplement* on December 9, 1986. Tate's writing for the *Village Voice* across the decade, and this essay in particular, played a key role in both imagining and interpreting a "New Black Culture," as the *VLS* headline read. Like Ellis, Tate's aesthetic sensibility was indebted to the black cultural nationalists of the 1960s and 1970s, but irreverently so. It was also deeply informed by what Nelson George just a few years later would identify as "a new post-soul access" (also on the pages of the *Village Voice*).[44] In contrast to the segregated institutions (e.g., Black Arts Repertory Theater, Broadside Press, *Negro Digest*) that supported black arts, culture, and criticism in earlier eras, "post-soul access," for George, underscored the newfound entrée that black culture workers (artists and critics) like Tate were making into "mainstream" American institutions in the decades that followed the end of Jim Crow.

The title of Tate's essay "Cult-Nats Meet the Freaky-Deke" linked the "black is beautiful" claims of 1960s cultural nationalists ("cult-nats") to the contemporary concern with celebrating black difference ("freaks"), which is to say, those versions of black art and identity that did not adhere to the expected orthodoxies of black authenticity. Rather than reactionary or a rejection the nationalist politics of the Black Arts movement, the essay credited the "postliberated" aesthetic of Tate's generation to the hardline Black Aesthetic of the "cult-nats." Drawing on the latest theories of postmodernism and poststructuralism, he paid little respect to the perceived divide between high and low culture, center and margins, the academic and the popular. New Black artists and critics, insofar as Tate helped to usher in this new aesthetic, seamlessly wed disparate sources (i.e., high and low, black and white, sacred and secular, theory and practice) in both their creative and critical work, and they celebrated the diversity of black identities.

Just as important, and perhaps more than any other black writer at the time, Tate also brilliantly blurred the line between theorizing and performing the New Black, and he did so to great effect. In this regard, his theory of the "New Black" attempted to fill a gap that he observed— namely, that "not many black critics have produced writing as fecund, eclectic, and freaky-deke as the art, let alone the culture itself." Accordingly, the content and form of his criticism sought to mirror the creative work he was busy interpreting. As Tate put it, "I decided that what black culture needs is a popular poststructuralism. . . . This whatchamajiggy is about how black aestheticians need to develop a coherent criticism to communicate the complexities of our culture."[45]

According to Tate, the emergence of the "freaky-deke" black artist and critic was evidence of the "maturation of a postnationalist black arts movement, one more Afrocentric and cosmopolitan than anything that's come before." As sources and models of this critical sensibility, Tate offered a litany that paired such seemingly dissonant figures as "Malcolm X and Jimi Hendrix . . . Rudy Ray Moore and Nam June Pak [sic] . . . Frederic Jameson and Reverend James Cleveland."[46] Each of the icons invoked offered something distinct to the New Black artist's heterodox cultural arsenal. Tate explained further:

These are artists for whom black consciousness and artistic freedom are not mutually exclusive but complementary, for whom "black culture" signifies a multicultural tradition of expressive practices; they feel secure enough about black culture to claim art produced by nonblacks as part of their inheritance. No anxiety of influence here— these folks believe the cultural gene pool is for skinny-dipping.[47]

In this "postliberated" and "postnationalist" vision, black artists and critics were free to formulate an aesthetic in which their individual agency appeared to be the sole authority for assessing what sources worked, for whom they could work, and what type of work they took up. Rather than bow to the racial orthodoxies or authenticity litmus tests of previous generations, for Tate "the text of blackness" was "a collection of sources—all making for a veritable postmodern bible of black visual culture."[48]

What made this aesthetic black, then, was that these artists deployed "cross-breeding aesthetic references" with an awareness of a tradition of black cultural expression and a keen sense of the current circumstances shaping black people's lives. Tate himself moved seamlessly from writing about prisons and police brutality to reflecting on Hip Hop and independent film, in part because black art itself covered this range of topics. Ultimately, Tate called for a cadre of individuated black subjects to help realize his dream of an institutionalized "popular black poststructuralism": a "bank trust" of black artists and intellectuals committed to reaching "mass audiences" and for whom no topic was out of bounds, no question sacrosanct. This collective, which he likened to a "black tower of Babel," would be united by a shared commitment to "total cultural black rule."[49] Interestingly (and ironically, Tate admitted), the one individual he suggested was moving in the right direction with regard to theorizing blackness was "a white man"—art historian and Yale professor Robert Farris Thompson. Thompson was instructive, Tate believed, because of his attention to a "Black Atlantic tradition" that connected "Africa and the New World, spiritually, aesthetically, and philosophically."[50]

In tracking the emergence of this New Black culture (and cultural criticism), references to religion and spirituality, at first glance, appear to be a conspicuous absence. In some places both terms evaded explicit reference (e.g., Michele Wallace) or seemed to disappear from the dialogue altogether. In other places, as with Adolph Reed's critic of the movement's academic wing, religion provoked a suspicion (or outright aversion) to the entire enterprise. For Tate, religion appeared as but one of many signifiers in a complex cultural matrix. Alongside historians, scientists, athletes, and economists, Tate identified a place for theologians in his collective. And black spiritual genius figured prominently in Tate's litany of New Black exemplars, which included the gospel music legend James Cleveland and the religious and political leader Malcolm X. More broadly, Tate pointed to Black Atlantic traditions as the primary spiritual source animating his vision for black cultural criticism. However, in another dose of irony, by wedding capitalist ("bank trust") and biblical ("tower of Babel") imagery, along with a hegemonic impulse ("cultural rule"), Tate's vision for the New Black was also in step, if unaware at the time, with a different set of religious logics (i.e., the Prosperity Gospel) that were increasingly dominant in black churches and American culture at the time.

In this way, New Black artists and critics often acknowledged, with some measure of ambivalence, the importance of religion (by a variety of names) as constitutive of the history of African Americans in the United States. They might also identify it as a source that simultaneously fomented and frustrated black political struggles. More often than not, however, New Black cultural criticism displayed a disconnect from, if not a misrecognition of, the ways in which black religious traditions continued to shape contemporary black cultural and social life. In this regard, Tate and others who called for a New Black might be understood as, at last, formulating a truly secular theory and performance of "the black." Yet a closer reading of the New Black reveals the persistence of a set of (Afro-)Protestant logics that, if a bit more subtly, had long held sway. The work of another up-and-coming critic, Joe Wood, helps to illustrate this point more forcefully. A regular contributor to the *Village Voice* and an editor at the New Press, Wood established himself as a significant player in New York City literary circles during the late 1980s and early 1990s. Wood's career was tragically cut short in 1999 when, at the age of thirty-four, he disappeared on a hiking trip in Washington State.[51]

In 1990 Wood penned an essay, "The Malcolm X Factor," which examined the appeal of El-Hajj Malik El-Shabazz to a generation of African Americans who came of age in the years after his assassination.[52] Two years later Wood extended the ambitions of his essay into an edited volume that brought together his skills as both a writer and an editor. *Malcolm X: In Our Own Image* (1992) captures well the complexities of black cultural criticism during the decade. It featured a roster of leading black academics—overlapping with Boynton's "new intellectuals"—including Hilton Als, Patricia Hill Collins, Angela Davis, Adolph Reed, Marlon Riggs, and Cornel West, among others. The volume was a response to the renewed interest in Malcolm X apparent among a new generation of black youth—evidenced in such phenomena as fashion (i.e., "X" hats and T-shirts), music (i.e., Hip Hop), and film (i.e., Spike Lee's 1992 biopic, *Malcolm X*). In addition to organizing the anthology, Wood revised his *Village Voice* essay into an introduction, "Malcolm X and the New Blackness," which helped situate the slain political and religious leader in the context of black culture and politics in the early 1990s.[53]

Blending cultural criticism and autobiography, Wood's introduction set the context for the book by outlining what Malcolm meant to him as a young black boy growing up in New York City in the 1970s and 1980s. His opening words, "When I was a child," conjured a passage from the Christian Bible's New Testament, 1 Corinthians 13, which is often referred to as "the love chapter." Beginning as such, Wood subtly signaled that the book's call for a mature, self-critical conversation about black identity, culture, and politics was grounded in a love for black people.[54] Educated at an elite private high school and an Ivy League university, Wood was well-schooled regarding the social construction of race. Accordingly, in the essay he interrogates his own identity and racial formation. As a teen, Wood shuffled back and forth from his family home in a predominantly black, working-class South Bronx neighborhood to the Riverdale Country School, located in a tony northern Bronx enclave. Separated by just a few miles, the two neighborhoods were culturally worlds apart, which created a good measure of racial dissonance for him as a teenager. As a young adult, Wood refused the logic of the racial binary and acknowledged both settings as formative to his identity even as he accented the ways that racism continued to order his life into adulthood.

Recognizing identity as both assigned and self-ascribed, without obscuring the sometimes life-and-death stakes in between, Wood recalled an incident in which he was on the receiving end of a racial slur:

> When I, for example, was stopped on Madison Avenue by that white cop with nigger on the tongue, I became Black. But I have also chosen to be Black, and determined to make my own name. "Race" is a dying category; Whiteness, and the Blackness it makes for itself, is dying too. We will seize the day and make a new Blackness.[55]

Wood's recollection centered around the tensions between the police officer's rendering of his racial identity, how he himself had "chosen to be Black," and his literary call for something new. Returning to the present, he articulated a commitment—on behalf of a new generation of black culture workers—to self-consciously construct a "new blackness" that both accounted for racial difference and acknowledged what Cornel West would diagnose the following year in his best-selling book, *Race Matters*, as "the pitfalls of racial reasoning."[56] Wood was clear that his experience was unexceptional. Although anecdotal, it was emblematic of a set of contradictory logics at a moment when a celebration of racial diversity (i.e., multiculturalism) could seem to be seamlessly coupled with state-sanctioned anti-black violence (e.g., Rodney King).[57]

As indicated by the book's subtitle, *In Our Own Image*, the anthology called attention to the ways that, following his death, Malcolm X was subsequently invested with infinite meaning(s). In his introduction, Wood likened Malcolm X's story to his own identity. It was a "mask" that he first authored, yet was continuously being reauthored by countless others. Perhaps surprisingly, Wood employed "spirit" as the key term for grasping the meaning of both Malcolm X specifically and the New Black more generally. In the 1990s, he argued, Malcolm X was being defined by a desire "to make a 'new' Black Man with 'true' Black spirit."[58] For Malcolm, in the flesh, this spirit took on an embodied, if evolving Muslim form—first reborn in the Nation of Islam, then evolving on to orthodox, or Sunni, Islam, and finally in founding the ecumenical Organization of Afro-American Unity. In life, Malcolm might be understood as traveling along a secularizing path on which religious difference was eventually bracketed under the more ecumenical, presumably secular rubrics of race politics and, later, human rights. Wood observed, however, that when Malcolm X and Alex Haley collaborated to tell his life story they agreed to give his narrative the "familiar shape of the Biblical Saul-to-Paul story."[59] In so doing Malcolm's Muslim identity in death was re-presented through a decidedly Christian mask, that is, the trope of a Christian conversion, a deeply evangelical story and one familiar to the American (consumer) public that would purchase the autobiography.[60] According to Wood, this bending of Islam into a Christian frame, coupled with the range of racial philosophies (from Nation of Islam to the Organization of Afro-American Unity), left the meaning of Malcolm's life "mostly empty, and available" for almost any interpretation.[61]

Wood's turn to the category of "spirit" not only aided his analysis of Malcolm X's legacy. It revealed much about the manner in which religious difference was often mediated in the context of New Black cultural criticism at the time. Similar to the autobiography's use of a Christian trope to frame Malcolm X's evolution, Wood turned to the history of Christian iconography to analyze Malcolm and the desire for "Black spirit" during the early 1990s. "Icons made Christianity portable," Wood explained. They provided believers with "a sense of communion, and simultaneously, a sense of 'authorship'—spirits, after all, converse with the individual, with you."[62] Malcolm X accordingly became an icon through his proliferation in popular culture, including Spike Lee's movie and the ubiquitous X paraphernalia (i.e., hats, posters, t-shirts) then available. Each of these cultural products, Wood averred, provided an occasion to commune with Malcolm X, who had become an icon of " 'real' black anger" and of " 'true' Black spirit," providing "Black believers" with some semblance of a "Black sanctuary."[63]

Wood wondered precisely what such practices of communion via consumption meant. "Are the buyers, African American or not, angry or not, Black believers?" Otherwise put, were those who consumed black spirit by wearing an X hat also believers in black freedom? Wood offered a provisional answer to his own question:

> Not necessarily, because Black spirit has never meant one thing, or anything concrete, which is its great power *and* failure. Spirit has no spine; it bends easily to the will of its buyer. Black spirit has many faces—it can mean anything from "angry" to "kind-hearted" to "cool." Even for those who purchase Malcolm with the spirit's current militance in mind, the meaning of the possession is very uncertain.[64]

Spirit's fluidity, for Wood, was both a blessing and a curse. To be sure, Malcolm as "spirit" and icon appealed to many more people than he did as a living and breathing black Muslim man. Yet, for Wood, accessing Malcolm's spirit came at the cost of emptying his life of any concrete meaning: namely, the black political struggles with which he was aligned. In terms of imagining a "New Blackness," spirit's decided strength was that it would not produce a restrictive racial orthodoxy, as religious doctrines—including the black nationalism of the Nation of Islam—are often imagined to do.[65] Black spirit was expansive enough to incorporate a heterodox array of "black" identities. Black spirit, as such, also seemed to suggest a broadening of the religious and racial logics that defined the Afro-Protestant orthodoxy associated with prior generations. Explicit or overt appeals to religion seem less essential to the aesthetics and politics of this "New Black." Spirit, in its undefined openness, aligned well with the celebration of diversity and difference so central to new theories of blackness. The fluidity suggested by the language of spirit, in Wood's telling, allowed for a public celebration of black individuality and plurality at once.

Yet Wood suggested that spirit's pliability was also cause for concern. Rather than the prize, Wood described spirit as a form of consolation. "In the absence of a viable ideology," he asserted, "we settle for spirit." "Black spirit" facilitated and sustained a variety of identities and practices that, in their plurality, failed to produce a concrete political ideology. Wood's ambivalence toward black spirit crystallized near the essay's end. In the midst of a moment that Tate described as "post-liberated," Wood called for a more sophisticated dialogue that accounted for the interworkings of culture and politics under the sign of "Black spirit":

> To help stop our blood from spilling, we still need Black People, the idea. And a people needs to feel a spirit and to possess its own icons: African America and all Black People need Malcolm. But Black spirit and icons (and culture) aren't enough to fix things. Our talk will lead us to a clear politics that takes into account our changing character, and directly addresses our problems. And beware: This new political thinking might—will—result in a complete re-working of the very idea of Black People.[66]

Spirit might be expansive enough to allow for a complicated vision of black identity that elides any narrow notion of racial authenticity. Wood seemed to suggest, however, that an investment in spirit might be the very thing frustrating efforts to achieve a political program or set of policies that effectively protected black people. Just as the market emptied Malcolm X's life of the politics that he was pursuing, Wood conceded that "Black spirit" was unable to prevent "our blood from spilling."[67] In acknowledging the abiding significance of spirit—be it Christian, Muslim, or some synthesis of the two—in black life, Wood suggested that the New Black culture and criticism was itself not yet the source of the secular black politics some hoped it might be.

Politics: #BlackLivesMatter, circa 2010s

Like the 1990s, the decade of the 2010s featured a flourishing of black literary and artistic expression that achieved both popular and critical acclaim. In 2016, for instance, a relatively long list of black writers— Elizabeth Alexander, Ta-Nehisi Coates, Gregory Pardlo, and Claudia Rankine among them—received many of the highest literary honors.[68] That same year, in a *New York Times Magazine* essay about the editor Christopher Jackson, one critic observed that a new "black literary movement" was underway.[69] Given all of the fanfare, one might be tempted to think of these developments as indicating the arrival of the newest Negro—that is, an even newer (or post-)black—renaissance. At the same time, the 2010s were undisputedly a period in which the United States and the world witnessed a pronounced resurgence of black protest politics. With a string of killings of unarmed black women and men—too many to enumerate here—caught on camera, the contradictions of the era came into clear focus during President Obama's second term in the White House. Indeed, the bitter distance between the hope attached to a black presidency that began the decade and the despair occasioned by a series of hypervisible black deaths that came to the fore just a few years later helped produce the hashtag #BlackLivesMatter and a new generation of black protest politics. Coupled with (and in stark contrast to) another wave of black artistic and cultural accolades, as a sustained form of social protest the Movement for Black Lives helped make the value and meaning of black people's lives a subject of interest to Americans of all colors.

In the realm of literature, from a crowded room of awardees Ta-Nehisi Coates surfaced as singular in his public significance, for both a liberal white audience and a new generation of black activists. Indicative of the century-long dilemma of the black artist, Coates's broader appeal seemed to be as much about the public's interest in race politics as it was the product of any particular analytical insight or literary innovation. To be clear, the content and form of Coates's creative and critical work became the object of fierce debate.[70] However, more to the point, the tone and tenor of his memoir *Between the World and Me* (2015) was received as representative of the times, thrusting the writer into the role of the reluctant racial commentator. Moreover, the text's appeal was indicative of the angst, anger, and, somewhat ironically, American ambitions of a generation of young black people (but also whites) coming of age during the 2010s.

Coates's literary powers could be witnessed, at least in part, in his affirmation of the value of black life by chronicling all of the ways in which black lives were still being made not to matter, now fifty years after the end of legal segregation. And one distinctive dimension of his prose—as a voice to (if not of) black millennials—was his professed disconnectedness from the church.[71] With his previous memoir, *The Beautiful Struggle* (2008), Coates had emerged squarely as writer and critic both in and of the Hip Hop generation, vocal in his disdain for the faith commitments associated with the civil rights era. As Jesse McCarthy notes, "he has an equivocal and sometimes hostile disdain for black religious tradition, a legacy from which he takes absolutely no solace."[72] In both books, Coates's gaze turns from religion to the brute material fact of the black body.

If it was Michael Brown's lifeless body lying in the street for four hours that helped galvanize a new social movement, Coates compellingly communicated the meaning of the black (male) body. And he did so, in his writing and speaking, in the affective register of one struggling for dear life to find his own breath—a more eloquent and elaborate articulation of the anthem that followed Eric Garner's final words: "I can't breathe."[73] Moreover, Coates's literary and journalistic reverence for everyday black life seemed to grant black bodies a kind of metaphysical weightiness. Absent any explicit theological claims, for Coates the black body itself is *the* sacred text. And he received a chorus of Amens—from black and white people alike, across the decade—as he preached his own particular gospel of blackness, and the anti-blackness to which it was opposed, in public.

If a simultaneous celebration of black literature and conspicuous consumption of black death struck readers as odd during the 2010s, it shouldn't have. Over the long haul, black creativity has charted a tradition of making the most sense, at least in the public imagination, when it is affixed to or interpreting racial crisis. Past and present, the structural arrangements and social effects of white supremacy, otherwise put, have provided the preconditions for black literary performance and protest politics alike. This is the long, if episodic, history that *Black is a Church* has attempted to narrate. The final decade of the nineteenth century was declared to be the dawn of a "Negro Renaissance" during a moment when the rule of the lynch mob was at an all-time high and racial segregation was endorsed by the nation's highest court. Indeed, Pentecostalism's inter-racial origin story is exceptional only because of *Plessy v. Ferguson*. And the ambitions that inspired the first World's Parliament of Religions can be grasped only in relationship to the conditions that required Ida B. Wells's *Red Record*. In this context, Victoria Earle Matthews argued before the First Congress of Colored Women that "race literature" would champion "true heroism" and advance "real Christianity."[74] Even earlier, it is impossible to comprehend the Afro-Protestant orthodoxy that first took shape in the slave narratives outside of the context of an Atlantic world network of abolitionists and against the backdrop of the nation's "original sin": the racialized institution of chattel slavery.

Over the long history of African American literary and artistic expression, culture has been commonly understood through the prism of (and in service to) race politics. And the measure of "true religion," in the context of black life, has almost always been black freedom. Over the years black cultural expression has appeared to become all the more visible, to the point of being granted movement status, in moments that have demanded and generated radical protest. Most emblematic, it was the tumultuous 1960s—a decade of civil rights activism, public assassinations, and Black Power politics—that gave us a Black Arts movement and, for that matter, black studies as an institutional enterprise. Then again, when has this not been the case? One could say that these are the perpetual conditions of modern black life—of politics pressing hard on the literary and of the arts attempting to lift the veil on the violently real constraints imposed by the fictions of race. One might wonder about the merits of a seemingly steady equation in which a singular and oppositional race politics appears ever ready to overdetermine black cultural expression, especially in view of the complexities of black literature and art and the distinctiveness of black politics as they evolve across time and place.[75]

Clearly there is no single answer to this query, but one need not search long for contemporary examples of the conundrum. On May 3, 2016, as the Nordic Resistance Movement processed through the streets of Borlänge, Sweden, black activist Tess Asplund jumped in front of the group of white male marchers and, with her right hand tightly clenched, shot her arm straight up in the air in defiance. Shortly thereafter, images of Asplund standing face to face with the marchers went viral.[76] The confrontation, ready-made for the Twitter-sphere, was spontaneously staged by an Afro-Swedish woman with a long record of antiracist activism. In addition to her closely shaved haircut, on this day she happened to be dressed, fittingly, in a jacket with black leather sleeves. Asplund's Black Power pose perfectly iconized the transnational dimensions of this new moment of black protest. It also confirmed Michele Wallace's observations, circa 1991, regarding the relationship between visual cultures and black politics.[77]

The history of black protest politics and aesthetics helps to explain the power of Asplund's pose, to be sure.[78] Though her image, fist in the air, harkened back to the racial iconography of the 1960s, the sight of her raised fist was strangely contemporary. After all, a team of Swedish filmmakers released *The Black Power Mixtape, 1967–1975* (directed by Göran Olsson, 2011) just five years earlier, repopularizing the movement's art and activism (and iconicity) around the globe. Her raised fist also made perfect sense in light of the more immediate context of 2016. After all, #BlackLivesMatter had gained so much traction the previous year that *Time* magazine shortlisted the movement for its 2015 "Person of the Year" award and described the moment as one in which a new freedom struggle "blossomed from a protest cry into a genuine political force."[79] As the noted scholar and activist Barbara Ransby observed, this cry of protest was emblematic of the "collective rage" of black and brown young people entering adulthood during the age of Obama. In turn, the Movement for Black Lives, as it is now often named, worked hard to harness this rage as a resource for bending the arc of the universe toward a twenty-first-century vision of racial justice.[80]

If xenophobia is what fueled the ambitions of Nordic Resistance in Sweden (and thus created the conditions for Asplund's counter-protest), similar issues were becoming increasingly apparent in the United States. Indeed, Donald Trump's rise to the presidency stoked the fires of a racial animus that had always kindled just below the surface of American political discourse and was rapidly making its way (back) into the mainstream.[81] Yet the rhetoric of Trump's presidential campaign became a target for #BlackLivesMatter activism only after organizers had already mobilized in response to the wave of police brutality and state-sanctioned anti-black violence that was being caught on video and broadcast around the world. As should be clear, this most recent wave of racial violence was by no means new. Yet the degree to which it made a claim on the public psyche—via representation and constant replay on traditional and new media—was no doubt novel.

Digital recording technologies, to be clear, have been deployed both by activists and the state to hold various kinds of institutions and publics accountable.[82] Although many have viewed this new cohort of activists' successful use of social media as a new organizing tactic, engaging media—television coverage specifically—to expose anti-black violence was also essential to the strategies employed during the 1960s. Stretching even further back, journalistic campaigns were the means through which Wells mounted a crusade against the rule of the lynch law at the end of the nineteenth century. Though commonly (and proudly) identified as "not your grandmother's civil rights movement," in truth the Movement for Black Lives is more of a continuation than a rupture in a tradition that has never been one single thing.[83] In this view, #BlackLivesMatter might better be understood as an updating of the platform rather than a complete reboot.

If the social media utilized in contemporary black activism reflected the natural evolution of methods and media technology, then perhaps the movement's substantive vision clarifies claims for its novelty. #BlackLivesMatter, generally speaking, is known for its public disavowal of the "politics of respectability"—a phrase historian Evelyn

Brooks Higginbotham coined to describe the organizing efforts of black Baptist women in the early twentieth century.[84] This forswearing of what is now often called "respectability politics" has worked, on one hand, to signal an alienation from and cynicism toward traditional (read: middle-class) black institutions and their organizing logics and, on the other hand, to affirm a notion of racial justice that embraces class, gender, and sexual difference. On each of these matters, #BlackLivesMatter has been cast as a radical reimagining of the black past and, specifically, as a full departure from "The Black Church."

In this regard, Coates's prose and #BlackLivesMatter's politics might appear to be cut from the same cloth. To be sure, the latter's feminist and queer politics and the former's overtly masculinist vision make for an awkward partnership. Yet it's a pairing that strangely resembles the complicated sexual and gender politics of black churches—sites in which women's leadership and hypermasculine performances have long been two sides of the same coin. Despite publicly professed commitments to a heteronormative male hierarchy, black churches have also been sites where women have wielded significant power and sexual difference has often been at least tacitly affirmed. Access to the podium and publishing could certainly stand to open up a bit more for black women and LGBTQ folks, to be sure. Yet, on this front, black literature and protest politics today are not as far removed from the traditions of Afro-Protestantism as they, more often than not, are thought to be.

Between the evolving ideals and strategic practices—the quotidian doings and utopian dreams—that have defined black literature and politics over the long haul, a much more complicated set of entanglements has animated the breaks and fissures in black social life. In previous generations, black churches provided a space to balance and mediate the tensions that defined black culture and politics and to hold together various kinds of black difference. Indeed, institutional Afro-Protestantism was often a space for cultivating political ambitions and artistic performances. Over time literature and politics came to be understood as diverging trajectories for activities that were once contained within the walls of an all-encompassing and first black institution, namely "The Black Church." And over the span of history, a long roster of black leaders, thinkers, and artists have repeatedly insisted that black churches ought to be remade by such modern, disciplinary logics. As we saw in chapter 2, perhaps no one did this more powerfully than W. E. B. Du Bois, but he was certainly not alone in calling for a "new religious ideal."[85]

Yet before black Christian churches emerged as a singular sociological construct (i.e., "The Negro Church") in the first half of the twentieth century, they were a geographically dispersed network of local congregations, with a range of complicated and contradictory theological doctrines, political orientations, and institutional affiliations. And this black church—that is, the history of heterodox Afro-Protestantism—resembled, in practice, what have more recently been described as the organizing logics of #BlackLivesMatter. Both #BlackLivesMatter and black churches began as movements defined by decentralized structural arrangements and constituted by an uneven ensemble of local agendas, actors, and organizations. During the 2010s, by both holding to a queer and feminist politics and eschewing respectability politics, #BlackLivesMatter exceeded the limits of a normative vision of blackness deemed desirable by the metrics of American democracy. And it was this very same measure to which Afro-Protestantism, an "invisible institution" under the terms of chattel slavery, originally aspired. At the same time, black Christians—clergy and laity, women and men, queer and straight—have played a significant role in the complex network of activism and organizing that is the Movement for Black Lives. Black churches hosted rallies, provided refuge for protestors, and offered solace to survivors of racial violence. Yet such facts, at a certain level, are beside the point—a sense of old things being reclaimed as new and being remade for a new moment.[86]

More interesting than the presence of Christian churches and preachers in today's black protest politics are the kinds of religious (or spiritual) work that have emerged as central in this moment—and to the movement itself. In this regard, #BlackLivesMatter has both decentered churches and made a claim for a different, yet not unfamiliar, kind of church. As the movement emerged, much was written about the "unorthodox" backgrounds of the three black women most often cited as founders of this leader-less (or leader-full) movement. At the time of the movement's emergence, Patrisse

Cullors's biography included a long-standing interest in "indigenous spirituality," which eventually led her to become an Ifa practitioner.[87] Alicia Garza identifies as Jewish but credited her approach to activism to Marxism, a characterization that casts her in opposition to religious belief of any kind. Ayo (formerly Opal) Tometi, by contrast, described herself as a "believer and practitioner of liberation theology."[88] In each case, their respective orientations toward religion were presented as extensions of a broader set of queer—which is to say, nonnormative—commitments. Yet again, by way of the biography of key figures in the movement, #BlackLivesMatter was defined by a refusal to abide by the traditional (black and American) authority of Christian churches *and* an embrace of spiritual and social practices that fall outside the bounds of "standard respectability discourses"—to borrow the phrasing of Richard Iton, the late scholar of black politics and popular culture. If anything, Iton's notion of a "Black Fantastic" aptly anticipates the kind of historically grounded, future-oriented, and heterodox fusion of the culture, politics, and spirituality on display in #BlackLivesMatter.[89]

Beyond debunking the myth of "The Black Church" or decrying respectability politics, church has provided black people—even in the context of the 2010s—with an institutional base, a space for organizing across ideological difference, and a horizon for (re)imagining the terms of black social life. In addition to public recognition within America's Protestant order, Afro-Protestantism has constituted a more expansive cultural and moral geography than the physical space and place occupied by a church building or the theological claims that are accepted as doctrinal orthodoxy. Here one thinks of the kind of cultural practices—which often present as religious, spiritual, and even "churchy"—that are intended to affirm black life and don't necessarily register on the radars of popular media or remain, by design, in the shadows of protests staged in public. Even when deployed in plain sight, social media has served multiple purposes and addressed multiple audiences at once. Within the Movement for Black Lives, social media has constituted a practical method for organizing specific, multisited demonstrations. Rather than a form of "hashtag activism" to be decried as superficial and unsubstantial, digital practices also fostered conversation, connection, and community and provided the conditions of possibility under the inescapable terms of twenty-first-century hypermediated realities for #BlackLivesMatter.

Rather than an alternative to or escape from the real world, black social life and #BlackLivesMatter are mutually constitutive.[90] During the decade of the 2010s, the steadily growing list of names of those whose lives were taken was often enumerated online via tweets, status updates, and stories. As acts of witness, digital practices often did the work of elegy and religious litany, blurring any easy line between the two. For instance, in the wake of Sandra Bland's death in a Texas jail cell, #SayHerName became one of the many secondary slogans that followed the original #BlackLivesMatter. Both of these hashtags were, in effect, mobilized to memorialize a life, affirm the conditions of black living in the present, forge social connection, and inspire further movement-building. In the case of #SayHerName, it also helped to overtly signal a commitment to gender equality as an organizing principle for a social justice movement that has featured (and in some cases privileged) black feminist and queer leadership.

Ultimately, in both its substance and form, many of the ideas and practices associated with #BlackLivesMatter, as it emerged during the 2010s, would seem to resemble a congregation that was birthed in the midst of the struggle for freedom—as an affirmation of life and a refusal of the social death that was American slavery. And the movement might best be understood as an effort to reclaim and reconstitute this religious tradition that gave rise to (but can never be conflated with) the institution of the church. For the Movement for Black Lives, the work of publicly affirming and sustaining black social life is prioritized alongside transforming the nation-state. In this view, black life itself—that is, all of black life—is the sacred prize. Church, if nothing else, has always been a sign of that prize.

Yet the affective dispositions, institutional structures, and imaginative horizons associated with Afro-Protestantism—that is, "The Black Church"—have been heterodox over the long haul, harnessing and mobilizing whatever resources were available to address the circumstances of black living and dying every day. Church, as such, has been concerned with making a claim upon the most "mainstream" of American ideas and institutions, including the nation-state itself. Since the American nation was founded, black churches have been preoccupied with citizenship and, accordingly, with making members into citizens. Yet with a clear sense of the state's inability to deliver on all that it promises, black churches have also, and always, been about the business of cultivating the capacity to conceive of a life on terms that don't neatly map onto established topographies. "The Black Church" has always constituted a space that suggested the possibility of what, as of late, has been identified as "otherwise."[91]

Afro-Protestantism as such—which is to say, church—has produced and constituted an imaginative terrain and a set of institutions, artistic and political at once, that set its first sights on transforming a violently anti-black system of social inequality even as it attempted to affirm and sustain the fullness of black lives. It has been oriented in this way by a utopian impulse, as it were, to imagine black life off the grid, as implausible as that might seem. It is true that churches, black and white alike, are creators and products of, as well as participants in, the modern discourses of race, gender, class, nation, and sexuality. Yet on another plain, blackness itself (under a variety of names) has circulated as a religious discourse, within and outside of the church. Sacred in its own right. Blackness, put otherwise, on a grid of its own. Afro-Protestant modernity, still.

Black activists, artists, and intellectuals—and, yes, preachers too—have known this all too well, carrying on this Afro-Protestant tradition up through the present with gestures prayerful and playful at once, as a sign of the deepest black devotion. On closer inspection, beyond black history hashtags and movement songs updated with the sonic landscapes of Hip Hop, #BlackLivesMatter and the writers who made this black literary moment laid claim to a tradition that has long made a claim for the sacredness of all black lives. For blackness, the black, as sacred. For the fullness of black life as something "holy, holy black."[92] And, in doing so, they continue to both bear the marks of and breathe life into something very CHURCH in the making.

When a memoir—penned by a scholar and poet—embraces the language of "light of the world" to elegize intimate love and loss.[93]

When a poet and professor names a book of verse *The New Testament*.[94]

When yet another poet recalls the formation of literary community and confesses that "for some of us it was church."[95]

When a journalist makes it just a bit more plain—in the aftermath of the 2015 mass murder in Charleston's Emmanuel AME Church—and affirms that "black folks are *my* church, preaching the value of black life is my ministry and blackness is my sanctuary."[96]

When a rapper—in a song that would become an anthem for a movement—declares, "If God got us, then we gon' be alright!"

Notes

Introduction

1. Ariana Huffington, "Announcing *HuffPost Religion*: Believers and Nonbelievers Welcome," *Huffington Post,* April 29, 2010.
2. Robert Wuthnow, *The Restructuring of American Religion: Society and Faith since World War II* (Princeton, NJ: Princeton University Press, 1988).
3. Huffington, "Announcing *HuffPost Religion*"; Hermann Hesse. *My Belief: Essays on Life and Art* (New York: Farrar, Straus and Giroux, 1973).
4. Robert Orsi, *Between Heaven and Earth: The Religious Worlds People Make and the Scholars Who Study Them* (Princeton, NJ: Princeton University Press, 2006), 177–204.
5. Paul Raushenbush, "Dear Religious (and Sane) America," *Huffington Post,* April 26, 2010.
6. Three years later, at a panel at the American Academy of Religion, Raushenbush would refer to his goal for the portal as "winning the internet for religion." Whatever "winning" might mean in this context, what's more interesting here is the kind of religion imagined and constructed in the launch of *HuffPost Religion.*
7. Eddie Glaude Jr., "The Black Church Is Dead," *Huffington Post,* February 4, 2010.
8. Glaude's post received ~1,900 likes and 765 shares. Chopra received ~1,000. Huffington and Raushenbush received 276 and 103 likes, respectively.
9. Eboo Patel, "The Pluralist Next Door," *Huffington Post,* April 26, 2010; Glaude, "The Black Church Is Dead."
10. Glaude, "The Black Church Is Dead."
11. Mark Anthony Neal, "A History of Black Folk on Twitter," YouTube, April 9, 2011, https://www.youtube.com/watch?v=GbPJNK4vw1s. See also Farhad Manjoo, "How Black People Use Twitter: The Latest Research on Race and Microblogging," *Slate Magazine,* August 10, 2010, https://slate.com/technology/2010/08/how-black-people-use-twitter.html.
12. "The Black Church Is Dead: Long Live the Black Church," *Religion Dispatches,* March 15, 2010.

13. Samuel Freedman, "Call and Response on the State of the Black Church," *New York Times,* April 17, 2010.

14. William D. Hart, "The Afterlife of the Black Church," *Religion Dispatches,* March 15, 2010.

15. Charles Long, "Perspectives for the Study of African-American Religion in the United States," in Charles Long, *Significations: Signs, Symbols and Images in the Interpretation of Religion* (Aurora, CO: Davies Publishing Group, 1999), 187–198. This essay was originally published in *History of Religions* 11, no. 1 (Aug. 1971). Henry Goldschmidt and Elizabeth McAlister, eds., *Race, Nation and Religion in the Americas* (New York: Oxford University Press, 2004).

16. Kathryn Lofton, "Black Church Blues: Parting with 'The Black Church,'" *Religion Dispatches,* July 3, 2009. Also see Curtis Evans quoted in Monique Parsons, "The History of the Black Church," National Public Radio, November 27, 2008.

17. Long, "Perspectives for the Study of African-American Religion in the United States," 188.

18. Long, *Significations,* 7.

19. Long, *Significations,* 7.

20. "The Black Church Is Dead—Long Live the Black Church."

21. Here I am thinking about, for example, Fred Moten's use of religious ideas and practices to theorize blackness, including "Manic Depression/Mantic Dispossesion: A Poetics of Hesitant Sociology/Black Topological Existence," unpublished manuscript (2021); Sylvia Wynter's appeal to black religions as a critique of Western constructions of "the human" in "Black Metamorphosis: New Natives in a New World," unpublished manuscript, Schomburg Center for Research in Black Culture, New York; and the unstated theology apparent in the Afro-pessimism metaphysic of anti-blackness in Frank B. Wilderson III. *Afro-Pessimism* (New York: Liveright, 2020). For an important and helpful effort to think through these trajectories in relationship to religious studies and theology, see J. Kameron Carter, guest editor, "Special Issue: Religion and the Future of Blackness," *South Atlantic Quarterly* 112, no. 4 (Fall 2013).

22. Kimberlé Crenshaw, "Mapping the Margins: Intersectionality, Identity Politics and Violence again Women of Color," *Stanford Law Review* 43, no. 6 (July 1991): 1241–1299.

23. A good example of an essay that brings religion into what might be understood as an intersectional analysis is Anthony Petro, "Race, Gender, Sexuality, and Religion in North America," *Oxford Research Encyclopedia of Religion* (February 2017): 1–33, https://doi.org/10.1093/acrefore/

9780199340378.013.488. Patricia Hill Collins and Sirma Bilge also integrate religion as a marker of social difference in their recent work, *Intersectionality* (New York: Polity, 2020).

24. Adolph Reed, *The Jesse Jackson Phenomenon: The Crisis of Purpose in Afro-American Politics* (New Haven, CT: Yale University Press, 1986), 41–60. For a more recent and sustained treatment of this problem, see Erica R. Edwards, *Charisma and the Fictions of Black Leadership* (Minneapolis: University of Minnesota Press, 2012).

25. For two works that capture this well, see Marla Frederick, *Between Sundays: Black Women and Everyday Struggles of Faith* (Berkeley: University of California Press, 2003); Fredrick Harris, *Something Within: Religion in African-American Political Activism* (New York: Oxford University Press, 1999).

26. Winston James, *Holding Aloft the Banner of Ethiopia: Caribbean Radicalism in Early Twentieth Century America* (London: Verso Books, 1999), 50, 76.

27. Robin D. G. Kelley, "'We Are Not What We Seem': Rethinking Black Working-Class Opposition in the Jim Crow South," *Journal of American History* 80, no. 1 (June 1993): 88. Ultimately, Kelley illuminates how a Marxist orthodoxy made it difficult for historians of the black experience to see how "the sacred and the spirit world," including Christianity, were a resource for black politics.

28. Louis Chude-Sokei, ed., "States of Black Studies," special issue of *Black Scholar* 44, no. 2 (Summer 2014). A word search of every article in this issue reveals that any variation of the word "religion" or "spiritual" shows up fewer than a handful of times. There are, to my mind, several more recent developments that suggest a broader engagement with religion, in the context of black studies, is afoot.

29. That the 2018 *Keywords in African American Studies* includes a chapter on religion by Rhon Manigault-Bryant (174–178) is a hopeful sign. Additionally, the widespread engagement with the work of Cedric J. Robinson, who dealt with religion across his body of work in creative and insightful ways, may also generate more nuanced approaches to religion. A sign of this promise can be seen in Erica Edwards's foreword to the new edition of Robinson's *The Terms of Order: Political Science and the Myth of Leadership* (Chapel Hill: University of North Carolina Press, 2016).

30. Here I am thinking in relationship to two works by theorists of great significance for religious studies and black studies, respectively: Jonathan Z. Smith, *Map Is Not Territory: Studies in the History of Religion* (Chicago: University of Chicago Press, 1993) and Sylvia Wynter, "On How We Mistook the Map for the Territory, and Re-Imprisoned Ourselves in

Our Unbearable Wrongness of Being, of Désêtre: Black Studies toward the Human Project" in *Not Only the Master's Tools: African-American Studies in Theory and Practice,* ed. Lewis R. Gordon and Jane Anna Gordon (Boulder, CO: Paradigm, 2006), 107–169.

31. For the first book to focus squarely on race and secularism, see Jonathan Kahn and Vincent Lloyd, eds., *Race and Secularism in America* (New York: Columbia University Press, 2016).

32. In referring to "the black" as such, I am referencing Stuart Hall's classic essay, "What Is This Black in Black Popular Culture?," in *Black Popular Culture: A Michele Wallace Project,* ed. Gina Dent (Seattle, WA: Bay Press, 1992), 21–33.

33. Jonathan Z. Smith, "Religion, Religions, Religious," in *Critical Terms for Religious Studies,* ed. Mark C. Taylor (Chicago: University of Chicago Press, 1998), 269–284.

34. For work in this vein, see Curtis Evans, *The Burden of Black Religion* (New York: Oxford University Press, 2008); Barbara Dianne Savage, *Your Spirits Walk Beside Us: The Politics of Black Religion* (Cambridge, MA: Belknap Press of Harvard University Press, 2008).

35. Jonathan L. Walton, *Watch This! The Ethics and Aesthetics of Black Televangelism* (New York: New York University Press, 2009), 27–33. For a discussion of broader uplift discourses, and the broader significance of black culture and politics, see Kevin Gaines, *Uplifting the Race: Black Leadership, Politics, and Culture in the Twentieth Century* (Chapel Hill: University of North Carolina Press, 1996).

36. See Josef Sorett, "'We Build Our Temples for Tomorrow': Racial Ecumenism and Religious Liberalism in the Harlem Renaissance," in *American Religious Liberalism,* ed. Leigh Schmidt and Sally Promey (Bloomington: Indiana University Press, 2012), 190–206.

37. For work that explores hemispheric and Africana approaches, see Josef Sorett, "African American Theology and the American Hemisphere," in *The Oxford Handbook of African American Theology,* ed. Katie G. Cannon and Anthony B. Pinn (New York: Oxford University Press, 2014), 415–430; Dianne M. Stewart Diakité and Tracey E. Hucks, "Africana Religious Studies: Toward a Transdisciplinary Agenda in an Emerging Field," *Journal of Africana Religions* 1, no. 1 (2013): 28–77.

38. For recent works that capture religious and geographic diversity in the black diaspora, see, for instance, Zain Abdullah, *Black Mecca: The African Muslims of Harlem* (New York: Oxford University Press, 2010); Yvonne Chireau, *Black Magic: The African American Conjuring Tradition* (Berkeley: University of California Press, 2003); Marla

Frederick, *Colored Television: American Religion Gone Global* (Stanford, CA: Stanford University Press, 2016); Paul Christopher Johnson, *Diaspora Conversions: Black Carib Religion and the Recovery of Africa* (Berkeley: University of California Press, 2007).

39. Sacvan Bercovitch, *The Puritan Origins of the American Self* (New Haven, CT: Yale University Press, 2011); Nan Goodman and Michael P. Kramer, eds., *The Turn around Religion in America: Literature, Culture and the Work of Sacvan Bercovitch* (New York: Routledge, 2011). See also Tracy Fessenden et al., eds., *The Puritan Origins of American Sex* (New York: Routledge, 2001).

40. Here my thinking regarding a "Protestant secular" is informed, especially, by the work of Tracy Fessenden, *Culture and Redemption: Religion, the Secular, and American Literature* (Princeton, NJ: Princeton University Press, 2008).

41. Cedric J. Robinson, *Black Movements in America* (New York: Routledge, 1997), 95–108.

42. Here I am thinking similarly to how Glaude describes the way black people used the language of Exodus to create a sense of "we-ness." See Eddie S. Glaude Jr., *Exodus: Race, Religion and Nation in Early Nineteenth Century America* (Chicago: University of Chicago Press, 1998), 16, 115. In addition to Glaude, for discussion of the varied approaches to black nationalism, see Wilson Jeremiah Moses, *The Golden Age of Black Nationalism* (New York: Oxford University Press, 1988) and *Classical Black Nationalism: From the American Revolution to Marcus Garvey* (New York: NYU Press, 1996); Tommie Shelby, *We Who Are Dark: The Philosophical Foundations of Black Solidarity* (Cambridge, MA: Belknap Press of Harvard University Press, 2007); Keisha N. Blain, *Set the World on Fire: Black Nationalist Women and the Global Struggle for Freedom* (Philadelphia: University of Pennsylvania Press, 2019).

43. James Melvin Washington, *Frustrated Fellowship: The Black Baptist Quest for Social Power* (Macon, GA: Mercer University Press, 1991).

44. Marlon B. Ross, *Manning the Race: Reforming Black Men in the Jim Crow Era* (New York: NYU Press, 2004); Maurice O. Wallace, *Constructing the Black Masculine: Identity and Ideality in African American Literature and Culture, 1771–1995* (Durham, NC: Duke University Press, 2002).

45. Amiri Baraka, " 'Black' Is a Country" (1962), in Amiri Baraka, *Home: Social Essays* (New York: Akashic Press, 2009), 101–106.

46. Cedric J. Robinson, *The Terms of Order: Political Science and the Myth of Leadership* (1980; Chapel Hill: UNC Press, 2016); Michel Foucault, *The Order of Things: An Archaeology of the Human Sciences* (1970; New York: Vintage, 1994).

Chapter 1

1. William L. Andrews, ed., *Sisters of the Spirit: Three Black Women's Autobiographies of the Nineteenth Century* (Bloomington: Indiana University Press, 1986), 1–22; Yolanda Pierce, *Hell without Fires: Slavery, Christianity, and the Antebellum Spiritual Narrative* (Gainesville: University Press of Florida, 2005).

2. By this I mean to point out that the category of aesthetics emerged to mark a fundamentally modern distinction between high and low art. In this view, art and aesthetics were viewed as elite forms, in service to the state (and previously, the church), divorced from the mundane artifacts, local contexts, and rituals of everyday life. Against this invidious distinction, which followed the movement of "art" out from the everyday to museum installations, John Dewey—in 1932 in the inaugural Williams James Lectures at Harvard—argued for the value of the arts in ordinary life. And it was the authority garnered by such logics that also led a number of black artists and intellectuals to claim that a great "race literature" might lend "the race" legitimacy on the stage of nations. See John Dewey, *Art as Experience* (1980; New York: TarcherPerigree, 2005). For a discussion of these questions in the context of black culture, see Josef Sorett, "African American Religion and Popular Culture," in *African American Religious Cultures*, ed. Anthony B. Pinn (Santa Barbara, CA: ABC-CLIO, 2009), 533–548.

3. Pierce, *Hell without Fires*, 3.

4. Theodore Parker, *The American Scholar*, ed. George Willis Cooke (Boston: American Unitarian Association, 1907), 37.

5. Victoria Earle Matthews, "The Value of Race Literature: An Address," *Massachusetts Review* 27, no. 72 (Summer 1986): 72.

6. Joanna Brooks, *American Lazarus: Religion and the Rise of African American and Native American Literatures* (New York: Oxford University Press, 2003), 6.

7. Tracy Fessenden, *Culture and Redemption: Religion, the Secular, and American Literature* (Princeton, NJ: Princeton University Press, 2006), 33.

8. See discussion in "Catechism and Conversion," chapter 3 of Albert Raboteau, *Slave Religion: The "Invisible Institution" in the Antebellum South* (New York: Oxford University Press, 1978), 95–150. Also see discussion of "conversion-brokered religion" in Clarence Hardy, *James Baldwin's God: Sex, Hope, and Crisis in Black Holiness Culture* (Knoxville: University of Tennessee Press, 2009), 17–36.

9. Here I am thinking in ways similar to Eddie S. Glaude Jr.'s argument concerning Exodus as a source through which black people constructed a "common grammar of faith" (*Exodus*, 3–18).

10. Vincent Lloyd, "Introduction," in Kahn and Lloyd, *Race and Secularism in America*, 1–22.

11. For academic approaches that figure religion in the development of black literature, see the following: Joanna Brooks, *American Lazarus: Religion and the Rise of African-American and Native American Literatures* (New York: Oxford University Press, 2003); Frances Smith Foster, *Witnessing Slavery: The Development of the Ante-Bellum Slave Narratives* (Madison: University of Wisconsin Press, 1994); Henry Louis Gates Jr., *Figures in Black: Words, Signs, and the "Racial" Self* (New York: Oxford University Press, 1987) and *The Signifying Monkey: A Theory of African American Literary Criticism* (New York: Oxford University Press, 1988); Ronald A. T. Judy, (*Dis)Forming the American Canon: African-Arab Slave Narratives and the Vernacular* (Minneapolis: University of Minnesota Press, 1993). For a popular coverage of this debate, see Dennis Maurizi, "Jupiter Hammon: The First Publishing African-American. Maybe," *Chicago Tribune*, June 28, 2002, https://www.chicagotribune.com/news/ct-xpm-2002-06-28-0206280238-story.html.

12. Gauri Viswanathan, "Secularism in the Framework of Heterodoxy," *PMLA* 123, no. 2 (2008): 466–476.

13. In attending to religion as the "content," or a prevailing theme, in the slave narratives, my thinking is shaped by the following works: Hayden White, *The Content of the Form: Narrative Discourse and Historical Representation* (Baltimore, MD: Johns Hopkins University Press, 1987); Werner Sollors, ed., *The Return of Thematic Criticism* (Cambridge, MA: Harvard University Press, 1993).

14. Gates, *The Signifying Monkey*, 135.

15. The first black Methodist Church (Bethel AME) was founded in 1787 and the first black Baptist church (First African Baptist) in 1784. See Albert Raboteau, *Canaan Land: The Religious History of African Americans* (New York: Oxford University Press, 2001), 29–46.

16. Gates, *The Signifying Monkey*, 132–133.

17. Gates, *The Signifying Monkey*, 138.

18. Gates, *The Signifying Monkey*, 139–183.

19. For discussion of secularism in its shaping of modern literary studies, two journal issues are especially helpful: *New Literary History* 38, no. 4 (August 2007); "Special Issue: Reading Secularism: Religion, Literature, Aesthetics," *Comparative Literature* 65, no. 3 (Summer 2013). One way to

read Gates's interpretation of Gronniosaw is that it suggests that secularization and Christianization were co-constitutive, well in advance of recent
debates about the substance and form of the secular.

20. The biblical quote that is used as the epigraph for Gronniosaw's narrative
makes this transformation explicit. (Whether he chose the epigraph himself, though, is a live question.) The idea in Isaiah 42:16 of moving from
darkness and obscurity into light and clarity is all right there in the epigraph: "I will bring the Blind by a Way that they know not, I will lead them
in Paths that they have not known: I will make Darkness Light before them
and crooked Things straight. These Things will I do unto them and not forsake them."

21. James Ukawsaw Gronniosaw, "A Narrative of the Most Remarkable
Particulars in the Life of James Albert Ukawsaw Gronniosaw, an African
Prince, as Related by Himself" (Chapel Hill: University of North Carolina
Academic Affairs Library, 2001), http://docsouth.unc.edu/neh/gronnio
saw/gronnios.html, 39.

22. Gil Anidjar, "The Idea of an Anthropology of Christianity,"
Interventions: International Journal of Postcolonial Studies 11, no. 3
(2009): 367–393.

23. Gates, *The Signifying Monkey*, 133, 135. Gronniosaw's story can also be
located within a subset in a genre of the slave narrative that Pierce has referred to as "spiritual narratives" (Pierce, *Hell Without Fires*, 1–12).

24. Gronniosaw, "A Narrative," 15.

25. David Wills, "The Rise of Black Evangelicalism: Acquiring a Taste for
Salvation," paper presented at Harvard Divinity School, 2002.

26. As Viswanathan notes, "Unlike tradition or orthodoxy, wonder has no institutional home, no anchoring mechanism that channels its expression in
determinate ways" ("Secularism in the Framework of Heterodoxy," 470).

27. Gronniosaw, "A Narrative," 10.

28. Gronniosaw, "A Narrative," 28.

29. Gates, *The Signifying Monkey*, 139.

30. Fessenden, *Culture and Redemption*, 103.

31. Gronniosaw, "A Narrative," 28, italics added.

32. For an excellent study of this subject, see Allyson Hobbs, *A Chosen
Exile: A History of Racial Passing in American Life* (Cambridge,
MA: Harvard University Press, 2016).

33. For a concise discussion of the limits of "belief," see Donald Lopez,
"Belief," in *Critical Terms for Religious Studies*, ed. Mark C. Taylor
(Chicago: University of Chicago Press, 1998), 21–35.

34. Such performances of black Christianity might be understood as in keeping with what Houston Baker identifies as demonstrating a mastery of the forms of "modernism," appropriations of a "mask" that cloaked nationalistic impulses within black religious culture. See Houston A. Baker Jr., *Modernism and the Harlem Renaissance* (Chicago: University of Chicago Press, 1987).

35. II Corinthians 5:17 (NRSV): "So if anyone is in Christ, there is a new creation: everything old has passed away; see, everything has become new!"

36. Charles Mills, *The Racial Contract* (Ithaca, NY: Cornell University Press, 1999), 1–8.

37. For a discussion of pluralism's prescriptive powers, see Pamela E. Klassen and Courtney Bender, "Introduction: Habits of Pluralism," in *After Pluralism: Reimagining Religious Engagement*, ed. Courtney Bender and Pamela E. Klassen (New York: Columbia University Press, 2011), 1–29. See also Tomoko Masuzawa, *The Invention of World Religions: How European Universalism Was Preserved in the Language of Pluralism* (Chicago: University of Chicago Press, 2005).

38. Gronniosaw, "A Narrative," 1–2.

39. Orsi, *Between Heaven and Earth*, 177–204.

40. For work that explores the convergence on race and theology in shaping modern thought, see J. Kameron Carter, *Race: A Theological Account* (New York: Oxford University Press, 2008); Willie Jennings, *The Christian Imagination: Theology and the Origins of Race* (New Haven, CT: Yale University Press, 2010).

41. Talal Asad, *Formations of the Secular: Christianity, Islam, Modernity* (Stanford, CA: Stanford University Press, 2003), 1–21. Mary Louise Pratt, *Imperial Eyes: Travel Writing and Transculturation* (New York: Taylor & Francis, 2003), 1–12.

42. Gates, *The Signifying Monkey*, 145. Gates suggests as much when he describes the narratives of John Marrant, John Cugoano (or Quobna Ottobah Cugoano), Olaudah Equiano, and John Jea as, among other things, different models of "black piety."

43. For a concise introduction and overview of each narrative discussed in this chapter (except for Omar ibn Said), see Gates, *The Signifying Monkey*. For an introduction to Said, see Ala A. Alryyes, "Notes on 'The Life of Oman ibn Said, Written by Himself' (1831)," in *The Multilingual Anthology of American Literature*, ed. Marc Shell and Werner Sollors (New York: New York University Press, 2000), 58–61.

44. John Marrant, "The Narrative of the Lord's Wonderful Dealings with John Marrant: A Black," in *Unchained Voices: An Anthology of Black Authors*

in the English-Speaking World of the 18th Century, ed. Vincent Carretta (Lexington: University Press of Kentucky, 2004), 110–133. For a more detailed account of John Marrant, see Brooks, *American Lazarus*, 87–113.

45. For a discussion of Indian captivity tales, see Richard Van Der Beets, *Held Captive by Indians* (Knoxville: University of Tennessee Press, 1973).

46. Marrant, "The Narrative," 114–116.

47. Marrant, "The Narrative," 118. For a full discussion of the ways in which black culture was formed on biblical terms, see Theophus H. Smith, *Conjuring Culture: Biblical Formations of Black America* (New York: Oxford University Press, 1995).

48. Marrant, "The Narrative," 113.

49. Marrant, "The Narrative," 122.

50. The narrative records four incidents when Marrant "burst out into tears" or "a flood of tears," and a fifth occasion in which Marrant promises that in heaven "God would wipe away all tears" ("The Narrative," 114, 117, 118, 122, 125).

51. Marrant, "The Narrative," 117–120, 127–128, italics added.

52. Thomas Fisher, *The Negro's Memorial, or Abolitionist's Catechism, Abridged* (1825; London: Forgotten Books, 2019).

53. Quobna Ottobah Cugoano, *Thoughts and Sentiments on the Evil of Slavery* (New York: Penguin, 1999), 17.

54. Cugoano, *Thoughts and Sentiments*, 17.

55. Cugoano, *Thoughts and Sentiments*, 62–67, italics added.

56. Cugoano, *Thoughts and Sentiments*, 63–64.

57. Cugoano, *Thoughts and Sentiments*, 63–64.

58. Gates, *The Signifying Monkey*, 150.

59. Cugoano, *Thoughts and Sentiments*, 65.

60. Gronniosaw, "A Narrative," 2.

61. Cugoano, *Thoughts and Sentiments*, 66–67.

62. Cugoano, *Thoughts and Sentiments*, 18, 98, 99, 145.

63. Cugoano, *Thoughts and Sentiments*, 64.

64. Here I am thinking about how the discourse of comparative religions developed from a distinctly Christian genealogy. See Masuzawa, *The Invention of World Religions*, 72–106.

65. In this way, Gronniosaw might also be read as affirming a Calvinistic doctrine of predestination.

66. Talal Asad, "Reading a Modern Classic: W. C. Smith's 'The Meaning and End of Religion,'" *History of Religions* 40, no. 3 (Feb. 2001): 205–222.

67. I recognize that Equiano's claim to an African birth has been contested, but here I am focused on the narrative structure of his book rather than

on the historical veracity of his claims. See Vincent Carretta, *Equiano, the African: Biography of a Self-Made Man* (New York: Penguin, 2005).

68. Carretta, *Equiano, the African*, 161–164. See Vincent Carretta, ed., *Olaudah Equiano: The Interesting Narrative and Other Writings* (New York: Norton, 2003), 132, 178–179.

69. Raboteau, *Canaan Land*, 65–84.

70. Frederick Douglass, *Narrative of the Life of Frederick Douglass, an American Slave*, in *The Classic Slave Narratives*, ed. Henry Louis Gates Jr. (New York: Signet Classics), 397–398.

71. Alryyes, "Notes on 'The Life of Omar ibn Said,'" 58–59. For a discussion of Muslim slave narratives, see also Judy, *(Dis)Forming the American Canon*, 149, 159–161. For new work on Said, see Yonat Shimron, "New Research Considers Writings of a Muslim Slave and Scholar," *Religion News Service*, February 7, 20-20, https://religionnews.com/2020/02/07/who-was-omar-ibn-said-new-research-reconsiders-muslim-slaves-writings/.

72. Alryyes, "Notes on 'The Life of Omar ibn Said,'" 83, 91.

73. Alryyes, "Notes on 'The Life of Omar ibn Said,'" 91.

74. Alryyes, "Notes on 'The Life of Omar ibn Said,'" 89.

75. Said does learn a new language (English), which is the inverse of Marrant's acquisition of the Cherokee tongue. Moreover, Said's narrative is in Arabic, which would suggest that this remained his primary language (and perhaps loyalty) even after an alleged Christian conversion.

76. Alryyes, "Notes on 'The Life of Omar ibn Said,'" 59.

77. Alryyes argues that the narrative "strongly indicates that Omar did not 'convert' in the sense that his masters and white visitors thought" ("Notes on 'The Life of Omar ibn Said,'" 60).

78. Alryyes, "Notes on 'The Life of Omar ibn Said,'" 58–61.

79. Tracey Hucks uses the term "multiple belonging" to describe African Americans who belong to more than one religious community/tradition at the same time. See "That's Alright . . . I'm a Yoruba Baptist," chapter 7 in Hucks, *Yoruba Traditions and African American Religious Nationalism* (Alberquerque: University of New Mexico Press, 2012).

80. For a discussion of literary authority within Islam, see Judy, *(Dis)Forming the American Canon*, 165–285.

81. For an overview of slavery in Africa, see Sean Stilwell, *Slavery and Slaving in African History* (New York: Cambridge University Press, 2014). In the years that follow a series of religiously inspired slave insurrections (e.g., by Nat Turner, Denmark Vesey, Gabriell Prosser), perhaps it was unsurprising that Said did not offer a critique of slavery writ large. Nat Turner's confession was published in 1831, the same year as Said's narrative. Said's

focus on the specific terms of enslavement could also be because of the longer history of slavery in the African Islamic world, where slaves were the spoils of war and the system. The terms of his enslavement were "unjust," but slavery, in general, was not necessarily considered evil. This would also explain why he considered his second master to be righteous. Owning slaves was not an issue, but the criteria for treating slaves in the African world was different. See also John Thornton, *Africa and Africans and the Making of the Atlantic World, 1400–1800* (London: Cambridge University Press, 1998), 72–97.

82. Jean McMahon Humez, ed., *Gifts of Power: The Writings of Rebecca Jackson, Black Visionary, Shaker Eldress* (Amherst: University of Massachusetts Press, 1981). *Gifts of Power* was not published until 1981, more than a century after Jackson's death.

83. For a discussion of black women preachers during the nineteenth century, see Andrews, *Sisters of the Spirit*.

84. Gates, *The Signifying Monkey*, 279n1. Gates notes similarities between John Jea's narrative and Jackson's, but he focuses more on the "uncanny resemblances" between Jackson's writing and the later work of Alice Walker, who reviewed *Gifts of Power* when it was first published in 1981. Humez argues that Jackson had not read other slave narratives and that her source materials were limited to the Bible and oral traditions such as testimony and visionary conventions (*Gifts of Power*, 45–47).

85. Humez details the process by which Jackson learned to trust her "inner voice" in *Gifts of Power* (15–27).

86. *Gifts of Power* was released in 1981, roughly a decade after the publication of Toni Cade Bambara's anthology *The Black Woman* (1970), which captured the rise of a nascent black feminism and called for the recovery of historical and contemporary sources of black women's writing. In this regard, what the publication of *Gifts of Power* did for Jackson was not unlike what Alice Walker did for Zora Neale Hurston during the 1970s.

87. For a discussion of the "politics of respectability," see Evelyn Brooks Higginbotham, *Righteous Discontent: The Women's Movement in the Black Baptist Church, 1880–1920* (Cambridge, MA: Harvard University Press, 1994), 185–230.

88. Glaude, *Exodus*, 19–43.

89. Joscelyn Godwin, *Upstate Cauldron: Eccentric Spiritual Movements in Early New York State* (Albany, NY: SUNY Press, 2015).

90. Gates, *The Signifying Monkey*, 142–169.

91. Gates, *The Signifying Monkey*, 164.

92. Two texts that have been helpful to my thinking about the convergence of race and colonialism in definitions of African American religious history are Jennings, *The Christian Imagination* and Sylvester Johnson, *African American Religions, 1500–2000: Colonialism, Democracy, and Freedom* (Cambridge: Cambridge University Press, 2015).

93. Bender and Klassen, *After Pluralism*.

94. Barbara E. Johnson, "'Response' to Henry Louis Gates, Jr., Canon-Formation, Literary History, and the Afro-American Tradition: From the Seen to the Told," in Houston A. Baker Jr., and Patricia Almond, *Afro-American Literary Study in the 1990s* (Chicago: University of Chicago Press, 1989), 43.

95. Saba Mahmood, *The Politics of Piety: Islamic Revival and the Feminist Subject* (Princeton, NJ: Princeton University Press, 2011).

96. Jon Butler, *Becoming America: The Revolution before 1776* (Cambridge, MA: Harvard University Press, 2000), 44, 186.

97. Ashis Nandy, *The Intimate Enemy: Loss and Recovery of Self under Colonialism* (New York: Oxford University Press, 1983).

98. Pratt, *Imperial Eyes*, 1–12.

Chapter 2

1. By this I mean to suggest that Afro-Protestantism developed into more than literary performances that figured the emergence of individual black subjects. It was also a social formation that shaped a set of shared knowledge and commonsense logics about the world. My thinking here is shaped by Foucault's idea of an "episteme." See Foucault, *The Order of Things*.

2. Rayford W. Logan, *The Negro in American Life and Thought: The Nadir, 1877–1901* (New York: Dial Press, 1954).

3. Henry Louis Gates Jr., "The Trope of a New Negro and the Reconstruction of the Image of the Black," in "America Reconstructed, 1840–1940," special issue of *Representations*, no. 24 (Autumn 1988): 129–155.

4. Robinson, *Black Movements in America*.

5. Steve Kramer, "Uplifting Our 'Downtrodden Sisterhood': Victoria Earle Matthews and New York City's White Rose Mission, 1897–1907," *Journal of African American History* 91, no. 3 (Summer 2006): 243–266.

6. Frances Smith Foster and Chanta Haywood, "Christian Recordings: Afro-Protestantism, Its Press, and the Production of

African-American Literature," *Religion & Literature* 27, no. 1 (Spring 1995): 15–33.

7. Raboteau, *Canaan Land*, 65–84.

8. Sutton Griggs, *Imperium in Imperio* (Cincinatti, OH: The Editor Publishing Co., 1899); Gates, "The Trope of a New Negro," 143–144.

9. David Douglas Daniels III, "The Cultural Renewal of Slave Religion: Charles Price Jones and the Emergence of the Holiness Movement in Mississippi" (PhD diss., Union Theological Seminary, May 1992).

10. Foster and Haywood, "Christian Recordings," 15–33.

11. Richard Hughes Seager, *The Dawn of Religious Pluralism: Voices from the World's Parliament of Religions, 1893* (Lasalle, IL: Open Court, 1999), 3–12. See also William Hutchison, *Religious Pluralism in America* (New Haven, CT: Yale University Press, 2003).

12. My thinking here is informed by Cedric Robinson's work on black social movements and black denominations specifically. But I am also thinking about how black people simultaneously participated in a range of distinct yet overlapping movements (*Black Movements in America*, 95–102).

13. For a discussion of Matthews, see Kerstin Rudolph, "Victoria Earle Matthews: Making Literature during the Woman's Era," *Legacy* 33, no. 1 (2016): 103–126; Gabrielle Foreman, *Activist Sentiments: Reading Black Women in the Nineteenth Century* (Champagne: University of Illinois Press, 2009), 132–136.

14. Victoria Earle Matthews, "The Value of Race Literature: An Address," *Massachusetts Review* 7, no. 72 (Summer 1986): 170–172.

15. Victoria Earle Matthews, "The Awakening of the Afro-American Woman: An Address Delivered at the Annual Convention of the Society of Christian Endeavor," San Francisco, July 11, 1897, https://collections.libr ary.yale.edu/catalog/10171939.

16. Victoria Earle Matthews, "The Value of Race Literature: An Address," *Massachusetts Review* 27, no. 72 (Summer 1986): 171–173.

17. See discussion of Douglass in chapter 1.

18. Henry Louis Gates Jr., "Harlem on Our Minds," *Critical Inquiry* 24, no. 1 (Autumn 1997): 1–12.

19. Victoria Earle Matthews, "Aunt Lindy: A Story Founded on Real Life," in *A.M.E. Church Review,* Online Archive of Nineteenth-Century U.S. Women's Writings, 1893 (no longer active). For more information, see http://dhhistory.blogspot.com/2015/05/the-online-archive-of-ninetee nth.html.

20. Kerstin Rudolph, "Victoria Earle Matthews's Short Stories," *Legacy* 33, no. 1 (2016): 159–160.

21. "And if a stranger sojourn with thee in your land, ye shall not vex him. But the stranger that dwelleth with you shall be unto you as one born among you, and thou shalt love him as thyself; for ye were strangers in the land of Egypt: I am the Lord your God" (Leviticus 19:33–34; KJV).

22. Kerstin Rudolph asserts that forgiveness in the Aunt Lindy stories figures as a form of resistance ("Victoria Earle Matthews: Making Race Literature," 12–17).

23. Matthews, "The Awakening of the Afro-American Women," 5–6.

24. For a discussion of uplift ideologies, see Kevin Gaines, *Uplifting the Race: Black Leadership, Politics and Culture in the Twentieth Century* (Chapel Hill: University of North Carolina Press, 1996).

25. W. E. B. Du Bois, *The Souls of Black Folk* (State College: Pennsylvania State University Press, 2006), 5.

26. Harriet Beecher Stowe, *Uncle Tom's Cabin* (1852; New York: Oxford University Press, 2002). Aunt Lindy's Christianity binds her in loyalty to the master that did her great harm under slavery, which is clearly similar to the title character in Stowe's *Uncle Tom's Cabin*, who sacrifices his own life to the violence of the overseer.

27. Rudolph, "Victoria Earle Matthews's Short Stories," 159.

28. Yvonne P. Chireau. *Black Magic: Religion and the African American Conjuring Tradition* (Berkeley: University of California Press, 2003), 11–34.

29. Frederick Douglass, *Narrative of the Life of Frederick Douglass, an American Slave*, ed. with an introduction by Deborah McDowell (Oxford: Oxford University Press, 1999), 66.

30. Charles W. Chesnutt, *The Conjure Woman* (1899), introduction by Robert Farnsworth (Ann Arbor: University of Michigan Press, 1969).

31. For a discussion of Hoodoo/Conjure, see Smith, *Conjuring Culture*; Chireau, *Black Magic*.

32. Chireau, *Black Magic*, 11–35.

33. For biographical entree into the black women's club movement, see Alison M. Parker, *Unceasing Militant: The Life of Mary Church Terrell* (Chapel Hill: University of North Carolina Press, 2020).

34. For a discussion of debates with an emphasis on religion, see William Hutchison, *The Modernist Impulse in American Protestantism* (Durham, NC: Duke University Press, 1992).

35. Matthews, "The Value of Race Literature," 172.

36. Richard Hughes Seager, *The World's Parliament of Religions: The East/ West Encounter, Chicago, 1893* (Bloomington: Indiana University Press, 1995), xxv–xxix; Carrie Tirado Bramen, *The Uses of Variety: Modern*

Americanism and the Quest for National Distinctiveness (Cambridge, MA: Harvard University Press, 2000), 250–292.

37. Anna R. Paddon and Sally Turner, "African Americans and the World Columbian Exposition," *Illinois Historical Journal* 88, no. 1 (Spring 1995): 19–36; Elliot M. Rudwick and August Meier, "Black Man in the 'White City': Negroes and the Columbian Exposition, 1893," *Phylon* 26, no. 4 (1965): 354; Frederick Douglass, "Preface," in Ida B. Wells, *The Reason Why the Colored American Is Not in the World's Columbian Exposition* (1893), as discussed in Paddon and Turner, "African Americans and the World Columbian Exposition," 19–36.

38. Ida B. Wells, *Daily Inter Ocean* (Chicago), June 28, 1893, as discussed in Paddon and Turner, "African Americans and the World's Columbian Exposition," 19.

39. I. Garland Penn is listed as "J. Garland Penn" in the reprint.

40. Ferdinand Lee Barnett, "The Reason Why," in Ida B. Wells, *The Reason Why the Colored American Is Not in the Columbian Exposition*, in *The Selected Works of Ida B. Wells-Barnett*, ed. Trudier Harris (New York: Oxford University Press, 1991), 134–135.

41. Frederick Douglass, "Preface," in Wells, *The Reason Why the Colored American Is Not in the World's Columbian Exposition*, in Trudier, *The Selected Works of Ida B. Wells-Barnett*, 54–55.

42. Barnett, "The Reason Why," 119.

43. As much as the Fair provided the occasion and target for its publication, *The Reason Why* is best understood as part of Wells's antilynching crusade; it was published shortly after *Southern Horrors* (1892), three years before *A Red Record* (1895), and seven years before *Mob Rule in New Orleans* (1900).

44. Douglass, "Preface," 55.

45. Douglass, "Preface," 57.

46. Amina Gautier, "African American Women's Writings in the Woman's Building Library," *Libraries & Culture* 41, no. 1 (Winter 2006): 55–81; William L. Andrews, Frances Smith Foster, and Trudier Harris, eds., "Victoria Earle Matthews," in *The Oxford Companion to African American Literature* (New York: Oxford University Press, 1997), 485. Somewhat surprisingly, Victoria Earle Matthews is not included in Paddon and Turner's list of African American participants at the Columbian Exposition, "African Americans and the World Columbian Exposition."

47. Seager, *The World's Parliament of Religions: The East/West Encounter, Chicago, 1893*, 3–14; Bramen, *The Uses of Variety*, 250–292.

48. Douglass, "Preface," 58.

49. For a discussion of the emergence of the idea of "world religions," see Masusawa, *The Invention of World Religions*.

50. The biblical story of the Tower of Babel can be found in Genesis 11:1–8.

51. Benjamin Arnett, "Christianity and the Negro," in Seager, *The Dawn of Religious Pluralism*, 138.

52. Arnett, "Christianity and the Negro," 138.

53. Arnett, "Christianity and the Negro," 138.

54. Fannie Barrier Williams, "What Can Religion Further Do to Advance the Condition of the American Negro?," in Seager, *The Dawn of Religious Pluralism*, 142.

55. Terence Keel, *Divine Variations: How Christian Thought Became Racial Science* (Stanford, CA: Stanford University Press, 2010).

56. Barrier Williams, "What Can Religion Further Do to Advance the Condition of the American Negro?," 143–144.

57. Walter R. Houghton, *Neely's History of the Parliament of Religions and Religious Congresses at the World's Columbian Exposition* (Chicago: Neely, 1894), 935–936.

58. Barrier Williams, "What Can Religion Further Do to Advance the Condition of the American Negro?," 148.

59. For a history of how atheism (and atheists) have figured in American society, see Leigh Eric Schmidt, *Village Atheists: How America's Unbelievers Made Their Way in a Godly Nation* (Princeton, NJ: Princeton University Press, 2016).

60. Barrier Williams, "What Can Religion Further Do to Advance the Condition of the American Negro?," 149.

61. Barrier Williams, "What Can Religion Further Do to Advance the Condition of the American Negro?," 149.

62. On Unitarians and the abolitionist movement, see Dean Grodzins, *American Heretic: Theodore Parker and Transcendentalism* (Chapel Hill: University of North Carolina Press, 2014); Paul E. Teed, *A Revolutionary Conscience: Theodore Parker and Antebellum America* (Lanham, MD: University Press of America, 2012).

63. Barrier Williams, "What Can Religion Further Do to Advance the Condition of the American Negro?," 143. See discussion of Douglass in chapter 1.

64. Frederick Douglass, "Impromptu Comments," in Seager, *The Dawn of Religious Pluralism*, 135.

65. J. R. Slattery, "The Catholic Church and the Negro Race," in Houghton, *Neely's History of the Parliament of Religions*, 602–604. See also William L. Portier, "*Pere Just's* Hero-Martyr Secularized: John R. Slattery's Passage

from Self-Sacrifice to 'Honest Manhood,'" *U.S. Catholic Historian* 17, no. 2 (Spring 1999): 31.

66. Douglass, "Impromptu Comments," 136. For more on Douglass's religious background, see David Blight, *Frederick Douglass: Prophet of Freedom* (New York: Simon and Schuster, 2018); Adelle M. Banks, "Five Religious Facts You Might Not Know About Frederick Douglass," *Religion News Service,* June 19, 2013.

67. For an introductory work on American Pentecostalism, see Cecil Robeck, *The Azusa Street Mission and Revival: The Birth of the Global Pentecostal Movement* (Nashville, TN: Thomas Nelson, 2006); Randall Stephens, *The Fire Spreads: Holiness and Pentecostalism in the American South* (Cambridge, MA: Harvard University Press, 2008).

68. Frank Bartleman, "How Pentecost Came to Los Angeles," in *Witness to Pentecost: The Life of Frank Bartleman,* ed. Donald W. Dayton (New York: Garland, 1985), 54, quoted in Leslie D. Callahan, "Fleshly Manifestations: Charles Fox Parham's Quest for the Sanctified Body" (PhD diss., Princeton University, 2002), 151.

69. On Pentecostal denominations, see Edith Blumhofer, *Restoring the Faith: The Assemblies of God, Pentecostalism, and American Culture* (Champagne: University of Illinois Press, 1993); Anthea Butler. *Women in the Church of God in Christ: Making a Sanctified World* (Chapel Hill: University of North Carolina Press, 2007); Calvin Harris, *The Rise to Respectability: Race, Religion, and the Church of God in Christ* (Fayetteville: University of Arkansas Press, 2015).

70. Daniels, "The Cultural Renewal of Slave Religion," 20.

71. For a survey of Afro-Pentecostalism, see Estrella Alexander, *Afro-Pentecostalism: Black Pentecostal and Charismatic Christianity in History and Culture* (New York: NYU Press, 2011).

72. Chireau, *Black Magic,* 5.

73. Daniels, "The Cultural Renewal of Slave Religion," 198–200. On Pentecostal theologies of race, see Douglas Jacobsen, *Thinking in the Spirit: Theologies of the Early Pentecostal Movement* (Bloomington: Indiana University Press, 2003), 260–285.

74. Charles Price Jones, *An Appeal to the Sons of Africa* (1902; Jackson, MS: Truth Publishing Co., 2000), 4.

75. Jones, *An Appeal to the Sons of Africa,* 105.

76. Regarding Du Bois and the development of sociology, see Aldon Morris, *A Scholar Denied: W. E. B. Du Bois and the Birth of Modern Sociology* (Berkeley: University of California Press, 2017), 6–54.

77. See David Levering Lewis, *W. E. B. Du Bois: Biography of a Race, 1968–1919* (New York: Henry Holt, 1993).

78. For work on Du Bois and religion, see Phil Zuckerman, ed., *Du Bois on Religion* (Walnut Creek, CA: Altamira Press, 2000); Barbara Dianne Savage, "W. E. B. Du Bois and 'The Negro Church,'" in "The Study of African American Problems: W. E. B. Du Bois's Agenda, Then and Now," special issue of *Annals of the American Academy of Political and Social Science* 568 (March 2000): 235–249; Jonathon S. Kahn, *Divine Discontent: The Religious Imagination of W. E. B. Du Bois* (New York: Oxford University Press, 2009); Edward Blum, *W. E. B. Du Bois: American Prophet* (Philadelphia: University of Pennsylvania Press, 2009).

79. Morris, *A Scholar Denied*, 55–99.

80. W. E. B. Du Bois, *The Souls of Black Folk*, Norton Critical Edition, ed. Henry Louis Gates Jr. and Terri Hume Oliver (New York: Norton, 1999), 5.

81. Du Bois, *The Souls of Black Folk*, 17.

82. Du Bois, *The Souls of Black Folk*, 16.

83. W. E. B. Du Bois, "The Strivings of the Negro People," *Atlantic Monthly*, August 1897.

84. Robert Gooding-Williams, *In the Shadow of Du Bois: Afro-Modern Political Thought in America* (Cambridge, MA: Harvard University Press, 2009), 4, 14, 57, 66, 145.

85. Kahn, *Divine Discontent*, 49–70.

86. Gooding-Williams, *In the Shadow of Du Bois*, 4.

87. Du Bois, *The Souls of Black Folk*, 148.

88. Du Bois, *The Souls of Black Folk*, 136–148.

89. Du Bois, *The Souls of Black Folk*, 137–138.

90. For a discussion of Du Bois's writing on Crummell, see Robert Gooding-Williams, *In the Shadow of Du Bois*; Stephanie Shaw, *W. E. B. Du Bois and The Souls of Black Folk* (Chapel Hill: University of North Carolina Press, 2015), 156–201.

91. Barrier Williams, "What Can Religion Further Do to Advance the Condition of the American Negro?," 146.

92. Du Bois, *The Souls of Black Folk*, 149.

93. Du Bois, *The Souls of Black Folk*, 149.

94. Du Bois, *The Souls of Black Folk*, 137, 173.

95. Du Bois, *The Souls of Black Folk*, 186.

96. See Frederick Davenport, *Primitive Traits in Religious Revivals: A Study in Mental and Social Evolution* (London: Macmillan, 1905). Davenport's

comparative study of revivals includes a chapter titled "The Religion of the American Negro."

97. Du Bois, *The Souls of Black Folk*, 153.

98. Du Bois, *The Souls of Black Folk*, 141.

99. Matthews, "The Value of Race Literature," 172.

100. Matthews, "The Value of Race Literature," 172.

101. Du Bois, *The Souls of Black Folk*, 11.

Chapter 3

1. W. E. B. Du Bois, *The Gift of Black Folk* (Garden City, NY: Square One, 2009), 154.

2. Du Bois, *The Gift of Black Folk*. 160.

3. Josef Sorett, *Spirit in the Dark: A Religious History of Racial Aesthetics* (New York: Oxford University Press, 2016), 19–54.

4. Jonathan Scott Holloway, *Confronting the Veil: Abram Harris, Jr., E. Franklin Frazier, and Ralph Bunche, 1919–1941* (Chapel Hill: University of North Carolina Press, 2002).

5. Benjamin E. Mays, *The Negro's God as Reflected in His Literature* (1938), ed. August Meier, Studies in Negro Life (New York: Atheneum, 1968).

6. Although Mays does not cite it in the bibliography of his dissertation, his dissertation seems to follow a model similar to V. F. Calverton's *The Newer Spirit: A Sociological Criticism of Literature* (New York: Boni and Liveright, 1925).

7. Between 1968 and 1973, several publishers reissued a paperback: Atheneum (1968, 1973), Negro Universities (1969), and Russell and Russell (vol. 11, Studies in American Negro Life, 1968). For a historical treatment of *The Negro's God*, see Randal Jelks, *Benjamin Elijah Mays, Schoolmaster of the Movement: A Biography* (Chapel Hill: University of North Carolina Press, 2012), 80–107; Savage, *Your Spirits Walk Beside Us*, 58–65. For a literary analysis of the book, see Qiana Whitted, *A God of Justice: The Problem of Evil in Twentieth Century Black Literature* (Charlottesville: University of Virginia Press, 2009).

8. Benjamin Elijah Mays, "The Development of the Idea of God in Contemporary Negro Literature" (PhD diss., University of Chicago, 1934).

9. T. S. Eliot, "Religion and Literature," in *The Faith That Illuminates*, ed. V. A. Demant (Leiden: E. J. Brill, 1935), 31–54.

10. For a short history of the field of religion and literature, see Giles Gunn, *The Interpretation of Otherness: Literature, Religion, and the American Imagination* (New York: Oxford University Press, 1979), 9–51.

11. Robert E. Park, "Negro Race Consciousness as Reflected in Race Literature," in *The New Negro: Readings on Race, Representation, and African American Culture, 1892–1938*, ed. Henry Louis Gates Jr. and Gene Andrew Jarrett (Princeton, NJ: Princeton University Press, 2007), 305–315.

12. Park, "Negro Race Consciousness as Reflected in Race Literature," 306.

13. See the discussion of *The Souls of Black Folk* in chapter 2.

14. Savage, *Your Spirits Walk Beside Us*, 22, 64. Savage notes that *The Negro's God* "received less notice" than *The Negro's Church*.

15. For a historical discussion of *The Green Pastures*, see Curtis J. Evans, *The Burden of Black Religion* (New York: Oxford University Press, 2008), 203–222.

16. Jelks, *Benjamin Elijah Mays*, 80–107. According to Jelks, the Institute for Social and Religious Research (ISSR) contributed roughly $3 million to various research projects, including several on African American religion. Other grant recipients included Howard University historian Charles Wesley and Carter G. Woodson.

17. W. E. B. Du Bois, *The Negro Church: A Report of a Social Study Made under the Direction of Atlanta University* (Walnut Creek, CA: Altamira Press, 1903); Benjamin E. Mays and Joseph Nicholson, *The Negro's Church* (New York: Institute of Social and Religious Research, 1933); Carter G. Woodson, *The History of the Negro Church* (Chapel Hill: University of North Carolina Press, 2018), first published in 1921. According to Evans, Du Bois first uses the term "The Negro Church" in his 1897 report "The Problem of Amusement" at the Atlanta University Conference for the Study of Negro Problems. Du Bois's *The Negro Church* was first delivered as a report to the eighth annual Conference for the Study of Negro Problems at Atlanta University.

18. As a writer, Zora Neale Hurston cast her lot with the younger guard of New Negroes who protested the impositions of race leaders like Du Bois and Alain Locke. See *Fire!! A Quarterly Devoted to the Younger Negro Artists* (1926); David Levering Lewis, *When Harlem Was in Vogue* (New York: Penguin, 1997). Similarly, she was part of a generation of anthropologists who charted new territory on matters of race and more. See Daphne Lamothe, *Inventing the New Negro: Narrative, Culture, and Ethnography* (Philadelphia: University of Pennsylvania Press, 2008); Charles King, *Gods of the Upper Air: How a Circle of Renegade*

Anthropologists Reinvented Race, Sex, and Gender in the Twentieth Century (New York: Anchor, 2020).

19. For a more recent historical treatment of such groups, see Judith Weisenfeld, *New World A-Coming: Black Religion and Religio-Racial Identity in the Great Migration* (New York: NYU Press, 2017).

20. Book note in the *New Yorker,* March 29, 1941, 71; V. F. Calverton, *Where Angels Dare to Tread* (New York: Bobbs-Merrill, 1941). V. F. Calverton was the pen name of the radical activist George Goetz. See Leonard Wilcox, *V. F. Calverton: Radical in the American Grain* (Philadelphia, PA: Temple University Press, 1992).

21. Arthur Huff Fauset, *Black Gods of the Metropolis* (1944; Philadelphia: University of Pennsylvania Press, 2002). For a recent book that takes inspiration from Fauset's study, see Edward E. Curtis IV and Danielle Brune Sigler, *The New Black Gods: Arthur Huff Fauset and the Study of African American Religions* (Bloomington: Indiana University Press, 2009).

22. Mays, *The Negro's God,* 245.

23. See my discussion of this in *Spirit in the Dark.*

24. Calverton, *The Newer Spirit.*

25. Mays, *The Negro's God,* 218.

26. Savage, *Your Spirits Walk Beside Us,* 205–237.

27. For a discussion of Mays's relationship with King, see Jelks, *Benjamin Elijah Mays.* See also: Benjamin E. Mays, *Born to Rebel: An Autobiography* (Athens: University of Georgia Press, 1987).

28. For a discussion of the organizing work of the Left in black communities, see Robin D. G. Kelley, *Hammer and Hoe: Alabama Communists during the Great Depression* (Chapel Hill: University of North Carolina Press, 2015).

29. Richard Wright, "Blueprint for Negro Writing," *New Challenge,* October 1937; Randal Jelks, "Masculinity, Religion, and Modernism: A Consideration of Benjamin Elijah Mays and Richard Wright," *Women, Gender, and Families of Color* 2, no. 1 (Spring 2014): 57–78.

30. Mays, *The Negro's God,* preface (no pagination).

31. Evans, *The Burden of Black Religion,* 203–222. Evans argues that the play actually helped white viewers negotiate their anxieties about the novel interracial mixing common in northern cities by appealing to nostalgia for a remote past in which blacks are at home in the rural South.

32. Mays, *The Negro's God,* preface.

33. Reverdy C. Ransom, "The Fraternal Council of Negro Churches in America," in *Yearbook of Negro Churches, 1935–36,* ed. Bishops of the A.M.E. Church (Wilberforce, OH: A.M.E. Church Publishing, 1936), 24,

quoted in Mary Sawyer, "The Fraternal Council of Negro Churches, 1934–1964," *Church History* 59, no. 1 (March 1990): 52.

34. Ann Douglas, *Terrible Honesty: Mongrel Manhattan in the 1920s* (New York: Farar, Straus and Giroux, 1995).

35. Sarah Azaransky, *The Worldwide Struggle: The International Roots of the Civil Rights Movement* (New York: Oxford University Press, 2017).

36. For work on the impact of Red Scare politics on the black writers and activists, see Mary Helen Washington, *The Other Black List: The African American Literary and Cultural Left of the 1950s* (New York: Columbia University Press, 2014).

37. For a discussion of the competing theologies of black civil rights activism, see Wallace D. Best, "The Right Achieved and the Wrong Way Conquered: J. H. Jackson, Martin Luther King, Jr. and the Conflict Over Civil Rights," *Religion and American Culture: A Journal of Interpretation* 16, no. 2 (Summer 2006): 195–226.

38. This chapter has already captured the growing literature on African American literature. Similarly, especially following the Renaissance of the 1920s, efforts to document and catalogue black literature during this period grew significantly. Mays was one of the very few to think across these fields.

39. Here I thinking about how the social and political context of Jim Crow shaped definitions of the Negro church, discussed here already, and African American literature. For discussion of the latter, see Kenneth Warren, *What Was African American Literature?* (Cambridge, MA: Harvard University Press, 2010).

40. For a discussion of how ideas about religion have shaped the telling of African American history, see Laurie Maffly-Kipp, *Setting Down the Sacred Past: African American Race Narratives* (Cambridge, MA: Harvard University Press, 2009).

41. In fact, such an approach led the earliest histories written on the Harlem Renaissance to label the cultural movement a success or failure in light of what kinds of political dividends black literature and the arts produced for black people. See Nathan Huggins, *Harlem Renaissance* (New York: Oxford University Press, 1971); Lewis, *When Harlem Was in Vogue*; Baker, *Modernism and the Harlem Renaissance*.

42. Lewis, *When Harlem Was in Vogue*, xxiii.

43. For a discussion of the Atlanta University publication series, see Lewis, *W. E. B. Du Bois: Biography of a Race*, 211–237.

44. David Levering Lewis, *W. E. B. Du Bois: The Fight for Equality and the American Century, 1919–1963* (New York: Henry Holt, 2000). The Swiss

sociologist Gunnar Myrdal, an "objective" outsider, was enlisted to document the U.S. race problem, which led to *An American Dilemma: The Negro Problem and Modern Democracy* (New York: Harper and Brothers, 1944).

45. Rayford Whittingham Logan, *African American National Biography*, ed. Henry Louis Gates, Jr. and Evelyn Brooks Higginbotham (New York: Oxford University Press, 2008). Kenneth Robert Janken, *Rayford W. Logan and the Dilemma of the African-American Intellectual* (Amherst: University of Massachusetts Press 1993); August Meier and Elliott Rudwick, *Black History and the Historical Profession, 1915-1980* (Urbana: University of Illinois Press, 1986).

46. Hazel Carby, *Race Men* (Cambridge, MA: Harvard University Press, 2000); Mia Bay et al., eds., *Toward an Intellectual History of Black Women* (Chapel Hill: University of North Carolina Press, 2015).

47. Editorial Board, "Apology," *Phylon* 1, no. 1 (1940): 3–5.

48. Richard J. Powell, *Black Art: A Cultural History* (New York: Thames and Hudson, 2003), 89.

49. Adam Green, *Selling the Race: Culture, Community and Black Chicago, 1940-1955* (Chicago: University of Chicago Press, 2009); Barbara Dianne Savage, *Broadcasting Freedom: Radio, War, and the Politics of Race, 1938-1948* (Chapel Hill: University of North Carolina Press, 1999).

50. Savage, *Broadcasting Freedom*, 91. See also Farah Jasmine Griffin, *Harlem Nocturne: Women Artists and Progressive Politics during World War II* (New York: Basic Civitas Books, 2013), 5–6; Green, *Selling the Race*, 161.

51. "The First Phylon Institute and Twenty-Fifth Atlanta University Conference," *Phylon* 2, no. 3 (1941): 275–288.

52. David A. Hollinger, *After Cloven Tongues of Fire: Protestant Liberalism in Modern American History* (Princeton, NJ: Princeton University Press, 2013); Matthew S. Hedstrom, *The Rise of Liberal Religion: Book Culture and American Spirituality in the Twentieth Century* (New York: Oxford University Press, 2012), 142–213.

53. For a short piece on "racial capitalism," see Robin D. G. Kelley, "What Did Cedric Robinson Mean by Racial Capitalism," *Boston Review*, January 12, 2017, https://bostonreview.net/articles/robin-d-g-kelley-introduction-race-capitalism-justice/.

54. Editorial Board, "Apology," 5. The editors' repeated use of the term "abolish" would seem to be a clear reference to slavery and how the editors understood the significance of this institution in shaping the primary economic problems of the twentieth century.

55. Savage, *Broadcasting Freedom*, 55–56. In the aftermath of World War II, international encounters across the lines of racial and religious difference

also took the form of the fledgling publication *Holiday*, which recast the conversation in the terms of tourism. See Michael Callahan, "A *Holiday* for the Jet Set," *Vanity Fair*, April 11, 2013, https://www.vanityfair.com/cult ure/2013/05/holiday-magazine-history. For a longer history of the spiritual visions occasioned by encounters, see Leigh Eric Schmidt, *Restless Souls: The Making of American Spirituality* (Berkeley: University of California Press, 2012).

56. Molly Worthen, *Apostles of Reason: The Crisis of Authority in American Evangelicalism* (New York: Oxford University Press, 2013).

57. Hutchison, *The Modernist Impulse in American Protestantism*; Samuel Moyn, *The Last Utopia: Human Rights in History* (Cambridge, MA: Harvard University Press, 2012).

58. Editorial Board, "Apology," 3. "A voice cries out: 'In the wilderness prepare the way of the Lord, make straight in the desert a highway for our God'" (Isaiah 40:3; NRSV).

59. Wendy L. Wall, *Inventing the "American Way": The Politics of Consensus from the New Deal to the Civil Rights Movement* (New York: Oxford University Press, 2008), 4.

60. Bender and Klassen, *After Pluralism* 1–30.

61. Evans, *The Burden of Black Religion*, 12.

62. Masuzawa, *The Invention of World Religions*.

63. Savage, *Your Spirits Walk Beside Us*; William D. Hart, *Black Religion: Malcolm X, Julius Lester, and Jan Willis* (New York: Palgrave Macmillan, 2008), 8.

64. Orsi, *Between Heaven and Earth*, 6.

65. Jamil Drake, *To Know the Soul of the People: American Folk Studies and Racial Politics of Popular Religion, 1900–1940* (New York: Oxford University Press, 2022).

66. "News and Notes," *American Journal of Sociology* 62, no. 3 (Nov. 1956): 332.

67. Edward Nelson Palmer, *Elder Michaux and His Church of God: A Sociological Interpretation*, Section 3, Row 6, Box 6, Folder 5, Fisk University Library.

68. John Eligon, "A Black Evangelist Who Opposed King," *New York Times*, April 2, 2018, https://www.nytimes.com/2018/04/02/us/black-evangelist-elder-michaux-opposed-dr-king.html.

69. Edward Nelson Palmer, "The Religious Acculturation of the Negro," *Phylon* 5, no. 3 (1944): 261.

70. Palmer, "The Religious Acculturation of the Negro," 265.

71. Melville Herskovits, *The Myth of the Negro Past* (1941; Boston: Beacon Press, 1990); Palmer, "The Religious Acculturation of the Negro," 264–265.

72. Venetria K. Patton and Maureen Honey, eds., *Double-Take: A Revisionist Harlem Renaissance Anthology* (New Brunswick, NJ: Rutgers University Press, 2010), 243.

73. Katharine Capshaw Smith, *Children's Literature of the Harlem Renaissance* (Bloomington: Indiana University Press, 2006). Nesby pastored St. John AME Church in Birmingham, and he taught and served as dean at Greater Payne University.

74. Effie Lee Newsome, "Early Figures in Haitian Methodism," *Phylon* 4, no. 1 (1944): 51–61. Newsome's privileging of Methodism over Catholicism is consistent with Robert Orsi's account of how the field of religious studies contributed to a discourse on good and bad religion in the United States (*Between Heaven and Earth*, 171).

75. Other articles in *Phylon* reveal a concern with toleration and religious freedom. See Marc Moreland, "Roger Williams: Discipline for Today," *Phylon* 6, no. 2 (1945): 137–140; Biller Geter Thomas and Ira De A. Reed, "France and the Traditions of Freedom," *Phylon* 4, Supplement: "Freedom in the Modern World: Four Broadcasts by the People's College of Atlanta University" (1943): 18–23.

76. Newsome, "Early Figures in Haitian Methodism," 55.

77. Newsome, "Early Figures in Haitian Methodism," 55.

78. For several works that examine the emergence of a Judeo-Christian sensibility, see K. Healan Gaston, "Interpreting Judeo-Christianity in America," *Relegere: Studies in Religion and Reception* 2, no. 2 (2012): 291–304 and *Imagining Judeo-Christian America: Religion, Secularism, and the Redefinition of Democracy* (Chicago: University of Chicago Press, 2019); Mark Silk, "Notes on the Judeo-Christian Tradition in America," *American Quarterly* 36, no. 1 (Spring 1984): 65–85; Kevin M. Schultz, *Tri-Faith America: How Catholics and Jews Held Postwar America to Its Protestant Promise* (New York: Oxford University Press, 2013); Ronit Y. Stahl, *Enlisting Faith: How the Military Chaplaincy Shaped Religion and State in Modern America* (Cambridge, MA: Harvard University Press, 2017). In chapter 3 of *Spirit in the Dark* I look at how this Judeo-Christian sensibility infused African American culture.

79. Savage, *Your Spirits Walk Beside Us*, 1–19.

80. Rene Maran, Monsignor Kiwanuka, and W. Mercer Cook, "An Interview with Monsignor Kiwanuka, Bishop of Massaka," *Phylon* 1, no. 1 (1940): 31–35.

81. Brent Hayes Edwards, *The Practice of Diaspora: Literature, Translation, and the Rise of Black Internationalism* (Cambridge, MA: Harvard University Press, 2003), 69. The same year that Mercer Cook translated Maran's

profile in *Phylon*, he also authored an essay on Maran in the *Journal of Negro History*. See Mercer Cook, "The Literary Contribution of the French West Indian," *Journal of Negro History* 25, no. 4 (1940): 520–530.

82. Maran's presentation of Kiwanuka reflects both the specific context of World War II and the longer Christian history of the category of religion. My thinking in this regard is informed by Talal Asad, *Genealogies of Religion: Discipline and Reasons of Power in Christianity and Islam* (Baltimore, MD: Johns Hopkins University Press, 1993), chapter 1.

83. Emile Durkheim, *The Elementary Forms of Religious Life* (1912), trans. Karen Fields (New York: Free Press, 1995).

84. S. Brent Plate, *Walter Benjamin, Religion, and Aesthetics: Rethinking Religion through the Arts* (New York: Routledge, 2004).

85. Maran, Kiwanuka and Cook, "An Interview with Monsignor Kiwanuka," 32.

86. Maran, Kiwanuka and Cook, "An Interview with Monsignor Kiwanuka," 33.

87. For two helpful treatments of race and American Catholicism, see John T. McGreevy, *Parish Boundaries: The Catholic Encounter with Race in the Twentieth-Century Urban North* (Chicago: University of Chicago Press, 1998) and Thomas Sugrue, *The Origins of the Urban Crisis: Race and Inequality in Postwar Detroit* (Princeton, NJ: Princeton University Press, 2014).

88. *Rerum Ecclesiae, Encyclical of Pope Pius XI on Catholic Missions to our Venerable Brethren, the Patriarchs, Primates, Archbishops, Bishops, and other Ordinaries in Peace and Communion with the Apostolic See*, February 28, 1926, Rome. https://www.vatican.va/content/pius-xi/en/encyclicals/documents/hf_p-xi_enc_28021926_rerum-ecclesiae.html.

89. Joseph Kiwanuka was consecrated as a bishop on May 25, 1939.

90. Maran, Kiwanuka and Cook, "An Interview with Monsignor Kiwanuka," 35.

91. For a book that is attentive to the significance of Catholicism for Negritude, see Gary Wilder, *Freedom Time: Negritude, Decolonization, and the Future of the World* (Durham, NC: Duke University Press, 2015).

92. Philip Butcher, "Introduction," in *The William Stanley Braithwaite Reader*, ed. Philip Butcher (Ann Arbor: University of Michigan Press, 1972), 1–7.

93. Elayne Oliphant, "Beyond Blasphemy or Devotion: Art, the Secular, and Catholicism in Paris," *Journal of the Royal Anthropological Institute* 21, no. 2 (May 2015): 352–373.

94. Gunn, *The Interpretation of Otherness*.

95. Gaines, *Uplifting the Race.*
96. Editorial Board, "Apology."
97. William Stanley Braithwaite, "Ascension," *Phylon* 1, no. 1 (1940): 54–55.
98. Braithwaite, "Ascension," 54. This recalls the sacred value attributed to literacy that Du Bois (as discussed in chapter 2) once described as "cabbalistic," a form of esoteric knowledge that black people pursued with religious fervor in the aftermath of Emancipation. See W. E. B. Du Bois, *The Souls of Black Folk* (New Haven, CT: Yale University Press, 2015), 8.
99. Hutchison, *The Modernist Impulse in American Protestantism.*

Chapter 4

1. Fred Moten, "The Case of Blackness," *Criticism* 1, no. 2 (Spring 2008): 177–218.
2. William D. Hart, "The Afterlife of the Black Church," *Religion Dispatches*, March 15, 2010.
3. "Black Faculty in Religion Departments at the Nation's Highest-Ranking Universities," editorial, *Journal of Blacks in Higher Education* 7 (1995): 28–31.
4. Since 1986 (following Long, Williams, and Scott) the AAR has elected four additional African American members as president: Peter Paris, Emilie Townes, Eddie Glaude, and Marla Frederick.
5. Henry Goldschmidt and Eliza McAlister, eds., *Race, Nation, and Religion in the Americas* (New York: Oxford University Press, 2004), 7.
6. Masuzawa, *The Invention of World Religions.*
7. Charles Long, interviewed by Carolyn M. Jones and Julia M. Hardy, "From Colonialism to Community: Religion and Culture in Charles H. Long's *Significations,*" Callaloo, no. 35 (Spring 1988): 258–271.
8. For accounts of that Christian/colonial genealogy, see Asad, *Genealogies of Religion*; David Chidester, *Savage Systems: Colonialism and Comparative Religions in Southern Africa* (Charlottesville: University of Virginia Press, 1996). For a concise account of this genealogy, see Smith, "Religion, Religions, Religious," 269–284.
9. Long, *Significations.* 7.
10. Charles Long, "Black Religion in America," Address at the 1980 annual meeting of the Society for the Study of Black Religion. (Gratitude to Larry Murphy for sending me a copy of this lecture on CD several years before

it was made available online at: https://radar.auctr.edu/islandora/object/ auc.120%3A0072).

11. On April 8, 1966, *Time* featured the cover story "Is God Dead?," which popularized debates concerning the challenges that scientific gains posed to traditional ideas about God. For a signal work that hailed the secularization thesis, see Peter L. Berger, *The Heretical Imperative: Contemporary Possibilities of Religious Affirmation* (Garden City, NY: Anchor, 1979).

12. Here I am thinking about the body of scholarship that followed the publication of Charles Taylor's *A Secular Age* (Cambridge, MA: Harvard University Press, 2007). An excellent primer for the interdisciplinary field of secularism studies can be found online at "The Immanent Frame," https://tif.ssrc.org/.

13. Bruno Latour, *We Have Never Been Modern*, trans. Catherine Porter (Cambridge, MA: Harvard University Press, 1993); Kahn and Lloyd, *Race and Secularism in America*.

14. Josef Sorett, "Secular Compared to What? The Trope of Black Sacred/Secular Fluidity," in Kahn and Lloyd, *Race and Secularism in America*, 43–73.

15. See the discussion of E. Franklin Frazier's debate with Melville Herskovits in Albert Raboteau, *Slave Religion: The "Invisible Institution" in the Antebellum South*, updated ed. (New York: Oxford University Press, 2004), 48, 55. A similar argument is posed for the contemporary era in the definition of a "black sacred cosmos" by C. Eric Lincoln and Lawrence Mamiya, *The Black Church in the African American Experience* (Durham, NC: Duke University Press, 1990).

16. Several more recent works extend Long's provocations, but they also highlight the degree to which Christian and African-derived religions are entangled. For example, see Chireau, *Black Magic*; Dianne M. Stewart, *Three Eyes for the Journey: African Dimensions of the Jamaican Religious Experience* (New York: Oxford University Press, 2005); James Noel, *Black Religion and the Imagination of Matter in the Atlantic World* (New York: Palgrave Macmillan, 2009); Hucks, *Yoruba Traditions and African American Religious Nationalism*.

17. In particular, Long highlighted then-recent works on slavery and American history, including John W. Blassingame, *The Slave Community: Plantation Life in the Antebellum South* (New York: Oxford University Press, 1979); Eugene Genovese, *Roll, Jordan, Roll: The World the Slaves Made* (New York: Vintage, 1976); and Lawrence Levine, *Black Culture and Black Consciousness: Afro-American Folk Thought from Slavery to Freedom* (1977; New York: Oxford University Press, 2007).

18. See, for example, Fessenden, *Culture and Redemption*; Janet Jakobsen and Ann Pellegrini, eds., *Secularisms* (Durham, NC: Duke University Press, 2008); John Lardas Modern, *Secularism in Antebellum America* (Chicago: University of Chicago Press, 2011); Philip Gorski et al., eds., *The Post-Secular in Question: Religion in Contemporary Society* (New York: NYU Press, 2012).

19. See my discussion of the slave narratives in chapter 1.

20. Jack E. White, "The Beauty of Black Art," *Time*, October 10, 1994.

21. The Historymakers: The Digital Repository for the Black Experience, "Jack E. White," February 28, 2013, https://www.thehistorymakers.org/biogra phy/jack-white.

22. Henry Louis Gates Jr., "Black Creativity," *Time*, October 10, 1994.

23. Gates, "Black Creativity," 75.

24. Gates, "Black Creativity," 74.

25. Gates, "The Trope of a New Negro."

26. Robert Boynton, "The New Intellectuals," *The Atlantic Monthly*, March 1995.

27. Boynton, "The New Intellectuals."

28. Adolph Reed, Jr., "What Are the Drums Saying Booker? The Current Crisis of the Black Intellectual," *Village Voice*, April 11, 1995, 31–36. For a treatment of Reed's critique of the black public intellectual, see Scott Sherman, "Fighting Words: Adolph Reed's Crusade against the New Black Intellectuals," *Lingua Franca*, March 1997, 38–48.

29. Reed, "What Are the Drums Saying Booker?"

30. For an excellent example of an effort to think across this division, see Cornel West, ed., "Religion and the Left," *Monthly Review: An Independent Socialist Magazine*, vol. 36, no. 3 (July–August 1984).

31. Kelley, " 'We Are Not What We Seem,' " 88.

32. Adolph Reed Jr., *The Jesse Jackson Phenomenon* (New Haven, CT: Yale University Press, 1986).

33. Michele Wallace, "Afterword: 'Why Are There No Great Black Artists?': The Problem of Visuality in African-American Culture," in *Black Popular Culture: A Michele Wallace Project*, ed. Gina Dent (Seattle, WA: Bay Press, 1992), 339.

34. Stuart Hall, "What Is This 'Black' in Black Popular Culture?," in Dent, *Black Popular Culture*, 21–33. Hall's opening essay to the volume captures well the push to rethink blackness as a hybrid form. He writes, "By definition, black popular culture is a contradictory space. It is a sight of strategic contestation. But it can never be simplified or explained in terms of simple binary oppositions that are still habitually used to map it out: high and

low; resistance versus incorporation; authentic versus inauthentic; experiential versus formal; opposition versus homogenization. There are always positions to be won in popular culture, but no struggle can capture popular culture for our side or theirs."

35. Among those who reviewed the book were two scholars of black literature: Hortense Spillers, *African American Review*, vol. 29, no. 1 (1995): 123–126; Jacquelyn Y. McLendon, "Review: When the Cultural is Political," *Women's Review of Books*, vol. 11, no. 8 (May 1994): 27–28.

36. Wallace, "Afterword," 345.

37. Wallace, "Afterword," 343.

38. Wallace, "Afterword," 344.

39. bell hooks, "Postmodern Blackness," *Postmodern Culture*, vol. 1, no. 1 (Sept. 1990).

40. Trey Ellis, "Notes on a Lifetime of Passing," *The New Yorker*, September 22, 2017.

41. Itabari Njeri, "Trey's Chi: Trey Ellis: He's Hot, He's Controversial and Breaking New Ground in Black Literature," *Los Angeles Times*, January 23, 1989.

42. Trey Ellis, "The New Black Aesthetic," *Callaloo*, no. 38 (Winter 1989): 236.

43. Nelson George, "Buppies, B-Boys, Baps, and Bohos," *Village Voice*, March 17, 1992; Maureen Mahon, *Right to Rock: The Black Rock Coalition and the Cultural Politics of Race* (Durham, NC: Duke University Press, 2004), 7.

44. Nelson George, *Post-Soul Nation: The Explosive, Contradictory, Triumphant, and Tragic 1980s as Experienced by African American (Previously Known as Black and Before That Negroes* (New York: Penguin, 2005), 142; Greg Tate, "Cult-Nats Meet Freaky-Deke," in Tate, *Flyboy in the Buttermilk: Essays on Contemporary Culture* (New York: Simon and Schuster, 1992), 198–210. This essay was originally published in the *Village Voice*, December 1986.

45. Tate, "Cult-Nats Meet Freaky Deke," 198.

46. Tate, "Cult-Nats Meet Freaky Deke," 207.

47. Tate, "Cult-Nats Meet Freaky Deke," 209.

48. Tate, "Cult-Nats Meet Freaky Deke," 207.

49. Tate, "Cult-Nats Meet Freaky Deke," 210.

50. Tate, "Cult-Nats Meet Freaky Deke," 206.

51. For writing that pays tribute to Wood and discusses the mystery surrounding his disappearance, see Major Jackson, "Surroundings More Congenial: The Perils of Hiking While Black," *Orion: People and Nature*, December 29, 2020; Lee Smith, "Gone but Not Forgotten," *Washington Examiner*, September 8, 2017.

52. Joe Wood, "The Malcolm X Factor," *Village Voice*, May 29, 1990. Wood begins the article with an invitation to a conversation between "brothers and sisters," and the essay proceeds to invite black people to think more critically about their investments in Malcolm X and to do more with his legacy than wear it as a brand.

53. Joe Wood, "Malcolm X and the New Blackness," in *Malcolm X: In Our Own Image*, ed. Joe Wood (New York: Anchor Books, 1994), 1–17. One of the biggest changes in the essay from the *Village Voice* version to the book introduction is that Wood seems to pivot from a black audience to an interracial audience in the book. His references to black people shifts from us/we language to they/them.

54. "When I was a child, I talked like a child, I thought like a child, I reasoned like a child. When I became a man, I put the ways of childhood behind me" (I Corinthians 13:11; New International Version). The essay, then, tells a story of Woods coming of age even as he calls for a more mature discussion of Malcolm X and race more generally.

55. Wood, "Malcolm X and the New Blackness," 15.

56. Cornel West, *Race Matters* (Boston: Beacon Press, 1993), 21–32.

57. Wood, "The Malcolm X Factor." In the original *Village Voice* essay Wood makes a point of distinguishing his vision for a New Black from multiculturalism, on one hand, and what Ellis identifies as a "cultural mullato," on the other. See Ellis, "The New Black Aesthetic," 235.

58. Wood, "Malcom X and the New Blackness," 7.

59. Wood, "Malcolm X and the New Blackness," 8–10.

60. Wood, "The Malcolm X Factor." Wood discusses this in greater detail in the *Village Voice* essay, explaining that Malcolm's desire was to have the autobiography serve as "the principle testament to Muhammad's Truth." For more background, see Alex Haley's epilogue to *The Autobiography of Malcolm X: As Told to Alex Haley* (New York: Ballantine, 1973), 390–463.

61. Wood, "Malcolm X and the New Blackness," 11–13.

62. Wood, "Malcolm X and the New Blackness," 4–5.

63. Wood, "Malcolm X and the New Blackness," 13.

64. Wood, "Malcolm X and the New Blackness," 6–7.

65. Wood, "The Malcolm X Factor." In the *Village Voice* article Wood explicitly states that he hoped the New Blackness would "move us away from the dubious religion of 'essential Blackness.'"

66. Wood, "Malcolm X and the New Blackness," 15.

67. Wood, "Malcolm X and the New Blackness," 16.

68. Elizabeth Alexander, *The Light of the World: A Memoir* (New York: Grand Central Publishing, 2015); Ta-Nehisi Coates, *Between*

the World and Me (New York: Speigel and Grau, 2015); Gregory Pardlo, *Digest* (New York: Four Way Books, 2014); Claudia Rankine, *Citizen: An American Lyric* (Minneapolis, MN: Gray Wolf Press, 2014).

69. Vinson Cunningham, "How Chris Jackson Is Building a Black Literary Movement," *New York Times Magazine*, February 2, 2016.

70. See, for instance, Concepción de León, "Ta-Nehisi Coates and the Making of a Public Intellectual," *New York Times*, September 29, 2017; Ismail Muhammad, "Cornel West's Reckless Criticism of Ta-Nehisi Coates," *Slate*, December 20, 2017.

71. Coates, *Between the World and Me*, 28.

72. Jesse McCarthy, "Why Does Ta-Nehisi Coates Say Less Than He Knows?," *The Nation*, November 15, 2015.

73. Julie Bosman and Joseph Goldstein, "Timeline for a Body: 4 Hours in the Middle of a Ferguson Street," *New York Times*, August 23, 2014, http://www.nytimes.com/2014/08/24/us/michael-brown-a-bodys-timeline-4-hours-on-a-ferguson-street.html.

74. See discussion of Matthews in chapter 2.

75. Vinson Cunningham, "Can Black Art Ever Escape the Politics of Race?," *New York Times Magazine*, August 20, 2015.

76. David Crouch, "Woman Who Defied 300 Neo-Nazis at Swedish Rally Speaks of Anger," *The Guardian*, May 4, 2016.

77. Wallace, "Afterword."

78. For a discussion of the politics of black fashion, see Tanisha C. Ford, *Liberated Threads: Black Women, Style, and the Global Politics of Style* (Chapel Hill: University of North Carolina Press, 2017).

79. Alex Altman, "Person of the Year: The Shortlist—Number 4, Black Lives Matter," *Time*, February 28, 2015.

80. Barbara Ransby, "The Class Politics of Black Lives Matter," *Dissent*, Fall 2015.

81. Sophia Tesfaye, "Violence Returns to the Trump Campaign: Black Protester Assaulted by Trump Supporters at 'New York Values' Rally," *Salon*, April 12, 2016.

82. John L. Jackson Jr., "Lights, Camera, Action!," *Public Culture* 28, no. 1 (Jan. 2016): 3–8.

83. Jelani Cobb, "The Matter of Black Lives," *The New Yorker*, March 14, 2016.

84. Higginbotham, *Righteous Discontent*, 185–230.

85. Du Bois, *The Souls of Black Folk* (State College: Pennsylvania State University Press, 2006), 136–148.

86. Nyle Fort, "The Religion of Protest," *The Cut*, January 31, 2022, https://www.thecut.com/2022/01/black-lives-matter-religion-spirituality.html.

87. Hebah Farrag, "The Role of Spirit in the #BlackLivesMatter Movement: A Conversation with Activist and Artist Patrisse Cullors," *Religion Dispatches*, June 24, 2015.

88. Tometi used to identify in this way in the bio on her website (opaltometi. org). One still finds "liberation theology" references in other bios of her, for example, Omega, "Opal Tometi," accessed September 13, 2022, https:// www.eomega.org/workshops/teachers/opal-tometi.

89. Richard Iton, *In Search of the Black Fantastic: Politics and Popular Culture in the Post–Civil Rights Era* (New York: Oxford University Press, 2008), 16–17. The point here is a privileging of heterodoxy, or what Nyle Fort refers to as "spiritual promiscuity."

90. Noah Berlatsky, "Hashtag Activism Isn't a Cop-Out," *The Atlantic Monthly*, January 7, 2015.

91. Tiffany Lethabo King, Jenell Navarro, and Andrea Smith, eds., *Otherwise Worlds: Against Settler Colonialism and Anti-Blackness* (Durham, NC: Duke University Press, 2020).

92. Amiri Baraka, "Foreword," in *Black Fire: An Anthology of Afro-American Writing*, ed. Amiri Baraka and Larry Neal (1968; Baltimore, MD: Black Classic Press, 2007).

93. Alexander, *The Light of the World*.

94. Jericho Brown, *The New Testament* (Port Townsend, WA: Copper Canyon Press, 2014).

95. Sophia Nguyen, "Elbow Room: How the Dark Room Collective Made Space for a Generation of African-American Writers," *Harvard Magazine*, March–April 2016.

96. Jamila Lemieux, "Trying to Forgive the Black Church," *The Nation*, July 2, 2015.

Bibliography

Abdullah, Zain. *Black Mecca: The African Muslims of Harlem*. New York: Oxford University Press, 2010.

Alexander, Elizabeth. *The Light of the World: A Memoir*. New York: Grand Central Publishing, 2015.

Alexander, Estrella. *Afro-Pentecostalism: Black Pentecostal and Charismatic Christianity in History and Culture*. New York: NYU Press, 2011.

Alryyes, Ala A. "Notes on 'The Life of Oman ibn Said, Written by Himself' (1831)." In *The Multilingual Anthology of American Literature*, edited by Marc Shell and Werner Sollors, 58–61. New York: New York University Press, 2000.

Altman, Alex. "Person of the Year: The Shortlist—Number 4, Black Lives Matter." *Time*, February 28, 2015.

Andrews, William L., ed. *Sisters of the Spirit: Three Black Women's Autobiographies of the Nineteenth Century*. Bloomington: Indiana University Press, 1986.

Andrews, William L., Frances Smith Foster, and Trudier Harris, eds. *The Oxford Companion to African American Literature*. New York: Oxford University Press, 1997.

Anidjar, Gil. "The Idea of an Anthropology of Christianity." *Interventions: International Journal of Postcolonial Studies* 11, no. 3 (2009): 367–393.

Asad, Talal. *Formations of the Secular: Christianity, Islam, Modernity*. Stanford, CA: Stanford University Press, 2003.

Asad, Talal. *Genealogies of Religion: Discipline and Reasons of Power in Christianity and Islam*. Baltimore, MD: Johns Hopkins University Press, 1993.

Asad, Talal. "Reading a Modern Classic: W. C. Smith's 'The Meaning and End of Religion.'" *History of Religions* 40, no. 3 (Feb. 2001): 205–222.

Azaransky, Sarah. *The Worldwide Struggle: The International Roots of the Civil Rights Movement*. New York: Oxford University Press, 2017.

Baker, Houston A., Jr. *Modernism and the Harlem Renaissance*. Chicago: University of Chicago Press, 1987.

Baker, Houston A., Jr., and Patricia Almond. *Afro-American Literary Study in the 1990s*. Chicago: University of Chicago Press, 1989.

Banks, Adelle M. "Five Religious Facts You Might Not Know about Frederick Douglass." *Religion News Service*, June 19, 2013.

Baraka, Amiri. "'Black' Is a Country" (1962). In Amiri Baraka, *Home: Social Essays*, 101–106. New York: Akashic Press, 2009.

Baraka, Amiri, and Larry Neal, eds. *Black Fire: An Anthology of Afro-American Writing*. Baltimore, MD: Black Classic Press, 2007. First published 1968.

Bartleman, Frank. *Witness to Pentecost: The Life of Frank Bartleman*. New York: Garland, 1985.

Bay, Mia, Farah J. Griffin, Martha S. Jones, and Barbara D. Savage, eds. *Toward an Intellectual History of Black Women*. Chapel Hill: University of North Carolina Press, 2015.

Bender, Courtney, and Pamela Klassen, eds. *After Pluralism: Reimagining Religious Engagement*. New York: Columbia University Press, 2011.

Bercovitch, Sacvan. *The Puritan Origins of the American Self*. New Haven, CT: Yale University Press, 2011.

Berger, Peter L. *The Heretical Imperative: Contemporary Possibilities of Religious Affirmation*. Garden City, NY: Anchor, 1979.

Berlatsky, Noah. "Hashtag Activism Isn't a Cop-Out." *The Atlantic Monthly*, January 7, 2015.

Best, Wallace D. "The Right Achieved and the Wrong Way Conquered: J. H. Jackson, Martin Luther King, Jr. and the Conflict over Civil Rights." *Religion and American Culture: A Journal of Interpretation* 16, no. 2 (Summer 2006): 195–226.

"The Black Church Is Dead: Long Live the Black Church." Editorial. Religion Dispatches (2010).

"Black Faculty in Religion Departments at the Nation's Highest-Ranking Universities." Editorial. *Journal of Blacks in Higher Education* 7 (1995): 28–31.

Blain, Keisha N. *Set the World on Fire: Black Nationalist Women and the Global Struggle for Freedom*. Philadelphia: University of Pennsylvania Press, 2019.

Blassingame, John W. *The Slave Community: Plantation Life in the Antebellum South*. New York: Oxford University Press, 1979.

Blight, David. *Frederick Douglass: Prophet of Freedom*. New York: Simon and Schuster, 2018.

Blum, Edward. *W. E. B. Du Bois: American Prophet*. Philadelphia: University of Pennsylvania Press, 2009.

Blumhofer, Edith. *Restoring the Faith: The Assemblies of God, Pentecostalism, and American Culture*. Champagne: University of Illinois Press, 1993.

Bosman, Julie, and Joseph Goldstein. "Timeline for a Body: 4 Hours in the Middle of a Ferguson Street." *New York Times*. August 23, 2014. http://www.nytimes.com/2014/08/24/us/michael-brown-a-bodys-timeline-4-hours-on-a-ferguson-street.html.

Boynton, Robert. "The New Intellectuals." *The Atlantic Monthly*, March 1995.

Braithwaite, William Stanley. "Ascension." *Phylon* 1, no. 1 (1940): 54–55.

Bramen, Carrie Tirado. *The Uses of Variety: Modern Americanism and the Quest for National Distinctiveness.* Cambridge, MA: Harvard University Press, 2000.

Brooks, Joanna. *American Lazarus: Religion and the Rise of African American and Native American Literatures.* New York: Oxford University Press, 2003.

Brown, Jericho. *The New Testament.* Port Townsend, WA: Copper Canyon Press, 2014.

Butcher, Philip, ed. *The William Stanley Braithwaite Reader.* Ann Arbor: University of Michigan Press, 1972.

Butler, Anthea. *Women in the Church of God in Christ: Making a Sanctified World.* Chapel Hill: University of North Carolina Press, 2007.

Butler, Jon. *Becoming America: The Revolution before 1776.* Cambridge, MA: Harvard University Press, 2000.

Callahan, Leslie D. "Fleshly Manifestations: Charles Fox Parham's Quest for the Sanctified Body." PhD diss., Princeton University, 2002.

Callahan, Michael. "A *Holiday* for the Jet Set." *Vanity Fair,* April 11, 2013. https://www.vanityfair.com/culture/2013/05/holiday-magazine-history.

Calverton, V. F. *The Newer Spirit: A Sociological Criticism of Literature.* New York: Boni and Liveright, 1925.

Calverton, V. F. *Where Angels Dare to Tread.* New York: Bobbs-Merrill, 1941.

Cannon, Katie G., and Anthony B. Pinn, eds. *The Oxford Handbook of African American Theology.* New York: Oxford University Press, 2014.

Carby, Hazel. *Race Men.* Cambridge, MA: Harvard University Press, 2000.

Carretta, Vincent. *Equiano, the African: Biography of a Self-Made Man.* New York: Penguin, 2005.

Carretta, Vincent, ed. *Olaudah Equiano: The Interesting Narrative and Other Writings.* New York: Norton, 2003.

Carretta, Vincent, ed. *Unchained Voices: An Anthology of Black Authors in the English- Speaking World of the 18th Century.* Lexington: University Press of Kentucky, 2004.

Carter, J. Kameron. Guest editor, "Special Issue: Religion and the Future of Blackness," *South Atlantic Quarterly* 112, no. 4 (Fall 2013).

Carter, J. Kameron. *Race: A Theological Account.* New York: Oxford University Press, 2008.

Chesnutt, Charles W. *The Conjure Woman.* 1899. Introduction by Robert Farnsworth. Ann Arbor: University of Michigan Press, 1969.

Chidester, David. *Savage Systems: Colonialism and Comparative Religions in Southern Africa.* Charlottesville: University of Virginia Press, 1996.

Chireau, Yvonne. *Black Magic: The African American Conjuring Tradition.* Berkeley: University of California Press, 2003.

Chude-Sokei, Louis, ed. "States of Black Studies." Special issue of *Black Scholar* 44, no. 2 (Summer 2014.)

Coates, Ta-Nehisi. *Between the World and Me.* New York: Speigel and Grau, 2015.

Cobb, Jelani. "The Matter of Black Lives." *The New Yorker,* March 14, 2016.

Collins, Patricia Hill, and Sirma Bilge. *Intersectionality.* New York: Polity, 2020.

Cook, Mercer. "The Literary Contribution of the French West Indian." *Journal of Negro History* 25, no. 4 (1940): 520–530.

Crenshaw, Kimberlé. "Mapping the Margins: Intersectionality, Identity Politics and Violence against Women of Color." *Stanford Law Review* 43, no. 6 (July 1991): 1241–1299.

Crouch, David. "Woman Who Defied 300 Neo-Nazis at Swedish Rally Speaks of Anger." *The Guardian,* May 4, 2016.

Cugoano, Quobna Ottobah. *Thoughts and Sentiments on the Evil of Slavery.* New York: Penguin, 1999.

Cunningham, Vinson. "Can Black Art Ever Escape the Politics of Race?" *New York Times Magazine,* August 20, 2015.

Cunningham, Vinson. "How Chris Jackson Is Building a Black Literary Movement." *New York Times Magazine,* February 2, 2016.

Curtis, Edward E., IV, and Danielle Brune Sigler. *The New Black Gods: Arthur Huff Fauset and the Study of African American Religions.* Bloomington: Indiana University Press, 2009.

Daniels, David Douglas, III. "The Cultural Renewal of Slave Religion: Charles Price Jones and the Emergence of the Holiness Movement in Mississippi." PhD diss., Union Theological Seminary, 1992.

Davenport, Frederick. *Primitive Traits in Religious Revivals: A Study in Mental and Social Evolution.* London: Macmillan, 1905.

De León, Concepción. "Ta-Nehisi Coates and the Making of a Public Intellectual." *New York Times,* September 29, 2017.

Dent, Gina, ed. *Black Popular Culture: A Michele Wallace Project.* Seattle, WA: Bay Press, 1992.

Dewey, John. *Art as Experience.* New York: TarcherPerigree, 2005.

Diakite, Dianne M. Stewart, and Tracey E. Hucks. "Africana Religious Studies: Toward a Transdisciplinary Agenda in an Emerging Field." *Journal of Africana Religions* 1, no. 1 (2013): 28–77.

Douglas, Ann. *Terrible Honesty: Mongrel Manhattan in the 1920s.* New York: Farrar, Straus and Giroux, 1995.

Douglass, Frederick. *Narrative of the Life of Frederick Douglass, an American Slave,* ed. With an introduction by Deborah McDowell. Oxford: Oxford University Press, 1999.

Drake, Jamil. *To Know the Soul of the People: American Folk Studies and Racial Politics of Popular Religion, 1900–1940.* New York: Oxford University Press, 2022.

Du Bois, W. E. B. *The Gift of Black Folk.* Garden City, NY: Square One, 2009.

Du Bois, W. E. B. *The Negro Church: A Report of a Social Study Made under the Direction of Atlanta University.* Walnut Creek, CA: Altamira Press, 1903.

Du Bois, W.E.B. *The Souls of Black Folk.* State College: Pennsylvania State University Press, 2006.

Du Bois, W.E.B. *The Souls of Black Folk*. Norton Critical Edition, ed. Henry Louis Gates Jr. and Terry Hume Oliver. New York: Norton, 1999.

Du Bois, W.E.B. "The Strivings of the Negro People," *Atlantic Monthly*, August 1897.

Durkheim, Emile. *The Elementary Forms of Religious Life*. 1912. Translated by Karen Fields. New York: Free Press, 1995.

Editorial Board, "Apology," *Phylon* 1, no. 1 (1940): 3–5.

Edwards, Brent Hayes. *The Practice of Diaspora: Literature, Translation, and the Rise of Black Internationalism*. Cambridge, MA: Harvard University Press, 2003.

Edwards, Erica R. *Charisma and the Fictions of Black Leadership*. Minneapolis: University of Minnesota Press, 2012.

Edwards, E. 2016. "Foreword." In *The Terms of Order: Political Science and the Myth of Leadership*, edited by C. Robinson. Chapel Hill: University of North Carolina Press, 2016.

Eligon, John. "A Black Evangelist Who Opposed King." *New York Times*, April 2, 2018. https://www.nytimes.com/2018/04/02/us/black-evangelist-elder-michaux-opposed-dr-king.html.

Eliot, T. S. "Religion and Literature." In *The Faith That Illuminates*, edited by V. A. Demant, 31–54. Leiden: E. J. Brill, 1935.

Ellis, Trey. "The New Black Aesthetic." *Callaloo*, no. 38 (Winter 1989): 236.

Ellis, Trey. "Notes on a Lifetime of Passing." *The New Yorker*, September 22, 2017.

Evans, Curtis J. *The Burden of Black Religion*. New York: Oxford University Press, 2008.

Farrag, Hebah. "The Role of Spirit in the #BlackLivesMatter Movement: A Conversation with Activist and Artist Patrisse Cullors." *Religion Dispatches*, June 24, 2015.

Fauset, Arthur Huff. *Black Gods of the Metropolis*. Philadelphia: University of Pennsylvania Press, 2002. First published 1944.

Fessenden, Tracy. *Culture and Redemption: Religion, the Secular, and American Literature*. Princeton, NJ: Princeton University Press, 2008.

Fessenden, Tracy. "'The Secular' as Opposed to What?" *New Literary History* 38, no. 4 (August 2007): 631–636.

Fessenden, Tracy, Nicholas F. Radel, and Magdalena J. Zaborowska, eds. *The Puritan Origins of American Sex*. New York: Routledge, 2001.

Fisher, Thomas. *The Negro's Memorial, or Abolitionist's Catechism, Abridged*. 1825. London: Forgotten Books, 2019.

Ford, Tanisha C. *Liberated Threads: Black Women, Style, and the Global Politics of Style*. Chapel Hill: University of North Carolina Press, 2017.

Foreman, P. Gabrielle. *Activist Sentiments: Reading Black Women in the Nineteenth Century*. Champagne: University of Illinois Press, 2009.

Fort, Nyle. "The Religion of Protest," *The Cut*, January 31, 2022, https://www.thecut.com/2022/01/black-lives-matter-religion-spirituality.html.

Foster, Frances Smith. *Witnessing Slavery: The Development of the Ante-Bellum Slave Narratives*. Madison: University of Wisconsin Press, 1994.

Foster, Frances Smith, and Chanta Haywood. "Christian Recordings: Afro-Protestantism, Its Press, and the Production of African-American Literature." *Religion & Literature* 27, no. 1 (Spring 1995): 15–33.

Foucault, Michel. *The Order of Things: An Archaeology of the Human Sciences*. New York: Vintage, 1994. First published 1970.

Frederick, Marla. *Between Sundays: Black Women and Everyday Struggles of Faith*. Berkeley: University of California Press, 2003.

Frederick, Marla. *Colored Television: American Religion Gone Global*. Stanford, CA: Stanford University Press, 2016.

Freedman, Samuel. "Call and Response on the State of the Black Church." *New York Times*, April 17, 2010.

Gaines, Kevin. *Uplifting the Race: Black Leadership, Politics, and Culture in the Twentieth Century*. Chapel Hill: University of North Carolina Press, 1996.

Gaston, K. Healan. *Imagining Judeo-Christian America: Religion, Secularism, and the Redefinition of Democracy*. Chicago: University of Chicago Press, 2019.

Gaston, K. Healan. "Interpreting Judeo-Christianity in America." *Relegere: Studies in Religion and Reception* 2, no. 2 (2012): 291–304.

Gates, Henry Louis, Jr. "Black Creativity." *Time*, October 10, 1994.

Gates, Henry Louis, Jr., ed. *The Classic Slave Narratives*. New York: Signet Classics, 2012.

Gates, Henry Louis, Jr. *Figures in Black: Words, Signs, and the "Racial" Self*. New York: Oxford University Press, 1987.

Gates, Henry Louis, Jr. "Harlem on Our Minds." *Critical Inquiry* 24, no. 1 (Autumn 1997): 1–12.

Gates, Henry Louis, Jr. *The Signifying Monkey: A Theory of African American Literary Criticism*. New York: Oxford University Press, 1988.

Gates, Henry Louis, Jr. "The Trope of a New Negro and the Reconstruction of the Image of the Black." In "America Reconstructed, 1840–1940." Special issue of *Representations*, no. 24 (Autumn 1988): 129–155.

Gautier, Amina. "African American Women's Writings in the Woman's Building Library." *Libraries & Culture* 41, no. 1 (Winter 2006): 55–81.

Genovese, Eugene. *Roll, Jordan, Roll: The World the Slaves Made*. New York: Vintage, 1976.

George, Nelson. "Buppies, B-Boys, Baps, and Bohos." *Village Voice*, March 17, 1992.

George, Nelson. *Post-Soul Nation: The Explosive, Contradictory, Triumphant, and Tragic 1980s as Experienced by African Americans (Previously Known as Black and Before That Negroes)*. New York: Penguin, 2005.

Glaude, Eddie S., Jr. "The Black Church Is Dead." *Huffington Post*, February 4, 2010.

BIBLIOGRAPHY 219

Glaude, Eddie S., Jr. *Exodus: Race, Religion and Nation in Early Nineteenth Century America.* Chicago: University of Chicago Press, 1998.

Godwin, Joscelyn. *Upstate Cauldron: Eccentric Spiritual Movements in Early New York State.* Albany, NY: SUNY Press, 2015.

Goldschmidt, Henry, and Elizabeth McAlister, eds. *Race, Nation and Religion in the Americas.* New York: Oxford University Press, 2004.

Gooding-Williams, Robert. *In the Shadow of Du Bois: Afro-Modern Political Thought in America.* Cambridge, MA: Harvard University Press, 2009.

Goodman, Nan, and Michael P. Kramer, eds. *The Turn around Religion in America: Literature, Culture and the Work of Sacvan Bercovitch.* New York: Routledge, 2011.

Gorski, Philip, David Kyuman Kim, John Torpey, and Jonathan VanAntwerpen, eds. *The Post-Secular in Question: Religion in Contemporary Society.* New York: NYU Press, 2012.

Green, Adam. *Selling the Race: Culture, Community and Black Chicago, 1940–1955.* Chicago: University of Chicago Press, 2009.

Griffin, Farah Jasmine. *Harlem Nocturne: Women Artists and Progressive Politics during World War II.* New York: Basic Civitas Books, 2013.

Grodzins, Dean. *American Heretic: Theodore Parker and Transcendentalism.* Chapel Hill: University of North Carolina Press, 2014.

Gronniosaw, James Ukawsaw. "A Narrative of the Most Remarkable Particulars in the Life of James Albert Ukawsaw Gronniosaw, an African Prince, as Related by Himself." Chapel Hill: University of North Carolina Academic Affairs Library, 2001. http://docsouth.unc.edu/neh/gronniosaw/gronnios.html.

Griggs, Sutton. *Imperium in Imperio.* Berkeley, CA: West Martin Press, 2022. First published 1899.

Gunn, Giles. *The Interpretation of Otherness: Literature, Religion, and the American Imagination.* New York: Oxford University Press, 1979.

Haley, Alex. *The Autobiography of Malcolm X.* New York: Ballantine, 1973.

Hardy, Clarence. *James Baldwin's God: Sex, Hope, and Crisis in Black Holiness Culture.* Knoxville: University of Tennessee Press, 2009.

Harris, Calvin. *The Rise to Respectability: Race, Religion, and the Church of God in Christ.* Fayetteville: University of Arkansas Press, 2015.

Harris, Fredrick. *Something Within: Religion in African-American Political Activism.* New York: Oxford University Press, 1999.

Harris, Trudier, ed. *The Selected Works of Ida B. Wells-Barnett.* New York: Oxford University Press, 1991.

Hart, William D. "The Afterlife of the Black Church." *Religion Dispatches,* March 15, 2010.

Hart, William D. *Black Religion: Malcolm X, Julius Lester, and Jan Willis.* New York: Palgrave Macmillan, 2008.

Hedstrom, Matthew S. *The Rise of Liberal Religion: Book Culture and American Spirituality in the Twentieth Century.* New York: Oxford University Press, 2012.

Herskovits, Melville. *The Myth of the Negro Past.* Boston: Beacon Press, 1990. First published 1941.

Hesse, Hermann. *My Belief: Essays on Life and Art.* New York: Farrar, Straus and Giroux, 1973.

Higginbotham, Evelyn Brooks. *Righteous Discontent: The Women's Movement in the Black Baptist Church, 1880–1920.* Cambridge, MA: Harvard University Press, 1994.

Hobbs, Allyson. *A Chosen Exile: A History of Racial Passing in American Life.* Cambridge, MA: Harvard University Press, 2016.

Hollinger, David A. *After Cloven Tongues of Fire: Protestant Liberalism in Modern American History.* Princeton, NJ: Princeton University Press, 2013.

Holloway, Jonathan Scott. *Confronting the Veil: Abram Harris, Jr., E. Franklin Frazier, and Ralph Bunche, 1919–1941.* Chapel Hill: University of North Carolina Press, 2002.

hooks, bell. "Postmodern Blackness." *Postmodern Culture* 1, no. 1 (1990). doi:10.1353/pmc.1990.0004.

Houghton, Walter R. *Neely's History of the Parliament of Religions and Religious Congresses at the World's Columbian Exposition.* Chicago: Neely, 1894.

Hucks, Tracey. *Yoruba Traditions and African American Religious Nationalism.* Alberquerque: University of New Mexico Press, 2012.

Huffington, Ariana. "Announcing *HuffPost Religion*: Believers and Nonbelievers Welcome." *Huffington Post,* April 29, 2010.

Huggins, Nathan. *Harlem Renaissance.* New York: Oxford University Press, 1971.

Humez, Jean McMahon, ed. *Gifts of Power: The Writings of Rebecca Jackson, Black Visionary, Shaker Eldress.* Amherst: University of Massachusetts Press, 1981.

Hutchison, William. *The Modernist Impulse in American Protestantism.* Durham, NC: Duke University Press, 1992.

Hutchison, William. *Religious Pluralism in America.* New Haven, CT: Yale University Press, 2003.

Iton, Richard. *In Search of the Black Fantastic: Politics and Popular Culture in the Post–Civil Rights Era.* New York: Oxford University Press, 2008.

Jackson, John L., Jr. "Lights, Camera, Action!" *Public Culture* 28, no. 1 (Jan. 2016): 3–8.

Jackson, Major. "Surroundings More Congenial: The Perils of Hiking While Black." *Orion: People and Nature,* December 29, 2020.

Jacobsen, Douglas. *Thinking in the Spirit: Theologies of the Early Pentecostal Movement.* Bloomington: Indiana University Press, 2003.

Jakobsen, Janet, and Ann Pellegrini, eds. *Secularisms.* Durham, NC: Duke University Press, 2008.

James, Winston. *Holding Aloft the Banner of Ethiopia: Caribbean Radicalism in Early Twentieth Century America*. London: Verso Books, 1999.

Janken, Kenneth Robert. *Rayford W. Logan and the Dilemma of the African-American Intellectual*. Amherst: University of Massachusetts Press, 1993.

Jelks, Randal. *Benjamin Elijah Mays, Schoolmaster of the Movement: A Biography*. Chapel Hill: University of North Carolina Press, 2012.

Jelks, Randal. "Masculinity, Religion, and Modernism: A Consideration of Benjamin Elijah Mays and Richard Wright." *Women, Gender, and Families of Color* 2, no. 1 (Spring 2014): 57–78.

Jennings, Willie. *The Christian Imagination: Theology and the Origins of Race*. New Haven, CT: Yale University Press, 2010.

Johnson, Paul Christopher. *Diaspora Conversions: Black Carib Religion and the Recovery of Africa*. Berkeley: University of California Press, 2007.

Johnson, Sylvester. *African American Religions, 1500–2000: Colonialism, Democracy, and Freedom*. Cambridge: Cambridge University Press, 2015.

Jones, Charles Price. *An Appeal to the Sons of Africa*. Jackson, MS: Truth Publishing Co., 2000. First published 1902.

Judy, Ronald A. T. *(Dis)Forming the American Canon: African-Arab Slave Narratives and the Vernacular*. Minneapolis: University of Minnesota Press, 1993.

Kahn, Jonathon S. *Divine Discontent: The Religious Imagination of W. E. B. Du Bois*. New York: Oxford University Press, 2009.

Kahn, Jonathan S., and Vincent Lloyd, eds. *Race and Secularism in America*. New York: Columbia University Press, 2016.

Keel, Terence. *Divine Variations: How Christian Thought Became Racial Science*. Stanford, CA: Stanford University Press, 2010.

Kelley, Robin D. G. *Hammer and Hoe: Alabama Communists during the Great Depression*. Chapel Hill: University of North Carolina Press, 2015.

Kelley, Robin D. G. "'We Are Not What We Seem': Rethinking Black Working-Class Opposition in the Jim Crow South." *Journal of American History* 80, no. 1 (June 1993): 75–112.

Kelley, Robin D. G. "What Did Cedric Robinson Mean by Racial Capitalism." *Boston Review*, January 12, 2017. https://bostonreview.net/articles/robin-d-g-kelley-introduction-race-capitalism-justice/.

King, Charles. *Gods of the Upper Air: How a Circle of Renegade Anthropologists Reinvented Race, Sex, and Gender in the Twentieth Century*. New York: Anchor, 2020.

King, Tiffany Lethabo, Jenell Navarro, and Andrea Smith, eds. *Otherwise Worlds: Against Settler Colonialism and Anti-Blackness*. Durham, NC: Duke University Press, 2020.

Kramer, Steve. "Uplifting Our 'Downtrodden Sisterhood': Victoria Earle Matthews and New York City's White Rose Mission, 1897–1907." *Journal of African American History* 91, no. 3 (Summer 2006): 243–266.

Lamothe, Daphne. *Inventing the New Negro: Narrative, Culture, and Ethnography*. Philadelphia: University of Pennsylvania Press, 2008.

Latour, Bruno. *We Have Never Been Modern*. Translated by Catherine Porter. Cambridge, MA: Harvard University Press, 1993.

Lemieux, Jamila. "Trying to Forgive the Black Church." *The Nation*, July 2, 2015.

Levine, Lawrence. *Black Culture and Black Consciousness: Afro-American Folk Thought from Slavery to Freedom*. New York: Oxford University Press, 2007. First published 1977.

Lewis, David Levering. *W. E. B. Du Bois: Biography of a Race, 1968–1919*. New York: Henry Holt, 1993.

Lewis, David Levering. *W. E. B. Du Bois: The Fight for Equality and the American Century, 1919–1963*. New York: Henry Holt, 2000.

Lewis, David Levering. *When Harlem Was in Vogue*. New York: Penguin, 1997.

Lincoln, C. Eric, and Lawrence Mamiya. *The Black Church in the African American Experience*. Durham, NC: Duke University Press, 1990.

Lofton, Kathryn. "Black Church Blues: Parting with 'The Black Church.'" *Religion Dispatches*, July 3, 2009.

Logan, Rayford W. *The Negro in American Life and Thought, 1977–1901*. New York: Dial Press, 1954.

Long, Charles. Interviewed by Carolyn M. Jones and Julia M. Hardy. "From Colonialism to Community: Religion and Culture in Charles H. Long's *Significations*." *Callaloo*, no. 35 (Spring 1988): 258–271.

Long, Charles H. *Significations: Signs, Symbols and Images in the Interpretation of Religion*. Aurora, CO: Davies Publishing Group, 1999.

McCarthy, Jesse. "Why Does Ta-Nehisi Coates Say Less Than He Knows?," *The Nation*, November 15, 2015.

Maffly-Kipp, Laurie. *Setting Down the Sacred Past: African American Race Narratives*. Cambridge, MA: Harvard University Press, 2009.

Mahmood, Saba. *The Politics of Piety: Islamic Revival and the Feminist Subject*. Princeton, NJ: Princeton University Press, 2011.

Mahon, Maureen. *Right to Rock: The Black Rock Coalition and the Cultural Politics of Race*. Durham, NC: Duke University Press, 2004.

Manigault-Bryant, R. "Religion." In: E. Edwards, R. Ferguson, and J. Ogbar (Eds.), *Keywords for African American Studies*. New York: New York University Press, 2018.

Maran, Rene, Monsignor Kiwanuka, and W. Mercer Cook. "An Interview with Monsignor Kiwanuka, Bishop of Massaka." *Phylon* 1, no. 1 (1940): 31–35.

Masuzawa, Tomoko. *The Invention of World Religions: How European Universalism Was Preserved in the Language of Pluralism*. Chicago: University of Chicago Press, 2005.

Matthews, Victoria Earle. "Aunt Lindy: A Story Founded on Real Life." In *A.M.E. Church Review*. Online Archive of Nineteenth Century U.S.

Women's Writings. New York: J.J. Little and Co., 1893. https://collections.
library.yale.edu/catalog/10267802.

Matthews, Victoria Earle. "The Awakening of the Afro-American Woman: An
Address Delivered at the Annual Convention of the Society of Christian
Endeavor." San Francisco, July 11, 1897. https://collections.library.yale.edu/
catalog/10171939.

Matthews, Victoria Earle. "The Value of Race Literature: An Address."
Massachusetts Review 27, no. 72 (Summer 1986): 170–185.

Maurizi, Dennis. "Jupiter Hammon: The First Publishing African-American.
Maybe." *Chicago Tribune*, June 28, 2002. https://www.chicagotribune.com/
news/ct-xpm-2002-06-28-0206280238-story.html.

Mays, Benjamin E. *Born to Rebel: An Autobiography*. Athens: University of
Georgia Press, 1987.

Mays, Benjamin Elijah. "The Development of the Idea of God in Contemporary
Negro Literature." PhD diss., University of Chicago, 1934.

Mays, Benjamin E. *The Negro's God as Reflected in His Literature*. Edited by
August Meier. Studies in Negro Life. New York: Atheneum, 1968. First
published 1938.

Mays, Benjamin E., and Joseph Nicholson. *The Negro's Church*. New York:
Institute of Social and Religious Research, 1933.

McGreevey, John T. *Parish Boundaries: The Catholic Encounter with Race
in the Twentieth-Century Urban North*. Chicago: University of Chicago
Press, 1998.

McLendon, Jacquelyn Y. Review. In: *Women's Review of Books*, vol. 11, no. 8
(1994).

Meier, August, and Elliott Rudwick. *Black History and the Historical Profession,
1915–1980*. Urbana: University of Illinois Press, 1986.

Mills, Charles. *The Racial Contract*. Ithaca, NY: Cornell University Press, 1999.

Modern, John Lardas. *Secularism in Antebellum America*. Chicago: University
of Chicago Press, 2011.

Moreland, Marc. "Roger Williams: Discipline for Today," *Phylon* 6, no. 2
(1945): 137–140.

Morris, Aldon. *A Scholar Denied: W. E. B. Du Bois and the Birth of Modern
Sociology*. Berkeley: University of California Press, 2017.

Moses, Wilson Jeremiah. *Classical Black Nationalism: From the American
Revolution to Marcus Garvey*. New York: NYU Press, 1996.

Moses, Wilson Jeremiah. *The Golden Age of Black Nationalism*. New York:
Oxford University Press, 1988.

Moten, Fred. "The Case of Blackness." *Criticism* 1, no. 2 (Spring 2008): 177–218.

Moten, Fred. "Manic Depression/Mantic Dispossesion: A Poetics of Hesitant
Sociology/Black Topological Existence." Unpublished manuscript, 2021.

Moyn, Samuel. *The Last Utopia: Human Rights in History*. Cambridge, MA:
Harvard University Press, 2012.

Muhammad, Ismail. "Cornel West's Reckless Criticism of Ta-Nehisi Coates." *Slate*, December 20, 2017.

Myrdal, Gunnar. *An American Dilemma: The Negro Problem and Modern Democracy*. New York: Harper and Brothers, 1944.

Nandy, Ashis. *The Intimate Enemy: Loss and Recovery of Self under Colonialism*. New York: Oxford University Press, 1983.

"News and Notes," *American Journal of Sociology* 62, no. 3 (Nov. 1956): 332.

Newsome, Effie Lee. "Early Figures in Haitian Methodism." *Phylon* 4, no. 1 (1944): 51–61.

Nguyen, Sophia. "Elbow Room: How the Dark Room Collective Made Space for a Generation of African-American Writers." *Harvard Magazine*, March–April 2016.

Njeri, Itabari. "Trey's Chi: Trey Ellis: He's Hot, He's Controversial and Breaking New Ground in Black Literature." *Los Angeles Times*, January 23, 1989.

Noel, James. *Black Religion and the Imagination of Matter in the Atlantic World*. New York: Palgrave Macmillan, 2009.

Oliphant, Elayne. "Beyond Blasphemy or Devotion: Art, the Secular, and Catholicism in Paris." *Journal of the Royal Anthropological Institute* 21, no. 2 (May 2015): 352–373.

"Opal Tometi," *Omega*. https://www.eomega.org/workshops/teachers/opal-tometi.

Orsi, Robert. *Between Heaven and Earth: The Religious Worlds People Make and the Scholars Who Study Them*. Princeton, NJ: Princeton University Press, 2006.

Paddon, Anna R., and Sally Turner. "African Americans and the World Columbian Exposition." *Illinois Historical Journal* 88, no. 1 (Spring 1995): 19–36.

Palmer, Edward Nelson. "The Religious Acculturation of the Negro." *Phylon* 5, no. 3 (1944): 260–265.

Pardlo, Gregory. *Digest*. New York: Four Way Books, 2014.

Park, Robert E. "Negro Race Consciousness as Reflected in Race Literature." In *The New Negro: Readings on Race, Representation, and African American Culture, 1892–1938*, edited by Henry Louis Gates Jr. and Gene Andrew Jarrett, 305–315. Princeton, NJ: Princeton University Press, 2007.

Parker, Alison M. *Unceasing Militant: The Life of Mary Church Terrell*. Chapel Hill: University of North Carolina Press, 2020.

Parker, Theodore. *The American Scholar*. Edited by George Willis Cooke. Boston: American Unitarian Association, 1907.

Parsons, Monique. "The History of the Black Church." *National Public Radio*, November 27, 2008.

Patel, Eboo. "The Pluralist Next Door." *Huffington Post*, April 26, 2010.

Patton, Venetria K., and Maureen Honey, eds. *Double-Take: A Revisionist Harlem Renaissance Anthology*. New Brunswick, NJ: Rutgers University Press, 2010.

Petro, Anthony. "Race, Gender, Sexuality, and Religion in North America." *Oxford Research Encyclopedia of Religion* (February 2017): 1–33. https://doi.org/10.1093/acrefore/9780199340378.013.488.

Pierce, Yolanda. *Hell without Fires: Slavery, Christianity, and the Antebellum Spiritual Narrative.* Gainesville: University Press of Florida, 2005.

Plate, S. Brent. *Walter Benjamin, Religion, and Aesthetics: Rethinking Religion through the Arts.* New York: Routledge, 2004.

Portier, William L. "*Pere Just's* Hero-Martyr Secularized: John R. Slattery's Passage from Self-Sacrifice to 'Honest Manhood.'" *U.S. Catholic Historian* 17, no. 2 (Spring 1999): 31–47.

Powell, Richard J. *Black Art: A Cultural History.* New York: Thames and Hudson, 2003.

Pratt, Mary Louise. *Imperial Eyes: Travel Writing and Transculturation.* New York: Taylor & Francis, 2003.

Raboteau, Albert J. *Canaan Land: The Religious History of African Americans.* New York: Oxford University Press, 2001.

Raboteau, Albert. *Slave Religion: The "Invisible Institution" in the Antebellum South,* updated ed. (New York: Oxford University Press, 2004)

Rankine, Claudia. *Citizen: An American Lyric.* Minneapolis, MN: Gray Wolf Press, 2014.

Ransby, Barbara. "The Class Politics of Black Lives Matter."*Dissent,* Fall 2015.

Ransom, Reverdy C. "The Fraternal Council of Negro Churches in America." In *Year Book of Negro Churches, 1935–36,* edited by Bishops of the A.M.E. Church, 24. Wilberforce, OH: A.M.E. Church Publishing, 1936.

Raushenbush, Paul. "Dear Religious (and Sane) America." *Huffington Post,* April 26, 2010.

Reed, Adolph, Jr. *The Jesse Jackson Phenomenon: The Crisis of Purpose in Afro-American Politics.* New Haven, CT: Yale University Press, 1986.

Reed, Adolph, Jr. "What Are the Drums Saying Booker? The Current Crisis of the Black Intellectual." *Village Voice,* April 11, 1995.

Robeck, Cecil. *The Azusa Street Mission and Revival: The Birth of the Global Pentecostal Movement.* Nashville, TN: Thomas Nelson, 2006.

Robinson, Cedric J. *Black Movements in America.* New York: Routledge, 1997.

Ross, Marlon B. *Manning the Race: Reforming Black Men in the Jim Crow Era.* New York: NYU Press, 2004.

Rudolph, Kerstin. "Victoria Earle Matthews: Making Literature during the Woman's Era." *Legacy* 33, no. 1 (2016): 103–126.

Rudolph, Kerstin. "Victoria Earle Matthews's Short Stories." *Legacy* 33, no. 1 (2016): 157–161.

Rudwick, Elliot M., and August Meier. "Black Man in the 'White City': Negroes and the Columbian Exposition, 1893." *Phylon* 26, no. 4 (1965): 354–361.

Savage, Barbara Dianne. *Broadcasting Freedom: Radio, War, and the Politics of Race, 1938–1948.* Chapel Hill: University of North Carolina Press, 1999.

Savage, Barbara Dianne. "W. E. B. Du Bois and 'The Negro Church.'" In "The Study of African American Problems: W. E. B. Du Bois's Agenda, Then and Now." Special issue of *Annals of the American Academy of Political and Social Science* 568 (March 2000): 235–249.

Savage, Barbara Dianne. *Your Spirits Walk Beside Us: The Politics of Black Religion*. Cambridge, MA: Belknap Press of Harvard University Press, 2008.

Sawyer, Mary. "The Fraternal Council of Negro Churches, 1934–1964." *Church History* 59, no. 1 (March 1990): 51–64.

Schmidt, Leigh Eric. *Restless Souls: The Making of American Spirituality*. Berkeley: University of California Press, 2012.

Schmidt, Leigh Eric. *Village Atheists: How America's Unbelievers Made Their Way in a Godly Nation*. Princeton, NJ: Princeton University Press, 2016.

Schmidt, Leigh, and Sally Promey, eds. *American Religious Liberalism*. Bloomington: Indiana University Press, 2012.

Schultz, Kevin M. *Tri-Faith America: How Catholics and Jews Held Postwar America to Its Protestant Promise*. New York: Oxford University Press, 2013.

Seager, Richard. *The Dawn of Religious Pluralism: Voices from the World's Parliament of Religions, 1893*. Lasalle, IL: Open Court, 1999.

Seager, Richard Hughes. *The World's Parliament of Religions: The East/West Encounter, Chicago, 1893*. Bloomington: Indiana University Press, 1995.

Shaw, Stephanie. *W.E.B. Du Bois and The Souls of Black Folk*. Chapel Hill: University of North Carolina Press, 2015.

Shelby, Tommie. *We Who Are Dark: The Philosophical Foundations of Black Solidarity*. Cambridge, MA: Belknap Press of Harvard University Press, 2007.

Sherman, Scott. "Fighting Words: Adolph Reed's Crusade against the New Black Intellectuals." *Lingua Franca*, March 1997, 38–48.

Silk, Mark. "Notes on the Judeo-Christian Tradition in America." *American Quarterly* 36, no. 1 (Spring 1984): 65–85.

Smith, Jonathan Z. *Map Is Not Territory: Studies in the History of Religion*. Chicago: University of Chicago Press, 1993.

Smith, Katharine Capshaw. *Children's Literature of the Harlem Renaissance*. Bloomington: Indiana University Press, 2006.

Smith, Lee. "Gone but Not Forgotten." *Washington Examiner*, September 8, 2017.

Smith, Theophus H. *Conjuring Culture: Biblical Formations of Black America*. New York: Oxford University Press, 1995.

Sollors, Werner, ed. *The Return of Thematic Criticism*. Cambridge, MA: Harvard University Press, 1993.

Sorett, Josef. "African American Religion and Popular Culture," in A. Pinn (Ed.), *African American Religious Cultures*. Santa Barbara, CA: ABC-CLIO, 2009.

Sorett, Josef. *Spirit in the Dark: A Religious History of Racial Aesthetics*. New York: Oxford University Press, 2016.

Spillers, Hortense. Review. In: *African American Review*, vol. 29, no. 1 (1995).

Stahl, Ronit Y. *Enlisting Faith: How the Military Chaplaincy Shaped Religion and State in Modern America*. Cambridge, MA: Harvard University Press, 2017.

Stephens, Randall. *The Fire Spreads: Holiness and Pentecostalism in the American South*. Cambridge, MA: Harvard University Press, 2008.

Stewart, Dianne M. *Three Eyes for the Journey: African Dimensions of the Jamaican Religious Experience*. New York: Oxford University Press, 2005.

Stilwell, Sean. *Slavery and Slaving in African History*. New York: Cambridge University Press, 2014.

Stowe, Harriett Beecher. *Uncle Tom's Cabin*. New York: Oxford University Press, 2002. First published 1852.

Sugrue, Thomas. *The Origins of the Urban Crisis: Race and Inequality in Postwar Detroit*. Princeton, NJ: Princeton University Press, 2014.

Tate, Greg. *Flyboy in the Buttermilk: Essays on Contemporary Culture*. New York: Simon and Schuster, 1992.

Taylor, Charles. *A Secular Age*. Cambridge, MA: Harvard University Press, 2007.

Taylor, Mark C., ed. *Critical Terms for Religious Studies*. Chicago: University of Chicago Press, 1998.

Teed, Paul E. *A Revolutionary Conscience: Theodore Parker and Antebellum America*. Lanham, MD: University Press of America, 2012.

Tesfaye, Sophia. "Violence Returns to the Trump Campaign: Black Protester Assaulted by Trump Supporters at 'New York Values' Rally." *Salon*, April 12, 2016.

"The First Phylon Institute and Twenty-Fifth Atlanta University Conference," *Phylon* 2, no. 3 (1941): 275–288.

The Historymakers: The Digital Repository for the Black Experience, "Jack E. White," February 28, 2013, https://www.thehistorymakers.org/biography/jack-white.

Thomas, Biller Geter and Ira De A. Reed, "France and the Traditions of Freedom," *Phylon* 4, Supplement: "Freedom in the Modern World: Four Broadcasts by the People's College of Atlanta University" (1943): 18–23.

Thornton, John. *Africa and Africans and the Making of the Atlantic World, 1400–1800*. London: Cambridge University Press, 1998.

Thurman, Wallace, ed. *Fire!! A Quarterly Devoted to the Younger Negro Artists*. New York: Martin Fine Books, 2022. First published 1926.

Van Der Beets, Richard. *Held Captive by Indians*. Knoxville: University of Tennessee Press, 1973.

Viswanathan, Gauri. "Secularism in the Framework of Heterodoxy." *PMLA* 123, no. 2 (2008): 466–476.

Wall, Wendy L. *Inventing the "American Way": The Politics of Consensus from the New Deal to the Civil Rights Movement*. New York: Oxford University Press, 2008.

Wallace, Maurice O. *Constructing the Black Masculine: Identity and Ideality in African American Literature and Culture, 1771–1995*. Durham, NC: Duke University Press, 2002.

Walton, Jonathan L. *Watch This! The Ethics and Aesthetics of Black Televangelism*. New York: New York University Press, 2009.

Warren, Kenneth. *What Was African American Literature?* Cambridge, MA: Harvard University Press, 2010.

Washington, James Melvin. *Frustrated Fellowship: The Black Baptist Quest for Social Power*. Macon, GA: Mercer University Press, 1991.

Washington, Mary Helen. *The Other Black List: The African American Literary and Cultural Left of the 1950s*. New York: Columbia University Press, 2014.

Weisenfeld, Judith. *New World A-Coming: Black Religion and Religio-Racial Identity in the Great Migration*. New York: NYU Press, 2017.

West, Cornel. "Introduction: Religion and the Left." Special issue of *Monthly Review: An Independent Socialist Magazine* 36, no. 3 (July–August 1984): 9–19.

West, Cornel. *Race Matters*. Boston: Beacon Press, 1993.

White, Hayden. *The Content of the Form: Narrative Discourse and Historical Representation*. Baltimore, MD: Johns Hopkins University Press, 1987.

White, Jack E. "The Beauty of Black Art." *Time*, October 10, 1994.

Whitted, Qiana. *A God of Justice: The Problem of Evil in Twentieth Century Black Literature*. Charlottesville: University of Virginia Press, 2009.

Wilcox, Leonard. *V. F. Calverton: Radical in the American Grain*. Philadelphia, PA: Temple University Press, 1992.

Wilder, Gary. *Freedom Time: Negritude, Decolonization, and the Future of the World*. Durham, NC: Duke University Press, 2015.

Wilderson, Frank B., III. *Afro-Pessimism*. New York: Liveright, 2020.

Wills, David. "The Rise of Black Evangelicalism: Acquiring a Taste for Salvation." Paper presented at Harvard Divinity School, 2002.

Wood, Joe. "The Malcolm X Factor." *Village Voice*, May 29, 1990.

Wood, Joe, ed. *Malcolm X: In Our Own Image*. New York: Anchor Books, 1994.

Woodson, Carter G. *The History of the Negro Church*. Chapel Hill: University of North Carolina Press, 2018. First published in 1921.

Worthen, Molly. *Apostles of Reason: The Crisis of Authority in American Evangelicalism*. New York: Oxford University Press, 2013.

Wright, Richard. "Blueprint for Negro Writing." *New Challenge*, October 1937.

Wuthnow, Robert. *The Restructuring of American Religion: Society and Faith since World War II*. Princeton, NJ: Princeton University Press, 1988.

Wynter, Sylvia. "Black Metamorphosis: New Natives in a New World." Unpublished manuscript, 2022.

Wynter, Sylvia. "On How We Mistook the Map for the Territory, and Re-Imprisoned Ourselves in Our Unbearable Wrongness of Being, of

Désêtre: Black Studies toward the Human Project." In *Not Only the Master's Tools: African-American Studies in Theory and Practice,* edited by Lewis R. Gordon and Jane Anna Gordon, 107–171. Boulder, CO: Paradigm, 2006.

Zuckerman, Phil, ed. *Du Bois on Religion.* Walnut Creek, CA: Altamira Press, 2000.

Index

For the benefit of digital users, indexed terms that span two pages (e.g., 52–53) may, on occasion, appear on only one of those pages.